GROUNDED-ENCOUNTER THERAPY:

PERSPECTIVES, CHARACTERISTICS, AND APPLICATIONS

L. ALEX SWAN

Order this book online at www.trafford.com
or email orders@trafford.com

Most Trafford titles are also available at major online book retailers.

Printed in the United States of America.

ISBN: 978-1-4907-1459-2 (sc)
ISBN: 978-1-4907-1460-8 (e)

Trafford rev. 11/23/2013

 www.trafford.com

North America & international
toll-free: 1 888 232 4444 (USA & Canada)
fax: 812 355 4082

Contents

Part 2: Psychotherapies and GET

Part 3: Explanation Examples of GET

Part 4: Application and Intervention Examples of GET

Preface

Colleagues who have reviewed the book <u>The Practice of Clinical Sociology and Sociotherapy</u> (1984, 1994) have welcomed the information and insights, but have made the point that the discussion and analysis of Grounded-Encounter Therapy (GET) was a beginning which needs more case examples and discussions of the ways in which GET can be used in discovery and treatment of problems of living that are lodged in a social context. There is no question that Clinical Sociologists need more sociodiagnostic and sociotherapeutic approaches to legitimize and validate their entrance and rightful place in the clinical field. GET is one such approach; no doubt there will be other approaches for Clinical Sociologists to use. This is the way it should be if the field is to become well established. Practitioners need approaches that are scientific that require, and allow for discovery for intervention and application. This is the essential weakness and inadequacy of the present psychotherapeutic approaches in use today.

This book is organized around several essential notions: Perspectives which underline the GET approach; The characteristics of GET; Explanatory Examples of GET in its discovery process, and Application and Intervention Examples. The book concludes with a few cases that demonstrate the discovery process of GET. The cases are mere examples because even though the symptoms presented might be similar, the context of the problem might be quite different in each case. The clinician must always be aware that the presenting problem is not usually the real problem; for the client they are real; but for the clinician the real problem must be discovered. This is the theme of Grounded Encounter Therapy (GET). It is also the fact that the Sociotherapist is capable of doing much more than build bridges to cope with trouble waters; he/she can get in the water and with the client discover what's troubling the waters. In the introductory chapter, we present some ideas regarding social thought and methods of discovery in Clinical Sociology. Various methods of knowing and the associated problems are discussed and analyzed. The process of thinking about problems of living and the methods of discovery; the nature and character of the real and presenting problems and their social context are significant matters to which Clinical Sociologists and every Clinician should pay special attention.

The theoretical perspectives that dominate contemporary sociological thinking are briefly presented in chapter one. Sociology, as the scientific study of society and of human behavior in group life, provides a variety of theoretical orientations that serve as frames of reference for viewing, understanding and making application. The theoretical perspective of human interactions and relationships are treated in chapter two, along with a discussion of the content of the self-image, properties of the self and style of conveyance of the properties. This theoretical understanding is especially important for sociotherapists who may be tempted to think in terms of personality when attempting to understand human interaction and relationship conflicts. There is an essential difference in the concept of the social self and the concept of the personality. The clinical understanding of Clinical Sociologists may be stifled if certain concepts are embraced and if certain theoretical perspectives are used. Clinical Sociologists and other therapists need broad assumptions about society and social behavior that provide a point of view for the study, discovery, understanding and treatment of specific problems.

In chapter three, a brief critical analysis is made of eight of the key psychotherapies that dominate the field today. What we have discovered is that each one of the therapeutic approaches treated has a predetermined definition of the nature of human problems which confines each to the problems within the scope of the definition. Problems that are outside the scope of the definitions cannot be addressed. Clients tend to have greater understanding and improvement in their situation and problems if the therapy they become involved in is consistent with the way they view, explain, and understand the problem and their conceptualization of how to correct it (Crane et. al., 1986). This is the reason that clients and all those implicated in the situation of the problem are involved in the sociodiagnostic process of discovery and in the devising of sociotherapeutic plans and strategies for change. It's also very effective in dealing with theoretical and therapeutic resistance.

In chapter four, the dilemma of psychotherapy and the way it is practiced is presented. It is argued that the Psychotherapeutic perspective is antithetical to the sociotherapeutic perspective. Further, the pre-determined explanations of problems, which are of a social nature; implicit in the basic philosophies and theoretical assumptions of the various psychotherapies are contrary to the scientific and methodological posture for discovering explanations of problems and their contexts.

Chapter five introduces Grounded-Encounter Therapy as a sociodiagnostic and sociotherapeutic approach. GET is defined, and the sociodiagnostic and sociotherapeutic processes and content are identified and the theoretical and methodological encounters that are necessary for GET to be effective are discussed. How to use GET, especially with groups, is outlined.

The characteristics of GET are specified in chapter six. The process and orientation of Grounding and Encounter are discussed, and the goals and basis for change are presented. This chapter makes the point that GET is a process which allows for the discovery of the problem(s) and its context which must be addressed theoretically and therapeutically if the problem (s) is to be solved. Further, it is argued that the treatment and the therapeutic techniques employed in the process are dictated by what is theoretically discovered about the problem and its context. Therefore, any approach which promotes a predetermined theory or explanation about a problem creates dysjuncture between theory and therapy which is dysfunctional to the understanding and resolution of the problem.

Classifying marriages and families is the primary focus of chapter seven. Types of marriages and types of families are discussed. Disengagement and distractions in marital relationships are presented and reasons for disengagement are discussed. It might be important to understand families in terms of their structure: the nuclear, extended and augmented. It might also be profitable to understand the family in terms of whether the father or mother dominates the family system. However, this chapter makes the point that for the purpose of therapeutic intervention and theoretical clarity, the most powerful way to understand the family is to focus on its internal dynamics by looking at member relationships and interactions. The organization and structure of the family are significant, but the kinds of relationships and the nature of the interactions between and among members have greater potential for understanding, clarifying, and intervening in family situations. This position allows Clinical Sociologists and Sociotherapists to focus not only on family problem issues, but also on family development issues.

Chapter eight, which focuses on institutional treatment and reentry of ex-convicts, is another example of what the Clinical Sociologists and Sociotherapists must pay attention to in order to be effective in discovering and treating problems of living. It is not enough for inmates to leave the prison environment; it is more significant that inmates want to, or express a desire to reenter society. The environmental context for reentry success must include efforts to prepare the various societal units/systems—family, school, job and the church for the inclusion of the ex-con. Many therapists focus exclusively on the individual without placing equal attention on the social situation out of which the ex-con comes and the social context within which he is placed.

Driving behavior provides an excellent way for understanding joint-action in relating and interacting. Driving takes place within the context of a group of drivers attempting to fit their action to the actions of others in the driving world. It is the nature of driving that the members of the driving public are embedded in a social situation created by the actions of others. Chapter nine identifies destiny-drivers, casual-caution drivers, and social-occasion drivers as the primary participants in the driving environment, and argues that it is when there is a breakdown in establishing joint-action among and between these drivers that accidents or conflicts in driving occur. Leftlaners—chronic, occasional, and convenient-mediators, parlor-room, dining-room, and library drivers are also discussed within the context of the driving world as potentially dangerous in that they make joint-action difficult to achieve in a social context where interaction is so intense and relationships are based upon indications, gestures, meanings, and designations from one driver to the other and others. Shot-gun driving is also problematic. This is driving done in a scattered manner instead of in an organized fashion. Movement from lane to lane to avoid others immediately before or behind one is rampant in many growing cities. Driving in a scattered manner does allow drivers to be more relaxed, reduce tension, etc., but it also makes it more difficult to establish joint-action, especially when the movement to scatter is not done for any other obvious reasons.

Chapter ten provides examples of various problems of living and how the GET therapist would seek to understand them and treat them. In other words, this chapter focuses on the application of specific knowledge about certain problems and the intervention postures of the therapist in attempting to manage, eliminate, or make adjustment to the problems within the context of their emergence. The point is confirmed in this chapter that presenting problems are not usually the real problems, but mere symptoms of the real problems which must be discovered through the sociodiagnostic process as the context of the problems is identified and discovered. Applying the knowledge gained and the explanatory insights obtained through the sociodiagnostic process to the social context of the problems enhances the resolution of the presenting and real problems.

Chapter eleven discusses the need for special and specific training and supervision of clinical sociologists to assure the acquisition of appropriate skills, abilities, integrity, and competencies that are essential to the scientific process of discovery and therapeutic intervention. This chapter also provides a few case examples of how to discover essential facts from the disclosure of clients, and the questions most appropriate for disclosure within particular settings. The problems are the clients' and they must disclose; they must discover, and they must decide to make application of the knowledge and understanding gained through the process. The sociotherapist is a facilitator of this process and uses his skills and certain techniques in achieving the goals of the process. The sociodiagnostic process should be conducted so scientifically that the clients see and understand what is happening in their social situation; how and what problems have emerged therefrom, and what the data discovered has to say about what to do to make changes in their situations and effect improvements in their interacting and relating. Most therapists seek to make their clients fit into their approach or predefined system. The initial struggle with the clients and the information they produce is to force them into seeing their problems and situations from the perspective defined by the approaches.

Success is accepted or acknowledged only when the client begins to see things from the perspective of the therapist and the particular approach dictating the session. This is not to suggest that clients do not have multiple problems, or that clients may not have problems in the areas of each of the modalities discussed here. However, it is not true to the scientific process of discovery for data to be skewed by therapeutic approaches that have a predetermined explanation of clients' problems. The data discovered must dictate explanations, understanding and possible solutions. To view clients and their situations from the particular therapeutic approach of the therapist is to stifle the process of discovery and exclude possibilities that might be beyond the dimensions of the particular approach.

GET provides a scientific way for discovering the nature of the social situation, explanations about the problems emerging from the social situation, and ways for making adjustment, choices, changing views, behavior, and the social situation. GET is not a hypothesis that requires testing. It is a scientific approach for discovery of theories and ways to change situations and behavior. GET argues the inclusion of those implicated in the situation out of which the problems emerged. Discovery dictates who are implicated and who are not.

Chapter twelve presents several cases showing how to discover the essential facts of a case making crucial observations.

Chapter thirteen addresses Sociological practice and its value to the survival and viability of the disruptive of sociology.

*   *   *

Foreword

This work is an effort to emphasize sociological practice. It represents an international movement of a growing number of sociologists to return to their roots and origin of searching for and applying sociological knowledge and understanding to problems of living for positive social change. The definition of Clinical Sociology mirrors the perspective of Wang-Yang-Ming (1472-1529), who said:

Knowledge is the beginning of practice; doing is the completion of knowing. Men of the present, however, make knowledge and action two different things and go not forth to practice because they hold that one must first have knowledge before one is able to practice. Each one says, "I proceed to investigate and discuss knowledge; I wait until knowledge is perfect and then go forth to practice it." Those who to the very end of life fail to practice also fail to understand. This is not a small error, nor one that came in a day. By saying that knowledge and practice are a unit, I am herewith offering a remedy for the disease.

In this work we define Clinical Sociology as the search for and the application of sociological knowledge, at various levels, from micro to macro, for the purpose of positive social change. This definition is in keeping with the view that the Clinical Sociologist must be a scientist first since he/she has to discover specific knowledge prior to its being applied and him/her being a practitioner. The definition also squares with the task of unifying the scientific and the professional aspects of clinical sociology so that the application and intervention is grounded and "that academians and practitioners who are committed to clinical research and clinical practice might work together to bring these aspects more closely together." This work also seeks to address another concern of a comparatively new field that of providing a "comprehensive overview of the field of clinical sociology, noting the context for clinical discovery (diagnosis) and treatment (therapy), the theoretical foundations for intervention, and the methods and techniques appropriate to group, community, organizational and societal change."

The claims which clinical sociology makes are lodged within the realities of the discipline of sociology. The legitimacy of the discipline to create knowledge and understanding and to explain human social behavior at the personal and societal levels validates clinical sociology. This means that the theoretical perspectives and methodological approaches of sociology give direction and scope to clinical sociology. Sociologists and sociology produce general knowledge, but clinical sociology and clinical sociologists attempt to produce specific knowledge regarding specific issues and problems. For Clinical Sociologists specific knowledge and understanding is the most appropriate for intervention and application.

Section one provides an understanding regarding the origin, history, and development of the field of clinical sociology. It is clear that when sociology began as a discipline in the USA, the main concern was the creation and discovery of knowledge for the purpose of intervention, and application. The great migration during this time, and the influx of residents from the southern regions of the United States who crowded the cities looking for jobs. Most of the men came alone without their families. They had escaped the south in record numbers not merely because they were looking for employment to support their families, but because of the real threat of lynching. When the families arrived, many soon after the husbands and fathers, the professional concern of sociologists was the welfare of the families and children. The Child Saving Movement began during this time and major developments in juvenile justice and delinquency resulted. Sociology, became for a good period, a discovery, intervention and application discipline. The works of the early sociologists, such as W.E.B. Dubois, were primarily focused on understanding and resolving and solving human social, relation and interaction problems. For Dubois, the issues for the families, from whom he collected data were broader and deeper then relational and interactional problems. The issues were fundamental to survival and progress as oppressed people.

"The Philadelphia Negro" represents the issues of concern to Dubois at the time, which have not been fully and adequately addressed to this point. In an attempt to compete with other academic disciplines, especially the social sciences, sociology and sociologists refocused their interests and concerns from intervention and application to purely academic and scientific. The duality of the discipline of sociology is defined by its content and territory we can pursue its duality separately and in combination.

Introduction

Social Thought and Methods of Discovery in Clinical Sociology

There are various models of social thought and methods of discovery that interact to assist us in understanding the human condition. There are various ways in which the human condition can be interpreted. Some guides to social thought divide thought about the human condition according to time and place, and others divide social thought according to different answers to a central question. It is out of our assumptions about the human condition that we define and make sense of reality. The broad conceptions we use to interpret and explain the human condition help us to become aware that we can make conscious choices about our lives and the various problems of living.

The Natural-Law perspective is one of the ways in which the human condition is explained and interpreted. This view sees human beings as an integral part of an orderly universe. Through divine revelation or reason, human beings can grasp the moral law that regulates their lives of which they cannot change. Human beings are thought to be ethically bound by the moral law that establishes a proper order to human existence although human beings might not always conform or adhere to that order. This type of thinking has its roots in ancient civilizations and was alive during the middle ages, and is alive today. Natural-law thinkers are very critical of social life which does not measure up to the moral standards they aspouse. They have clear descriptions of the kinds of human relations that do measure up to these standards and those that do not. A natural law for many religious and/or Christian people is the commandment to love thy neighbor as thyself. The argument is that human beings may break this natural law in many instances, but they cannot change it since God is the one who instituted it.

Another way the human condition is interpreted and explained is by the monistic model. This is also referred to as the one-factor

1

model. According to this view, a simple organizing factor can explain and interpret the human condition. All of the activities of the human being are understood in terms of the working of certain key forces that operate under one overriding concept. If it is believed, for example, that human beings have a primary drive to have power over others, then every human relation and interaction is viewed in terms of the person's power drive. In those cases where the demonstration of power is not obvious, even the expression of love is viewed as a concealed attempt to dominate and impose the will (Blau, 1967).

Other monistic theories of the human condition view economic factors, relations between the sexes, racial factors, and climate as primary. Whenever we attempt to give a precise answer to a question, we are engaging in reducing human activity to a simple factor. Greed, lust for power, desire for love, desire for approval, the desire to survive are some of the simple-factors to which the explanation of the human condition has been reduced. Contrary to the monistic model, the pluralistic model argues that multiplicity of factors are involved in the interpretation of the human condition. In order to fully understand and explain the human condition, all of these factors must be taken into account. The individual or the group is viewed as a unique combination of factors that is never repeated. While those who advocate natural law are searching for and applying the natural laws that should be followed by human beings in order for their conditions to be good, pluralists are trying to discover and apply the factors they believe determine human behavior.

The process conception of the human condition promotes the notion that events in the human condition can be best understood by organizing them around a simple human process. It is within this process that individuals continuously create and recreate the conditions and situations under which we live, interact, and relate. The process model presents an image of the human condition in which human beings have freedom that is expressed in the multiple possibilities for future action. At the same time, they face conditions in the present that somewhat limit the possibilities. The process model does not see a world of moral laws in the absence of human choice.

All social thought models have problems. This must be understood by Clinical Sociologists. All of the models presented above are based on a different image of the human condition. These are not the only types of social thought, but they are the four that have appeared most frequently in the history of civilization in the East and the West. Which type of social thought is most sound and debatable? The most widespread perspective and for a long time, the most dominant is the natural-law which answered the question, what is the good life by saying, it is the fulfillment of some basic human needs human beings have identified. There are very few sociologists who represent the natural law perspective today. In fact, scientific sociology has always rebelled against the natural law theories of society. Religious visions of natural law still survive and have been joined by theories of the "normal" or healthy self.

Methods of Knowing

There are a variety of sociological theories and sociological social psychological theories that undergird the practice of Clinical Sociology and psychosociotherapy. What might not be clear or well established are the various methods of discovery in the process of sociodiagnosis. Clinical Sociology is grounded in the body of knowledge created by the disciplines of sociology and sociological social psychology out of which have emerged an array of theoretical perspectives that attempt to explain human social behavior. However, Clinical Sociologists need explanations that are specific to the particular system (individual, family, group, community, society, organization, etc.) that they seek to explain and change. Consequently, they must employ certain methods of discovery so that specific explanations that are related to the particular system's condition can emerge. The question that must be raised then is: How do we arrive at a fairly complete vision of the system's condition? Some therapists or clinicians listen to their clients and relate what they hear to a theoretical perspective that they are comfortable with or a particular perspective that they have clung to since graduate school. But if they are to be effective, they have to employ methods that would allow the perspective to emerge in the process of discovery, and they have to employ methods that are appropriate in so doing. When we see the system's condition from any explanatory perspective other than the explanation that emerges during the process of discovery, there is the tendency for distortion and misapplication. The explanation must be partial to the systems' reported and discovered condition and not the result of pre-packaged interpretations that come from the most cherished sources of sociological information. The quality and type of information is very important since application and systems' commitment in clinical settings are based upon beliefs. In this work, method is used to refer to a series of regularized acts pursued to gain previously unknown information and knowledge from the systems. The focus is on the specific content of the knowledge and the means of gaining the knowledge are fully in awareness.

The Problems of Methods

Using a method is like fishing. Therefore, the type of hook, line, bait, and even rod one uses depends upon the variety of clients or systems that present themselves and their reported condition, rather than the kind of knowledge one is after. The method has to be specific to the given species of system, but the particular knowledge cannot be specified in advance. Methods must be chosen to facilitate adequate and appropriate discovery because certain methods are more appropriate for gaining some kinds of knowledge and with certain systems than are others. These motions are crucial because the clinical sociologist must be concerned with the applications to be made from the knowledge gained through the discovery process with particular systems. This process must be an authentic activity because the results really matter. The clinical sociologist has to be concerned about the uses to which the findings are made. In the sense that the initial goal of the clinical sociologist is to discover, this goal should dictate the method to be employed. The clinical sociologist will therefore use a particular method that seems appropriate or most likely to help solve the problem or give new information.

The clinical sociologist must answer a number of questions before deciding on a method of discovery. What is being presented and by whom? What needs discovering? Why is the system presenting itself? If the answers are to change, to understand, or to function more effectively, then we can properly select the appropriate method. After we have made the determination of a method, the next task is to try to achieve such a close relation between the problem and the method that all aspects of the presenting problem can be approachable by the method. If the problem is illegitimate, then the method will be inadequate. It is important to realize that the clinical sociologist is a scientist before being a therapist. Essential facts about the system and its conditions must be discovered before application is made.

The fact that sociology has no single paradigm and has a number of methods, is bemoaned by some and applauded by others. A paradigm is established in a science when there is such agreement on problem and method. There are those social scientists who view the natural sciences as being successful in this regard; consequently, they argue that the social sciences should emulate the natural sciences. The argument is that sociology should be grounded on a small set of axioms about human behavior and those axioms should be tested for consistency and accuracy and then applied by sociologists. This kind of paradigm is difficult to bring into existence because of the nature of human freedom and the free will which human beings exercise in behaving. So in the true sense of paradigms, sociology does not have paradigms simply because of the nature of its focus—human social behavior. Sociology has visions of the human situation which have immediate impact on human activity contrary to the adaptation of one paradigm rather than another. It is this impact on human activity that makes it undesirable for sociology to have paradigms because they do not allow us to see changes in activity in everyday life. Adopting on vision of the human situation rather than another does change one's everyday activity. Those who would like to have paradigms in sociology and are disappointed by the many methods in use, argue that all important questions would be answered when the proper method is found. They further argue that the very fact that there are so many methods indicates that the "right" one has not yet been discovered. No one method seems to provide the key to the discovery of knowledge. All important questions are not always answered but it is important to recognize which questions need answers.

The variety of methods in sociology have proved necessary for scientific inquiry, and can be essential in the process of discovery in sociodiagnoses with different systems. Further, employing various methods can increase the validity of findings and improve the accuracy in application. Human science and human existence suggest that human beings are continually reshaping their situations. Human beings make choices, judgments and decide about their conditions, and their surroundings and then act to alter the surroundings and conditions or their responses to them.

Classifying Methods of Discovery

There are a variety of ways to classify methods of discovery. Methods may be classified on the basis of the degree to which they incorporate precise measurement. Certain methods can produce information that can be described in mathematical symbols and certain methods can produce information that can be stated in terms of everyday language. Methods may be used to illuminate the process of understanding the system that presents itself. Methods can be classified in terms of the degree to which the systems are involved with the sociotherapist in creating information. In the process of discovery, in a clinical sense, methods that can be used by all parties in an attempt to understand and clarify visions of the human condition are those that are really crucial. Clinical sociologists should seek to employ methods of discovery that would involve all parties that are implicated in the situation. The creation of information should not involve only the clinical sociologist as scientist. The cooperation of the parties involved makes the difference in the effort of the sociotherapist in significantly involving the systems in the process of disclosure and discovery of knowledge.

Sociologists have developed all kinds of methods for gathering information. The classification ranges from those methods in which clinical sociologists analyze and reshape information gathered by others about problems related to their clients, to methods in which clinical sociologists create and discover with their clients the information and knowledge themselves. <u>Historical, demographic, participant observation, non-participant observation, survey, depth-interview, and experimental small-group methods</u> are the methods available to clinical sociologists for creating knowledge about systems' conditions and problems. No one method is inherently better or worse than another, but one is more or less appropriate to answer given questions. The clinical sociologists must always seek to employ the most appropriate method to arrive at a fairly complete vision of the human condition within the social setting or context of the clients. Any method we employ must allow us to be factual about what happened or is happening. The method should help us in avoiding contradictions or in our being consistent. We will confuse our clients if we are inconsistent in what we say, describe and conclude. The method must allow for adequacy in the quality of the human situation so that some sense can be made regarding the aspects of the human activity. The image we get of the human situation must be comprehensive, significant and grounded in consistent reporting of the facts. The method used must also allow for the vision or image of the human situation to reveal new possibilities for action.

Most information about the human condition comes to us through various sources and with built-in interpretations. Even clinical sociologists tend to adopt a mixture of these interpretations as their own image. It must be remembered that the methods we use to discover the situation and activities are to assist us in discovering specific information and knowledge for direct utility. Consequently, we have to avoid bringing to the process predetermined and built-in interpretations. We have the process and data to tell us what is going on in the setting. Sociology is the science of the human condition, but it has no single paradigm and, thus it has several different methods. There seems to be no right method that is capable of answering all of the important questions or adequate to the discovery of all knowledge—specific or general. The validity of our findings is not related so much to the use of more than one method, but more to the selection of the most appropriate. The human condition is always changing because human beings who create their conditions are continually shaping and reshaping their situations. Human beings are always in the process of self-understanding, and they make judgments and alter their responses in the process.

Methods of discovery can be classified in several ways. One way is to classify it in terms of the degree to which it incorporates precise measurement. Information that can be described in mathematical terms and symbols are considered to be the employment of "Hard" methods, and information produced that can only be described or stated in everyday language is resulting from "Soft" methods. For the clinical sociologist, the aim of all methods of discovery is self-understanding and the understanding of the situation. To some degree, all methods have the potential for all to be a part of the creation of specific information of the clients and the socio-therapist or the psychotherapist should be to clarify the situation and views of the situation in which the clients are involved, and out of which the problems emerge.

The historical method is used in a limited manner by the sociotherapist. But there are historical facts and patterns that could illuminate the structure and process of social relations and interactions that are important to the process of discovery. The demographic approach is related to the historical method which allows for statistical data to be collected, organized, and analyzed. The historical method of discovery helps the sociotherapist to establish a general picture of the clients and their situation which is crucial or the basis for discovering specific knowledge. Patterns of relationships and interactions can be discovered, and a general idea of the social context in which clients are operating can be determined. Before the sociotherapist can go any further, or use another method of discovery, the social context and patterns must be determined. The primary aim in using the historical method is to bring the social context and the kinds of human relations and organizations in which clients established, into clear focus. An imaginative synthesis of the quantitative information provided by the demographic approach, and the qualitative information provided by historical method establishes a basic view of the human condition of the clients.

The sociotherapist will use the participant method in many cases, especially in group situations. In this method, the sociotherapist is present and becomes a member of the client-group. The purpose is to illuminate the structure and process of social actions by carefully observing what goes on in the client-group. It takes much effort and time to truly gain entrance into the client-group, but the sociotherapist must start immediately to gain entrance as a participant. The sociotherapist can do more observing than participating or can be present in the client-group as the therapist and not be a part of it. The sociotherapist must determine what is best, at the time, given the circumstances, to collect data and make discovery.

The sociotherapist also employs the survey method of discovery which involves the asking of specific questions of the clients about aspects of their situation. Here everyone implicated in the situation, along with the sociotherapist, is deeply involved in encountering each other, relative to the questions asked, for the creation of information. The questions may be embarrassing and very personal, and they may be questions the clients may have never thought about before being asked by the sociotherapist. Taking this method a step further, the sociotherapist may use the depth interview method to ask open-ended and general questions in order to find out underlying attitudes about given issues and perspectives relative to the attitudes and issues. By using these two methods, the sociotherapist can obtain specific and general information about the clients and their social situation. In all cases, the sociotherapist must use methods that have the greatest potential for involving everyone in the process of creating information and knowledge about the human beings and their social setting.

Knowledge About Human Action and Society

Knowledge about human behavior and society is only as accurate as the assumption on which it is based. All studies of human society and of human action in society are guided by images, or pictures, about the nature of society and about the nature of human beings as actors in society. The picture a clinician has of society and of the human being determines what he observes, the question she asks, her methodology, and ultimately the character of the knowledge that is formulated for application to the problems being addressed. Most images of man and society assumed in social science are inaccurate. Because a clinician's images of man and society so greatly influence his discovery and application, his images must be as realistic as possible. The assumptions on which most clinicians make discoveries and applications are based on unrealistic images of man and society.

It is the view of most clinicians that human conduct is determined by things that force the human being to act in a particular way. In fact, knowledge in the social sciences is based upon this imagery. There have been attempts to change that imagery over the years, but this is still the prevailing view. The human being is seen as a neutral organism upon which casual factors act to determine her behavior, an organism whose action is therefore a product of the various forces acting on it. Therefore, in order to accumulate knowledge and make discoveries about the human actors, the scientist-practitioner seeks to identify the antecedent conditions that cause human behavior. Because of the deterministic assumptions, there is the belief that social laws exist which can be formulated on the following model: <u>Given a particular man with a particular internal organization or make-up, under particular social or environmental circumstances, he will behave in a particular and predictable way</u>. This belief in the existence of laws of human behavior is the most important background image employed in the social and behavioral sciences. This image is altogether erroneous.

In the different sciences, different antecedent conditions are chosen as being the cause of human action. The choice of causes of human action is one of the most important distinctions between sociology and psychology. For psychologists, the determinants of a person's behavior are lodged inside him. In different fields of psychology, behavior is assumed to be caused by different antecedents. Causes of behavior are identified as need dispositions, organic drives, conscious or unconscious motives, attitudes, sentiments, ideals, and/or feelings. Because people are believed to engage in conduct as a result of one or more of these internal conditions, the task of the scientist-practitioner is to find them and describe them. So if he believes that actions result from attitudes, he will focus on attitudes. If she assumes that organic drives cause behavior, she will focus on organic drives. If he believes that ideas determine action, he will relate the ideas of the actors to the behavior he observes. Sociologists look for societal rather than internal psychological causes of human behavior, causes lodged not in the individual but in the group to which the individual belongs. Norms, values or roles and status are often selected, for example, as the casual basis of behavior.

Many scientists-practitioners have not been able to account for behavior by using only one casual explanation, and some have tried to combine or synthesize different sets of determining conditions. One such effort has led to a synthesis of Marxian class doctrine with Freudian psychology. Another syntheses, effectively presented by the sociologist Talcott Parsons, views the human being as having an internal organization that is the result of the external social organization's becoming lodged inside of him. While there has been an increasing tendency to combine sociological with psychological perspectives, all of these efforts seem fruitless. The reason for this is that the nature of human group life has been viewed incorrectly. Human beings are participants in group life or are participants in social action. A human group consists of people who are acting; therefore, a society consists of people who are living. Most scientists do not start from the view that <u>action is the basis of human society</u>. Instead, they view the group as an established organization—a social culture, plus a whole series of guides and prescriptions called culture. Thus, in this view, the human group is based on a combination of social structure, plus a whole series of guides and prescriptions called culture. This view of social organization is the dominant concept in sociology today. It holds that society consists not of people acting, but instead of an organization inside which people act, which is responsible for their action. The social organization consists of the status hierarchy and of a collective possession and sharing of values and norms which are part of the culture. The status system, and the values and norms held in common by the group, have a casual influence on the behavior of the members of the group. As a consequence of holding this view, most scientists-practitioners have endeavored to understand the nature of culture and social structure.

This view of society is opposed to the social psychological concept of what is basically the nature of the human group. The society posited by the structural view is essentially frozen, because structures must be abstracted out of ongoing group activities. In reality, <u>the essence of society lies in action, in ongoing activity</u>. This is the basic assumption that underlies this work and the perspective of GET. Society is interaction because the action that goes on in group life is in fact interaction; therefore, human society consists of people engaged in interaction. The action of every separate person is part of a larger system in interaction, a collective action. In human interaction, the participants engage in a process of interpreting one another's activity, and the response of each person is made, not directly to what he perceives in the activity of the other, but to the meaning he attributes to the other's activity. Among human beings interpretation is often used to direct action. Responses are usually chosen based on reflective interpretation. Interpretation takes place between the action perceived by a person and the action the person takes in response. Interpretation allows for the development of differential responses; the response, instead of being dictated in advance by what is indicated or designated, can be built up in different directions as the person interprets and gives meaning to what is being indicated or to the gesture. Interaction between human beings, therefore, is a creative process and is not a simple matter of interstimulus and response. Participants in group action do not merely elicit from one another pre-established types of behavior which simply need to be released. Instead, they have to work out responses to the actions they perceive. Each person tries to figure out what the other's action signifies before he responds with his own actions. He is able to plan his response rather than just react. This perspective seems to be a richer view of human action which has been investigated and thought of from the sociological social psychological perspective that focuses on social interaction and the perceptions of situations by human beings in interaction. The perspective being established here is very significant because humans are social beings and nearly everything we do in our lives takes place in the company of others. Few of our activities are truly solitary. Consequently, studying the way we are able to interact with one another, and what happens when we do, should be one of the most fundamental concerns of clinicians who intervene in human problems of living.

With some degree of seriousness social scientists have demonstrated a special interest in the social aspect of human existence. Naturalistic and individualistic explanations have been two of the most resilient non-social approaches to human behavior. Rather than seeing social behavior as the product of interaction, these theories have concentrated on presumed qualities inherent in individuals. Naturalistic explanations suppose that all human behavior, including social interaction, is a product of inherent dispositions we possess as human animals. The essential notion is that, humans, like animals, are biologically programmed by nature. Individual explanations argue that human are individual and different. Consequently, explanations of human behavior must always rest ultimately on the particular and unique psychological qualities of individuals. Sociological explanations are in direct opposition to these kinds of approaches. Nonetheless, the study of the individual in society and society's influence on the individual is the focus of sociology and psychology. These two disciplines have differing definitions, levels of analysis, methodologies and theories of social psychology; yet there is some overlapping. The reason that GET expresses a sociological social psychological perspective is that there are great similarities and interchanges between the two viewpoints which strengthen and broaden the view of the behavior of individuals in group life. Our basic perspective is that human beings live group life. Further, both the microsocial processes, the events concerning individuals and groups of individuals; and the macrosocial processes, the events concerning larger groups, such as the political, economic and religious groups of society are the focus of inquiry and understanding.

According to Stephen & Stephen (1985), sociological social psychology has two different perspectives: symbolic interactionism and the personality and society perspective. The sociological definition of social psychology concerns itself with (1) social experiences stemming from the individual's participation in social groups; (2) interaction with others; (3) the effects of the cultural environment on both social experiences and interaction with others; and (4) the emergence of social structure from these interactions. The sociological social psychological view strongly promotes the notion that the individual and the social environment (setting) must be studied together. The self, meaning, socialization, small groups, language, roles; the relationship between individual characteristics such as attitudes, values, traits, properties of the self, etc., and the characteristics of the setting, society, or social situation must be assessed with a view to create a synthesis of information and knowledge. In other words, social interaction and the mutual influence and the social situation on the individual and the social situation must be the focus for discovery and intervention.

Because of the weaknesses in each discipline (Sociology and Psychology), combining the approaches offers the balance needed to view the individual and human behavior in a more complete context. There is much evidence of complementary information; they converge to present an understanding of human behavior that accounts for both individual behavior in its social context and group behavior. W.I. Thomas wrote several years ago that, "If men define situations as real, they are real in their consequences" (1923). The subjective world of the individual and the situation as perceived by the individual are the basis of the cognitive interpretations of reality and on subsequent behaviors based on these interpretations.

Conclusion

Because we argue in this work that the mental problems people face are primarily difficulties they are having in coping with stresses and everyday life or with the problems of living, we advance a social-psychological perspective. However, the definition is a sociological definition of social psychology rather than a psychological definition of social psychology. Over the years, we have identified distinguishing characteristics and different philosophical basis between psychology and sociology. On the one hand, one deals with the personal system, the other deals with the social system; one concerns itself with those determinants of behavior that arise from within the individual, and the other is concerned with the effects of the environment, or social settings on the individual; one looks at the behavior of people by means of studying them as individuals, and the other takes a look at behavior within the context of the society in situations which the individuals find themselves. There is a growing number of psychologists especially, community psychologists who believe that their subject should have more to say about person-to-societies and have become interested in utilizing more sociological and organizational concepts in their thinking.

The sociological definition is concerned with "social experiences stemming from individuals' participation in social groups; interactions with others; the effects of the cultural environment on the social experiences and interactions with others, and the emergence of social structure from these interactions"(Stephen & Stephen, 1985, p. 4). Clinical sociologists stress groups and group behaviors, rather than mere individuals and individual behaviors. Thus, social interactions are the primary focus along with the mutual influence of the society on the individual and the individual on the society. The individual and the social setting or the social situations must be studied together for clinical and intervention or application purposes.

All models of social thought and methods of discovery must, for clinical sociologists, have the potential for creating knowledge for direct utility. Doing this requires a scientific process where facts about the situation, and information about the activities, events, interactions, and relationships are determined and discovered. What is made of the data collected and the organizing of the data are crucial to the explanations or theories generated therefrom. Developing specific theoretical perspectives and establishing an understanding of what are the presenting and real problems set the stage for developing plans, strategies and schemes for application, intervention, and change. GET offers clinical sociologists the technique and process for creating theory for direct utility, or for therapeutic purposes. Clinical sociologists must come to understand that a good and effective practitioner is also a good scientist, and that the treatment of any problem of a social nature requires the creation and application of specific knowledge that is obtained from the clients and their social situation/setting which is the proper context of the real and apparent problems.

It is assumed by GET that theory and methods have essential relationships. This is the reason that GET argues that theory must be grounded in the social context of the clients, and that therapy must be grounded in the theories that emerged from the social context of the clients' problems and difficulties. This must be the process if the theory and therapy are to have direct utility. The relationship between theory and therapy eliminates the possible dysjuncture between the creation of knowledge and its application to the clients' problems. It allows for constant verification and validation of the explanations that emerge, and in turn the explanations suggest the methods most appropriate for intervention and treatment. The creation of data for organization and the invention of explanations, and the direction to and devising of methodological strategies appropriate to the task of discovery and application are also enhanced and facilitated by the relationship between theory and methodology. Those who do not understand this relationship are doomed to make grave mistakes in assisting clients in discovering, understanding and changing themselves and their situations. The process of GET assists clients in understanding their real problems, and helps them look for answers themselves. In this way, they are empowered to take control of their situations and their destinies.

References

Blau, Peter M.
  1967 <u>Exchange and Power in Social Life</u>. New York: Wiley

Stephen, Cookie White, and Walter G. Stephen
  1985 <u>Two Social Psychologies: An Integrative Approach.</u>
  Homewood, Illinois: The Dorsey Press.

Thomas, W.I
  1923 <u>The Unadjusted Girl.</u> New York: Little, Brown.

Theoretical Frames of Reference

Chapter 1

*   *   *

Theoretical Frames of Reference

Introduction

Social scientists use theories for explaining discovered data. Theories also stimulate discovery. The discovery process can begin with a hunch, and idea, or an existing theory, out of which hypotheses are formed or questions are raised. To test hypotheses, or answer questions, clients are observed and asked questions and data are collected. The discovered information is ultimately interpreted in terms of theory. Theories, therefore, are end products and serve also as the basis for future discovery. Sociology, as the scientific study of society and of human behavior in group life, provides a variety of theoretical orientations that serve as frames of references for viewing and understanding behavior and society.

Sociological theories are said to be deficient in some respects. The fundamental deficiency is how they reflect the images of human beings and the nature of human action (Blumer, 1969). The importance of the theoretical orientations discussed in this chapter is that all therapeutic approaches depict images of human beings and the nature of human behavior. The fact is that like the sociological perspective, the therapeutic approaches suffer from the same fundamental deficiency in how they view human behavior and the nature of human action.

Theories are explanations of group life and individual behavior in society. These theories are usually expressed as a set of propositions interrelated and consistent with each other with concepts that are definable, with the potential for verification and generalization. The therapist has to participate in the process of creating and developing

19

explanations and understanding. These explanations that are discovered in the process of social diagnosis have to be specific and particular to the problems and social context of the clients. At times there might be the need to invent explanations, and other times there might be the need simply to refine or reconstruct explanations already in existence. The activity of therapists of all varieties in this regard has more to do with refining and reconstructing existing explanations than with creating or inventing specific and particular explanations. What is ideal is for therapists to create and invent explanations that are informed by one or more theoretical orientations.

Because all therapeutic strategies have theoretical orientations, the use and application of theory is an important clinical posture. Many clinicians practicing today have not developed this posture in their work. Some believe that a theoretical posture is unnecessary because there are too many explanations or frames of reference that exist; and others argue that to embrace any particular frame of reference limits therapeutic intervention. It is evident that many therapists do not really understand the role of theory in understanding, explaining and treating human social problems.

Sociological Frames of Reference

There are five or six theoretical frames of reference that dominate sociological knowledge. Functionalism, conflict theory, symbolic inter-actionism, social exchange, phenomenology and ethnomethodology are contemporary perspectives of social reality that have their roots in classical perspectives of society and human social behavior. For example, Compte, Spencer and Durkheim laid the foundation for the functional perspective. They were concerned with the problem of maintaining social order and assuming harmony in society. Functionalism is evident in Durkheim's analysis of religion (Durkheim, E 1961). Because religion appeared to Durkheim to be a universal phenomenon, he argued that religion had some vital social functions among which is a system of values and rituals that serve to unite a community and maintain social solidarity. This theoretical perspective is grounded in the belief that society is a complex of interdependent and interrelated institutions which contribute to the social order and its stability.

The structural-functional frame of reference has been used to analysis family life-styles and the family as a system. Clinical sociologists who are conservative in their orientation will find this frame of reference helpful and suited to their theoretical taste. Those who embrace this perspective argue that this approach establishes a framework for looking at and understanding the relationship between and among individuals within the family and the influences and impact of other systems such as religion, education, etc., on the family as a social system. This frame of reference can be seen in the works of Malinowski (1939, 1945), and the gestalt position which focuses on the relation between a whole and its parts. In contemporary sociology, this perspective is represented in the works of Talcott Parsons (1951) and in Anthropology in the works of A. R. Radcliffee Brown (1952).

Functionalists, especially structural-functionalists stress the importance of studying the general setting of life without detaching it from any particular aspect of life. The same emphasis is made in the functional branch of psychology, especially the gestalt position which is an organized whole in which the parts are distinguishable but are interdependent. When structural-functionalists talk about the family as a social system, they are referring to the interdependence of the parts of the family in a definite pattern of organization, and the ways in which the social structure of the family, or more specifically, how its social units are arranged. Structural-functionalists describe and analyze a society, a subculture within the society, or a subsystem of the society in terms of the parts and their interrelationship and interdependency. Because each part acts and reacts upon each other, each part is seen in relationship to the whole. Both macro functional analysis (large scale system) and micro functional analysis (small scale system) are concerned with explaining the parts of the structure, the relationship between the parts of the structure and the structure as a whole. Further, the concern is with functions and results of the relationship established by the parts. The only distinction that is made is in the size (large or small) of the unit (system) selected for understanding, analysis and intervention.

Functionalism is grounded in the belief that society is a complex of interdependent and interrelated institutions which contribute to the social order and its stability. The primary focus of the theory is on social equilibrium, and the component elements of society are analyzed in relation to their functions in maintaining the social system. This theoretical approach has become very influential in sociological analysis, especially after its marriage with structuralism which argues that the social structure must be analyzed and viewed in terms of its functional contribution to the social cohesion of certain patterns of social relations. According to functional theorists, human beings tend to respond to the requirements of society, and in so doing they find their place in the social order and remain there; whatever change is experienced by the individual is prescribed by society. This view of human beings and society suggests that individuals are passive responders to society which is the active agent. What is permitted and possible is defined and determined by society, and individuals conform to societal expectations under pressures from the social order.

Functionalists see society as a (social) system balanced and with boundaries that are to be maintained if the system and its various parts are to be kept balanced. Functionalists tend to allow for slow alterations and see change in any element of the system affecting the other parts as well because all elements are interdependent and interrelated. The church, the family and the school are examples of the various parts of the social system that function in an interrelated manner to keep the social order functional. For functionalists a function is determined by the system and influences the system of which it is a part in a positive manner. In this way, the function of the system also helps to determine the nature and character of the system. In other words, functions perpetuate social systems that determine human social behavior.

Talcott Parsons developed the concept of social system to emphasize the functional imperatives for the maintenance of social systems (1952). He identified four imperatives or prerequisites which are necessary for maintaining social systems. Nations, communities, families, schools, etc., must have an adaptive imperative, a goal attainment imperative, an integrative imperative, and a latent pattern maintenance and tension management imperative (1951). Adaptation has to do with the system's ability to adapt to its environment-social and non-social—which impacts the system and in turn the system impacts the environment. The goal attainment imperative functions to satisfy individual and collective needs by bringing together and allocating social roles and scarce resources. The harmonization of the various structures and their interrelated activities, goals, values, and norms is the function of the integrative imperative, and the latent pattern maintenance and tension management imperative entails learning about the values, goals, and social roles of the system and the means for their attainment and motivational support. Functionalists see the family, schools, the police, the courts and other social control agents carrying out this function. In the Parsonsian scheme, and equilibrium state of the social system is achieved when taken as a whole, the structures are integrated and harmony is experienced with each other. For Parsons, the single most important imperative is the adaptation function.

Robert K. Merton (1936), another key structural-functionalist, places emphasis on the consequences of given social practices of the social system. He is more concerned with explaining how certain social practices such as punishment, division of labor, etc., help to sustain the social order or the system. Merton emphasizes the latent functions of social practices—those practices that individuals do not recognize the functions, or do not intend the social consequence of their behavior. He argues that there are unanticipated consequences which occur when people behave, especially in an attempt to change the social system (1936).

Merton extends his functional analysis to suggests that all systems have both functional and dysfunctional aspects. While the majority of the parts or elements are functional which perform a positive service and help maintain a balanced state in the system, there are those dysfunctional elements that are negative and have negative effects. Is crime dysfunctional to society? It is dangerous, damaging and threatening to the system. However, Durkheim argued that crime is functional to society in that it strengthens the moral order by bringing attention to the significance and importance of the laws. Merton also makes a distinction between manifest functions and latent functions. His argument is that the social usefulness of some elements or events is not always obvious. The latent functions represent those social purposes served unknowingly and unconsciously by the participants of certain actions. The manifest functions are those that produce social consequences that are intended and expected (1956). In pointing out that a system could have dysfunctional aspects, Merton dissociates himself from Parsons who believed that all existing institutions are functional for society.

For functionalists, explanations of human behavior are based on the operations of the social system. Social behavior is viewed and analyzed from the standpoint of social structure. They perceive structural elements of the social system as elements of a model of social reality that characterize society, and to this extent is a model of objective reality. The assumption that there is an objective reality is imperative to the concept of society as a social system, because structural functionalists believe that the structure of society exist independently of the social processes occurring within the structure, and that the elements of the model of objective reality reside outside the human interpretative process which characterizes the structure of society. The basis for explaining social behavior and understanding social action is to observe, describe and theorize about the structure of society and the regularities of the structural characteristics of the system within which social actions occur.

Critics have argued that this approach to theorizing is conservative because it is concerned with system maintenance. Other critics have argued that the structural-functional approach tends to promote a model of human social action akin to that of the stimulus-response model in psychology. Another criticism of the approach is the disequilibrium in society can be functional rather than dysfunctional, and that a practice that is functional for social equilibrium in society might be dysfunctional for some groups of the society (McGree, 1980).

Social Conflict Orientation

There are those who see no real difference in the conflict frame of reference and the structural-functional perspective (Coser, 1967). Yet, there are others who share the view that the frames of reference are quite different (Dahrendrof, 1958, 1968). It might also be argued that the conflict perspective is the flipside of the structural-functional perspective. We will discuss the conflict frame of reference from the view that it is an entirely separate theoretical orientation. The basic position is that conflict is natural and expected in human interaction and in social system: Functionalists view conflict as bad, disruptive, and strongly stress equilibrium, system maintenance, order and control, and balance. The conflict orientation promotes managing and resolving conflict rather than avoiding or treating it as negative. Conflict, if faced, and managed can be the basis for improvements in the interaction, increased strength in the social system and more satisfying, meaningful, and rewarding experiences may be derived.

Conflict theory is grounded in the works of Karl Marx (1964) who argued that the private ownership of property in particular, and economic organization in general, create class conflict (Mills, 1948; Dahrendrof, 1959). When applied to the family, the conflict orientation views the husband as the bourgeois and the wife as the proletariat. However, the context for clarity of this position is the capitalist society in which the family is defined as a basic unit which is thought to be the main source of female oppression (Engles, 1902.) The conflict frame of reference views mothers, wives, and females as persons oppressed in the family system by husbands, males, and fathers who dominate them in family relations. It is argued that when the oppressed in the family becomes aware of their dominated condition, they will take collective action to achieve change and a redistribution of power, money, and other resources that would equalize the relationship. Conflict, therefore, which is inevitable in family relations and interpersonal interactions, results in change in decision making, economic and financial matters, marital adjustment and other issues in marital and family relations.

Two varieties of conflict theorizing can be identified in the worker of Georg Simmel and Karl Marx (Turner, 1957), and in the works of contemporary theorists, Ralf Dahrendorf and Lewis A. Caser (Turner, 1957). Conflict theorizing places emphasis on open struggle between individuals, groups, communities, families, cities, nations, etc., over values, meanings, property, income, wages, power and the like. Social conflict exists when there is disagreement, discontent, and fighting over issues and concerns that are important and significant to the people involved. In the presence of social conflict, harmony, consensus and the equilibrium functionalists are concerned with is threatened or absent. Marx argued that conflict is inevitable in society. He suggests that the various groups are polarized around their conflicting interests. The primary groups that are in conflict in capitalists societies are the dominant and the dominated or subjugated. The dominant group attempts to maintain the social order and the subjugated attempts to bring about structural changes in the arrangements of the system and in the redistribution of resources.

We can view social conflict as opposition in human social life. There is much confusion regarding the nature and character of this opposition, which has influenced the definition of social reality. Many sociologists do not see conflict as the basis of all human social arrangements, although they have brought some attention to the nature and function of social conflict in social life (Coser, 1956; Dahrendorf, 1958). In their attempt to focus on the integrative nature of social conflict, they have come to appear as functionalist in their analysis. Conflict is seen as having functional value to society because of its potential to bring society together and establish social solidarity. Continuing contest between groups and individuals over scarce resources, rewards, and power makes possible stability in the social order and in relationships. In other words, these conflict functionalists view social conflict as struggle and competition—as a mechanism to ensure social progress and the assurance that the fittest individuals in society survive.

The subordinates are subordinated out of a necessity to promote and secure societal needs. In another sense Georg Simmel argued that there are occasional conflicts, as in the case of marriages and families, where conflict serves the purposes of the release of tension, and makes possible harmony for collective sharing and bearing of difficulties. In such an event, the marriage or the family continues. In the case of an external opponent, conflict serves to bring groups together and allows for the closing of ranks among groups in society against outside opponents. So there are conflict theorists who emphasize the value of conflict to the maintenance and progress of the social order. What should become evident to students as they compare functional and conflict theorizing is that they place emphasis on social organization and its forces that determine and impact the social life of individuals, groups, communities and societies.

Symbolic Interaction Orientation

The emphasis on social organization and its forces that determine the fate of groups, communities, etc., is not the viewpoint of symbolic interactionalism. Increasingly, many sociologists are looking at the issue of the person-in-situations and, the formation and development of the self. William James, George Herbert Mead, and Charles Horton Cooley are the intellectuals who set the theoretical ground work in these matters. These men argued that the human self has the potential of being an object to itself. The attitude one develops toward oneself is largely dependent on the way others react and act toward him/her. Cooley developed the notion of the "looking-glass" self to explain the socialization of infants who interact with others who provide meaning of the infants' selves through their responses to them. This process entails preverbal and nonverbal gestures and social signs and symbols. Both Cooley and Mead pointed out that the self is socially defined in terms of social symbols which are committed to the infants to their acts, and gestures which are taken by them to represent what their selves should be.

Three basic elements of the self have been identified by Cooley (1970). The first he notes is the individual's understanding or imagination what his/her appearance is to other people; the

27

understanding of the judgments others will make of the apparent self, and the individual's response to these understandings and judgments. As the individual interacts with significant others in his/her social world, the socially derived symbolic meanings of the self become the determinant of the individual's actions. The theoretical position of symbolic interaction is that social interaction between individuals is reciprocal expectations of each other's behavior that are symbolically defined and constitutes the basis of social life. In other words, symbolic interaction is the process of interaction between individuals conducted at the symbolic level.

Mead emphasized the role of society in shaping the individual's sense of self suggesting that human beings are fully human through the interaction between themselves and society. Mead placed great emphasis on language and the role of language in the process of socialization. As the child interacts with others (the particular others, such as parents, and the generalized others) through play and later symbolically, he/she internalizes social attitudes and achieves a fully human mind. The development of the mind, therefore, is a social process.

It was Herbet Blumer who labeled the two basic forms of human interaction as symbolic and non-symbolic. Mead identified the first as the use of the significant symbol, and the second as the conversation of gestures (Blumer, 1969). In symbolic interaction the participants engage in a process of interpreting one another's activity. The response of each other is made, not directly to what he/she perceives in the activity of the other, but to the meaning he/she attributes to the other's activity. In non-symbolic action the participants respond to one another's activity directly and unreflectively. Their responses are in the nature of immediate reactions to the actions of the other, as these actions are perceived. When the response is chosen on the basis of reflective interpretation, symbolic interaction is taking place. Interpretation on a symbolic level takes place between the action perceived by a person and the action the person takes in response.

Interpretation allows for the development of differential responses; the response, instead of being dictated in advance by the gesture, can be built up in different directions as the person interprets and gives meaning to the gesture. Interaction between human beings is therefore not a simple matter of interstimulus and response, but is a creative process. Participants in group action do not merely elicit from one another pre-established types of behavior which simply need to be released. Instead, they have to work out responses to the action they perceive. Each person tries to figure out what the other's action signifies before he/she responds with his/her own action. He/she is able to plan his/her response rather than just react.

Symbolic interactionists view society as consisting of people engaged in interaction. All of the action of each individual takes place in a context of interaction. Interaction is a presentation of action which at the same time is a request for a reaction. Orderly social interaction takes place when the different lives of activity of the different actors mesh smoothly. Symbolic interactionists argue that the most important interaction takes place on the symbolic level, primarily by means of gesture. A gesture is part of an action which stands for the rest of the action for what is to come. Both words and movements are gestures. Gestures are basic to interaction, because people respond to what they expect others to do, as well as to what others have already done. Three identifiable parts of symbolic interaction are noted: 1) the designation or indication in the form of an act or gesture; 2) the interpretation of the designation; and 3) the devising of a response on the basis of the interpretation.

By definition, a gesture always implies two things: 1) it implies what will be the remainder of the action of the person who makes it, and is in this sense a prelude to further action; 2) it implies that there will be a particular response to it by the person to whom it was made. Because by this definition a gesture cannot take place in the absence of another person, it is intrinsically joint action. Another point which is essential to symbolic interaction theory is the matter of role taking. It is argued that in order for participants in interaction to fit their actions together, they must understand the meaning of one another's gestures, and must interpret the gestures similarly. The whole process of interaction depends upon the ability of the human being to take the role of another, or to take that other person's point of view. The actor making the designation must be able to see himself in the position of the person who responds, so that he/she will get the response he/she is asking for. To the extent to which people fail to put themselves in the place of others, interaction breaks down. Communication, in symbolic interaction terms, is the ability of people to take one another's roles and in this way to understand what others are thinking and planning to do.

Symbolic interaction is a social-psychological frame of reference with the particular focus on socialization and the development of the self. The process by which the individual internalizes the values, norms, patterns of behavior and ways of viewing things, and how the individual obtains a self are of primary concern to symbolic interactionists. Human beings are viewed as having the ability to create symbols, assign meaning, define their situation, interpret theirs and others behavior, and select and devise alternative modes of response. Symbolic interactionism promotes observable action as significant to the process of understanding and knowing. Therefore, this frame of reference embodies both a theoretical perspective and methodological orientation. In obtaining a sense of what is happening in the world of reality, such techniques as interviews, direct observation, listening to the views of others, using letters and diaries, securing accounts of life histories, consulting public records, and conducting group discussions for ascertaining subjective meanings are used. It is important to this theoretical perspective that we ascertain the meanings for the actions of others by noting the symbols and appropriately interpreting the gestures in interaction among and between socialized human beings.

In an attempt to understand marriages and families, we must do so within the context of the social setting or situation and the society in which they exist. The problems, the conversations, the definitions given to situations, the gestures and interaction, the relationships, or the nature of the marital and family arrangements are appropriately understood within a social context. Therefore, it is important to know the symbols and shared meanings that dominate the interaction and activities of individuals in relationships. The frame of reference promotes the view that human beings can do much more than simply respond to objective stimuli. Human beings can take note of, interpret, take the role of the other, assign meaning to, and select a response in the process of interaction. The interactionist framework views the family as a unit of interacting selves in the process of fitting their action to the action of others (Burgess, 1926; Turner, 1970; Styker, 1972; Burr et.al., 1979; Blumer, 1969).

Social Exchange Orientation

Social exchange takes place on a daily basis between human beings. Many exchanges are taken for granted, including economic and social, because they are institutionalized. In the majority of cases economic exchanges are predetermined, and in many social matters exchanges are uncertain relative to the return. In both areas, however, reciprocity is expected and realized. Social exchange, as a theoretical orientation, attempts to explain why certain behavioral outcomes occur given a set of structural conditions and interactional capabilities and potentialities.

Two different perspectives on social exchange are presented by George C. Homans (1958, 1961) and Peter M. Blau (1964). Homans position is that human social behavior is based on exchange. In other words, people relate to each other on the basis of what each person expects to gain from the other. Relationships in the social world seem to be dominated by the principle that giving is done in anticipation of what is expected in return. Several studies have used this perspective to indicate that social behavior is based on exchange or a reciprocity of services that individuals provide to one another (Gouldner, 1974). Reading carefully the works of Homans, it becomes evident that his focus is on small groups while the concern of Blau is with social institutions.

Blau points out that social exchange is based on emergent properties in interpersonal relations and social relations which are relationships between elements in a social structure. The action of each person depends upon those of the other. Therefore, social relations are the joint product of the actions of interacting individuals. When a service is rendered, the exchange situation starts,

31

and expressed gratitude is the expected response of the recipient which is interpreted by the person rendering the service as a reward. The extension of additional services is contingent upon the reward, and in the process of this exchange a social bond is established. In the event that no reward is expressed the interaction is terminated. Characteristic of most social interaction which leads to social exchange is the focus on ends of goals that can be achieved through interaction and the search for means to achieve those goals.

Blau differs significantly with Homans in that Blau argues that not all exchange can be explained in terms of actual behavior. Exchange can also be subjective and interpretive. In this sense Blau shares the symbolic interactionist perspective which sees interaction as a creative process between actors not within individuals or in external forces. Social exchange theorists argue that the best way to understand human social behavior is to view it as an exchange which is a process of selection on the part of the participants based upon an examination of the cost, risks, and rewards of alternative courses of action. Homans admits to the influence of experimental psychology on his work. He states, "We believe that the propositions of behavioral psychology are the general explanatory propositions of all social sciences" (1961, 1967). Consequently, Homans attempts to explain social interaction in terms of the behavioristic learning theory. He argues "that every human action is determined by its relative profitability to the actor: the actor seeks to increase his rewards and decrease his cost in his interaction with other actors. It is the differences between rewards and costs that constitute the profit to any actor of his social action: Profits = Rewards—Costs" (Douglas, 1973, 1974). Homans saw power in psychological explanations of human behavior and argued that the universal motive that causes society to function was the self interest of individuals. People modify their behavior in terms of the reinforcement (negative or positive) provided by their environment. For Homans, individuals interacting and exchanging rewards and punishment constitute the social world. Approval, esteem, love, affection plus materialistic tokens are considered incentives to action and social exchange. The performance of an activity is based upon the perceived value of the reward.

The exchange perspective does not only promote the notion that if you scratch my back, I'll scratch yours, or the formula of give a little and take a little, it also suggests that giving is established or continued also on the basis that failure to do so will cause the termination of services being rendered. This argument strengthens the notion that giving is done in anticipation of what will be given in return or for what services are already being rendered. The assumptions that are made in social exchange theory are:

> Most gratifications of humans have their source in the actions of other humans (spouse, children, friends, colleagues, fellow workers).
>
> New associations are entered into because they are expected to be rewarding and old associations continue because they are rewarding.
>
> As we receive rewards or benefit from others, we're under an obligation to reciprocate by supplying benefits to them in return.
>
> In general, giving is more blessed than receiving, because having social credit is preferable to being socially indebted (Wallace & Wolf, 1980: 16).

These assumptions underline and establish the basis for the social exchange perspective.

Phenomenological and Ethnomethodlogical Orientations

Phenomenology as a theoretical perspective is establishing itself among sociologists who are coming to recognize that social meanings are the essential determinants of social action. Phenomenologists view meanings as being complex and problematic to understand if they are not determined and examined in everyday life situations. Because phenomenology starts with the individual and his/her own conscious experience avoiding prior assumptions, it is held that it has a philosophical impact on sociology. It seeks to examine phenomena as they are perceived or as they are recognized in their immediacy by social actors.

According to the phenomenological theory, individuals create and define society. They provide a context that establishes in their mind a sharing of the social order. The task of sociology is to determine and examine the process by which and how individuals as social actors create society and the social order. Phenomenologists assume the position of the individual in the process or take the point of view of the social actor in an attempt to understand the process by temporarily changing the individual's perceptions of social reality.

The field of phenomenological sociology has been influenced by Alfred Schutz (1899-1959); Edmund Husserl (1859-1938), and Max Weber. However, the recent work of Peter Berger and Thomas Luckmann has made a modern contribution by suggesting that as people go about their everyday tasks social reality is created (Berger and Luckmann, 1967). In other words, the essential premise of their work is that "reality is socially constructed and the sociology of knowledge must analyze the process in which this occurs." Knowledge, for Berger and Luckmann is derived from the structure of the common sense world of everyday life as well as from ideology and theorizing.

It is through the process of socialization that people come to accept everyday reality and legitimated institutions. Phenomenologists argue that normal everyday acts become so habitualized and accepted that no one ever or rarely thinks to question them. In their attempt to emphasize the subjective nature of the human experience of reality, phenomenologists argue that society and social reality do not exist as individuals create them and offer definitions agreed upon of what they have created. A serious question for students is: Does society exist except as individuals subjectively imagine it? In everyday life reality is shared with persons in face-to-face interaction. Situations and acts become so routine that they are taken for granted reality. People accept the social order they create and the set of institutions that are defined by interacting individuals, become society. In this sense, phenomenologists sound much like structural-functionalists who link human conduct to institutions and social systems theory, especially how they view institutions as having control over human behavior. For phenomenologists, institutions have a validity and objective reality that are independent of human consciousness, yet they are products of human consciousness in a phenomenological sense.

Phenomenologists argue that the purpose of society is to determine how society, the social order or the social world is created and maintained by human beings. A way they propose to do this is to examine interaction situations in everyday life. Many people view ethnomethodology as a branch of phenomenology which attempts to provide the sociological method for studies of how human beings acting in society create and understand the basis for their action.

Harold Garfinkel is credited with coining the term to refer to the methods of studying the everyday living practices of people in society (Garfinkel, 1967). The emphasis in this method is on the meanings as understood by the social actors themselves. The attempt of the ethnomethodologist is to get inside of the social actor's own frame of reference to understand how he/she in a situation actually makes decisions and carries out courses of action. Ethnomethodology holds that sociology should be primarily concerned with the study of what people take to be everyday reality. Further, "Ethnomethodological studies suggest that when there is no appropriate common sense solution and the social actor has no comparable previous experience to draw on, he will become suggestible, acceding to whatever source provide guidance that seems to provide a way out that will be judged socially correct by others who may be observing. The main concern of social actors seems to be finding a solution that will not make them appear to have lost control of the situation or to have failed to do what most people would judge "right" under the circumstances" (Frank, 1967).

Ethnomethodology has forced sociologists to "examine the extent to which they impose a view of social reality on the rather than endeavoring to understand the often strange and illogical ways in which social actors actually act" (Frank, 1967). Ethnomethodologists use the technique of surprise interruption, disturbance of the routine flow of social life and contrast what happened before and after the interruption. Examples of experiments are responding truthfully to a cashier who asks "how are you doing?" or, pausing at a table of a stranger in a restaurant and taking a sip from his drink. The reaction these actions receive exposes the rules for "normal" behavior. Phenomenologists believe the social order takes for granted the reality of everyday life and its social meanings. This natural stance toward everyday life to which sociologists seek to apply sociology is labeled by David Matza as naturalistic sociology (Matza, 1969). Those sociologists who reject this stance argue that it relegates sociology to a common sense form of thinking. If phenomenology is to be theoretical, or offer explanations of everyday social life, it must take a theoretic stance which requires the sociologists to describe, analyze and objectively observe the experiences of social actors to convert into scientific data for purposes of constructing, generating and testing scientific theories about everyday life. In other words, phenomenology sociologists must analyze the fundamental properties of everyday life from a theoretical and scientific perspective which differs from the common sense stance.

Berger and Luckmann see the construction of plausible and rational meanings in everyday life by social actors as basic, and suggest that this common sense knowledge is the foundation of the everyday life of individuals. According to Berger and Luckmann (1967): "The world of everyday life is not only taken for granted as reality by the ordinary members of society in the objectively meaningful conduct of their lives. It is a world that originates in their thoughts and action, and is maintained as real by them." The ways in which sociologists investigate ways members of society construct for each other rational and fundamental properties of the everyday lives are the concerns of the ethnomethodologists (Garfinkel, 1967).

Theoretical Summary

There are a number of theoretical approaches used in the study of the family. There is an increasing interdisciplinary development in the field of marriage and the family even though in the social sciences, sociology seems closer in theoretical orientation and content focus. Since the middle of the 20th century, findings of earlier studies have been summarized, social research methodology had been refined, and theory building has been of primary concern. The frames of reference that are briefly presented here constitute the dominating contemporary theoretical orientations in sociology. All of the frames of reference permit the viewing of human behavior and society in a certain way. They all provide propositions that are logically and systematically interrelated to explain human behavior in group life.

Structural-functional frame of reference shows the social system as the basic autonomous unit and the family as a subsystem of the social system. All systems and subsystems have interdependent and interrelated parts of structures that have certain social consequences or functions for the individual and/or society. Structural-functional analysis seeks to explain the structures (parts) and the relationship between the parts and the system or subsystems as a whole. Further, it seeks to explain the functions that result from the relationship established or formed by the parts. Social conflict frame of reference has been given much attention over the years. A growing number of social scientists have come to accept the notion that conflict is natural and inevitable and is a major factor that can lead to social change. Many who are specialists in marital and family relations are applying this frame of reference to an understanding of these relationships. The process of socialization and the development and formation of the self are the major concerns of symbolic interaction frame of reference. The essential notion in this perspective is that human beings act toward objects on the basis of the meaning the objects, including the self, have for them which come through interaction and modified through interpretation. This means then, that human beings are social beings and must be understood in social context.

Social exchange, as a frame of reference, provides an understanding of why certain behavioral outcomes occur providing certain sets of structural conditions and interactional potentialities occur. There is a behavioral frame of reference and an interactionist frame of reference within the broad frame of reference of social exchange. However, they both subscribe to the essential premise that all contacts among men rest on the scheme of giving and returning the equivalence. This concept suggest that, for the most part, people's interactions and behavior toward one another are best understood and analyzed as an exchange of goods and services based on the assessments of the cost and rewards of alternative courses of action.

References

Blau, Peter
   1964 Exchange and Power in Social Life. New York: Wiley.

Blumer, Herbert
   1969 Symbolic Interactionism: Perspective and Method. Berkeley:
   University of California Press.

Burgess, Ernest W.
   1925 "The Growth of the City." In R. E. Park and E. W. Burgess,
   eds. The City. Chicago: University of Chicago Press, pp. 47-62.

Durkheim, Emile
   1951 Suicide. Glencoe: Free Press.

Coser, Lewis
   1956 The Future of Social Conflict. Glencoe: Free Press.

Colley, Charles Horton
   1964 Human Nature of the Social Order. New York: Shocken
   Books.

Dahrendrof, Ralf.
   1959 "Out of Utopia," American Journal of Sociology, vol. 64
   (Spetmeber): 115-127.

Douglas, J. D.
   1968 The Social Meaning of Suicide. Princeton, NJ: Princeton
   University Press.

Engles, Friedrich
   1942 The Origin of the Family, Private Property of the State.
   New York: International Publishers.

Frank, Andre Gunder
1967 <u>Capitalism and Underdevelopment in Latin America</u>. New York: Monthly Review Press.

Garfinkel, Harold
1967 <u>Studies in Ethnomethodology</u>. Englewood Cliff, New Jersey: Prentice Hall

Gouldner, Alvin W.
1970 <u>The Coming Crisis of Western Sociology</u>. New York: Basic Books.

Homans, George Casper
1961 Social Behavior: In Elementary Form. New York: Harcourt Bruce & World.

Hussel, Edmund
1961 <u>Ideas; General Introduction to Pure Phenomenolgy</u>. The Hague, Netherlands: N. Nighoff.

Matza, David
1969 <u>Becoming Deviant</u>. Englewood Cliff, New Jersey: Prentice-Hall.

Marx, Karl
1967 <u>Capital, Vol. 1</u>. Translated by S. More and E. Aveling. New York: International.
1959 <u>Class and Class Conflict in Industrial Society</u>. Stanford, California: Stanford University

Maliniwski, Baonislaw
1944 <u>The Scientific Theory of Culture</u>. Chapel Hill, North Carolina: University of North Carolina Press.

Merton, Robert K.
1957 <u>Social Theory and Social Structure</u>. Glencoe: Free Press.

Mills, C.W.
1959 The Sociological Imagination. New York: Oxford University Press.

McGrace, T. G.
"The Persistence of the Proto-Proletariat: Occupational Structures and Planning of the Future of Third World Cities." In Third World Urbanization. J. Abu-Lughard and R. Hay, Jr.; eds. Chicago: Maasofa Press.

Parsons, Talcott
1951 The Social System. New York: The Free Press.

Radcliffe, Brown
1965 Structure and Function in Primitive Society. New York: The Free Press.

Styker, Sheldon
1980 Symbolic Interaction. A Social Structural Version. Mento Park, CA: Benjamin Cummings.

Turner, Jonathan H.
1979 Functionalism. Mento Park, CA: Benjamin Cummings.

Weber, Max
1949 The Methodology of the Social Science. Glencoe: Free Press.

Human Interaction, the Self and Personal Relationships

Chapter 2

*   *   *

Human Interaction, the Self and Personal Relationships

The Nature of Human Interaction

In order for us to understand contemporary relationships, we have to understand the nature of human interaction and the concept of the self. Because we have accepted the notion that we interact with others on the basis of our concept of others (especially significant others) concept of us, we have failed to realize that human beings have the ability to indicate to others how they want others to see them, thus having the ability to interact with others on the basis of their concept of themselves. Moreover, implicit in the nature of human interaction is the ability of the individual to assume as many selves as there are others. Consequently, I can interact with each of you on the basis of how I want each of you to see me, and each of you can interact with me on the basis of how you see me, or your concept of me, or how you want me to see you. All of this is possible because human beings live group life. Because human group life consists of human beings interacting together, they must of necessity fit their actions to the actions of each other in relationships. This perspective is important since it is the very nature of relationships that the individuals are embedded in a social situation or setting created by the action of each other.

Consequently, establishing joint action in relating or interaction is imperative in growing, developing, satisfying, functioning relationships. Joint action is fitting of the lines of action together which is the context for understanding patterns of interaction, conflicts, and relationships between human beings. Because the action that goes on in contemporary relationships is in fact interaction, contemporary relationships consist of individuals engaged in interaction. The action of each person is part of a larger system of interaction, a collective action. Contemporary relationships therefore are embedded in a social setting created by their collective action. Interaction in this setting is a presentation of action, which at the same time is a request for a reaction. Orderly social interaction in contemporary relationships takes place when the different lines of activity of the different individuals mesh smoothly. Most professionals ignore the process of human interaction itself. They tend to focus merely on causes which precede interaction and view social interaction as an area in which these causes of human action work themselves out. The process of interaction operates in its own right to lead to the formation of behavior; in the process, participants interpret one another's acts and formulate their own actions on the basis of the meaning they derive from the interpretation. In order for individuals to fit their action together, they must take each other's roles and understand the indications designated by each other and have relatively common interpretations and share similar meanings of objects in their social world, including themselves as objects (Blumer, 1969).

Communication, therefore, between human beings is the ability of each to take one another's roles and in this way understand the behavior of each other. This process enhances joint action. We can conclude then, that contemporary human relationships are not simply an aggregation of separate organisms acting independently. The actions of an individual member in relationships are necessarily connected with the actions of the other member or members in the relationships. Every act must be adapted to the actions of other persons involved in the act. The essence or bottom line of relationships is that the individual, as she constructs her act, must take into account the behavior of the other member or members who are implicated in the act. Contemporary human relationships must be viewed as an ongoing process in which all the members take one another into account, and fit their lines of action together. A breakdown is experienced in relationships when the contrary takes place. What is also significant to this theoretical perspective for understanding and intervening in contemporary human relationships is the concept of the self and its significance in the process of human interaction. I realize that we have been hooked on the "looking glass" concept as we have been on the S-R concept, but we have to go beyond the looking glass self concept to fully understand human relationships.

The Concept of the Self

Human beings are capable of making objects of themselves and can deal with themselves as with any other objects. Moreover, every person sees himself as a certain kind of object, defines himself in a certain way and handles himself on the basis of his self definition. The meaning of all objects are based upon the ways people act toward the objects. Accordingly, the object a person makes of himself is based upon his perception of the ways others act toward him. Consequently, the meaning of all objects is socially derived. A person can see himself by taking someone else's role and looking at himself from outside himself, from the point of view of the other. In Freudian theory the roles of father and mother are crucial in a child's development. Freudian theory presupposes that a child takes the roles of his parents, and formulates his self conceptions from the viewpoints of those roles. However, a child engages in many diverse associations and identifications. Life and the advent of television have greatly increased the variety and scope of the roles a child can learn to assume. A child, therefore, takes many roles during the course of his development, and the cumulative effect on his self definition of his taking all these roles far transcends the effect of his taking the special roles of his father and mother. There are many influences on the development of the self conception of a child and it is not logical to assign as much importance to contrary theories.

The formation of a stable and secure identity, or self definition, is more difficult today than it was in the past. It is almost a truism that today adolescents and young adults have a difficult time "finding themselves." To search for identity means to be unsure what kind of an object one is. A person is a different object from the viewpoint of each position or role from which he looks at himself. In recent years the number and variety of roles from which young people can view themselves have increased. Young people, therefore, might find it difficult to select particular viewpoints from which to make stable and secure objects of themselves. People act toward objects on the basis of the meanings the objects have for them. Hence, a person's actions can be based, in part, on the kind of object he is to himself. Because a person is an object to himself, he is able to act toward himself and to interact with himself. This means that he can make gestures, or indications and so on.

A common example of self interaction is carrying on a conversation with oneself. Another example is memory, which is not merely a resurgence of images into the consciousness but a process of pointing out images to oneself. A person can interact with himself without making overt indications, and he can therefore create a private world. There is a tendency in social science to differentiate between the private world of the mind and the outer world of social interaction. But self interaction and social interaction are essentially the same process; the fundamental difference between them is that the private world of the mind is not open to observation from the outside. Self interaction is an important means by which a person controls his actions in the external world. He confronts the world on the basis of his ability to make indications to himself: the only things in his environment he can deal with and those he can point out to himself. People act on the basis of what they define the meanings of those objects to be. People act not only on the basis of how they define objects in their environments, but also on the basis of how they define themselves as objects.

The kind of object a person makes of himself depends on roles he takes in looking at himself. A person defines his self conception by taking the roles of other people and groups and looking at himself from the point of view of these roles. The role of the social group is also a very important perspective from which the person defines his self conception. The individual takes the roles of individuals, groups

46

such as teams, and these roles also influence his self conception, particularly in the earliest stages of his development. Later, however, there seems to be a point of independence.

Problems of the self are related to the object a person has made of himself. For example, a person can be dissatisfied with himself because he sees himself as two objects, the object he is and the object he ought to be; the person gets into this situation by defining himself from the perspectives of two incompatible roles. There are today so many diverse and conflicting roles that a person takes in order to define himself might not be fully compatible with one another. If they are not, the person will make inconsistent and conflicting objects of himself, and will be uncertain of his real identity. He may feel a sense of purposelessness or a sense of being lost. His quest for identity will consist essentially of efforts to arrive at a stable and consistent definition of himself as an object. The person can resolve personal problems such as the search for identity only by working through the process by which the self is formed. The roles a person takes in making an object of himself are not necessarily conventionalized roles (Shibutani, 1968). A person can create a unique generalized other from the social milieu and define himself from this unique perspective. Not all soldiers, college professors, nurses, and therapists see themselves in the same ways most of the members of their respective professions see themselves. Most people do adopt conventional roles, but it is possible for the self to address and guide itself in unusual ways.

Because a person can be an object to himself, he can engage in interaction with himself. A person's life is a continuing process in which he makes indications to himself, and so on. The human being is different from all other organisms because he is able to "stand over against" his environment. He can approach and handle both his environment and himself through the process of self interaction; he needs simply to respond to casual forces in his environment. Because a person can point out objects to himself, he can handle, inspect and deal with them, and take them into account in building up his conduct. People's actions are meaningful to the extent that they construct their actions with regards to the subjects in their environment. Human consciousness consists of people's making indications to themselves, that is, pointing objects out to themselves.

To have a self is to be able to make an object of oneself. To have a self, an individual must be able to interact with himself. This means that a person who has a self can see himself, or communicate with himself, as if he were an object outside himself. The self can stand outside of itself, look at itself, and address itself as an entity. A person can say to herself, "I don't feel well today," "I have a good future ahead," or "I'd better stop smoking or I'm a dead duck." The implication of this view is that if a person is aware of himself as an object, and other objects in his social world, he does not simply respond to them. He defines the objects, and in the process can delay his action; during the delay he can construct, or think through the action he will take. The person therefore can stand over against an object and make a choice among the possible responses (Blumer, 1969).

This also means that one does not exist as a self only by approaching himself from outside himself. One can also interact with himself on the basis of his concept of himself. The correct image the person holds of herself is the view she holds of her total self. Because the individual is capable of making herself an object, she can interact with herself and seek to develop certain properties of the image content through collective action, especially within the context of the human relationships which enhance the interaction with other persons in her social world. As I have indicated, human beings are capable of interacting with others both on the basis of their perceptions of others' perceptions of them, and on the basis of their perceptions of themselves. The latter point speaks to the independence one can exercise after a certain point in the process of socialization when the individual controls what is taken into account and what is internalized during interaction. This is also the point at which individuals seek to control the definition of themselves by developing a behavioral style to convey what they judge to be a true image of themselves, or the property of image they want others to interact with in the process of developing that part of their image content.

Properties of the Self and Style of Conveyance

The self consists of a number of properties which constitute the content of the image of the individual. These properties interact and are associated in such a way that makes a whole. The individual knows or can know her total image content and others know and see certain properties of the image content through interaction. Very rarely, if at all, does another know the total image content of the other. Because the individual interacts with a variety of persons, she alone gets to know or is in a position to know, as a result of having to bring certain or all of the properties into play, the full range of her image content. On the other hand, those she interacts with get to know only those properties which are necessary to be employed during the periods of interaction. This means that the individual can control how she is perceived by others and interact with the others on the basis of how she sees herself, or how she wants others to see her, rather than to continue to interact with others on the basis of how they see her or what she thinks they think of her. This is possible because the image has a variety of properties.

Properties of the image are at various stages of development. They are developed out of social settings and situations of interaction on a regular basis with significant individuals, or periodically with persons who are not so significant. Therefore, a number of persons will come to see the individual differently based upon the setting or situation and the property of the image content which is called into play and displayed during the process of interaction. The meanings that are assigned to each other and the significance of the situation to the individuals involved, form the basis for action and behavior in those social settings and during those situations. If a certain property is not satisfactorily developed for a given situation or setting, the individual will seek to develop the property, or will develop a more appropriate or adequate style of conveyance. There are times when the property is developed but the style of conveyance to others is inappropriate and inadequate. Consequently, there are times when the wrong indications are made and must be corrected instantly or very soon thereafter, if distortions are to be clarified, smooth interaction experienced, relationships are not collapsed, and role taking and conversations are not broken down.

This process speaks to the notion that one has the ability to indicate to himself the responses he expects from others in a given situation, or setting. In this context, it is very important to have an appropriate and adequate style to convey to others in your social setting the nature of a property of the image content irrespective of the stage of its development. It must be understood also that in certain situations and social meetings, the person(s) to whom the properties are being indicated might reject the indications. It is when there is a rejection of, ignoring of, or being unaware of these indications, for whatever reason(s), regarding the properties of the image by others in the social setting or situation, that breaks down in interaction and relationships occur. If the property or properties are indicated often enough, or during the most appropriate circumstances and settings, there is bound to be acceptance of the image content and the projected self. Through the process of socialization an overlapping network of properties are developed through interaction. During the process of socialization, questions regarding the content of properties are made, and interpretation and meanings established. At some point in the process, which varies from individual to individual, a degree of independence is achieved in what is internalized, where the individual assumes the responsibility for the definitions of self and the selection of properties which are significant and important for interaction and relationship in the individual's social world. It is also out of this process of independence that a style of conveyance is developed for the purpose of making indications (Swan, 1984).

Everyone has a particular style that is related to the self in relation to the individual and the collective properties of the image content. Our properties might be the same, but might vary in degree(s) of development, and our styles of conveyance are usually different from individual to individual. This is very evident in interaction and relationships; for example, how and when love or affection, or kindness, as properties of the image content of the self are conveyed. The temptation and the mode of contemporary human relationships is for each to see the other in a particular way not allowing for all of the properties of the self to be displayed or conveyed in interaction in different settings and situations. We limit the expression of the self and are tempted to think our relating partners have what has commonly been referred to as split personalities. The fact is that the individual has and can convey various competing and conflicting properties of the self depending on the situation, setting, or individuals involved.

Meaning and the Self in Relationships

Meaning makes the individual. Every person has a meaning and it is this particular meaning that makes him the particular person he is. Because a man is a banker, he is a special kind of person, different from a tailor. People act toward each other according to the meanings they have for each other. When two people attribute different meanings to themselves and to each other as objects in interaction, they will most likely have misunderstandings. The meaning of the individual is given by the way the people act toward the individual and how the individual defines himself. The ways people act toward each other define the meaning of the individual for them. Meaning is not only intrinsic to an individual, but is also conferred upon him by others and by the individual himself. Meaning arises in relationships between human beings and specifically in the disposition of human beings to act toward one another in particular ways. This means that the individual can have different meanings for different people, and people will act toward an individual on the basis of what the individual means to them. President Obama has very different meanings for different people, and therefore these different people will act quite differently toward him.

Meaning is a social product; it develops in the process of human interaction. People who do not know the meaning of certain people can learn what they mean by watching the ways in which other people act toward them, the way they define them with their action. For example, a child learns the meaning of a chair by watching older

51

people use chairs; he learns the meanings of all the objects in his environment as he sees other people signify the meanings by using the objects or otherwise expressing a relation to them. Even the pain of a toothache, which most people expect would be perceived in the same way by anyone, is a social product. Insofar as the victim becomes aware of his toothache-points it out to himself—the pain is an object and the victim gives it a meaning. This meaning varies enormously, depending on what group the victim of the toothache belongs to. If he lives in a primitive tribe, he may think of the toothache as the result of the magic of an enemy or a witch doctor. In contemporary society, people think of a toothache as the result of the decay of nervous tissue in the tooth (Berger and Luckman, 1966).

In order to understand human action and interaction, we must understand what meanings people impute or convey to each other when they relate. The claim that meanings are not inherent but are conferred by human action raises several important questions. To what extent is man free to define others in his world? To what extent can others force him to modify his definitions if the definitions do not correspond to the reality of others? Human beings have real existence outside the minds of others. They do offer resistance to human action and can limit, in this way the meanings which can be imputed to them. Nevertheless, human beings do not exist only in the minds of others. The meaning of an individual may be conferred by others, but the individual also has a meaning of self that might be independent of the meanings conferred. The fact that meaning is given to individuals by the way others are prepared to act toward them does not mean, however, that individuals as objects exist only in the minds of others. Individuals have meanings of themselves and seek to convey these meanings during interaction and in relationships with others. In the process of interaction, people make indications to one another about how they should act toward each other. This understanding is usually absent in the interpersonal interaction in contemporary human relationships.

What is being said in this theoretical outline is that conflicts and problems often arise in contemporary human relationships when there is disjuncture between the perceptions of the selves of those in interaction; a breakdown in the style of conveying the properties of the self; distortion of meanings of each other; and where there is lack of knowledge and understanding of the social context that dominates the interpersonal and interactional patterns of behavior in relationships. Key questions that emerge from this orientation are: What is the nature of the group life experience we represent? What is our concept of ourselves and of each other? What do we mean to each other, and what meanings do we have of others relative to the meanings we have of ourselves? Have we made functional the negative definitions of ourselves by society?

Our sense of self and the worth and meaning of individuals as selves provide the basis for social interaction between human beings. Conflicts emerge when the sense of self is different from the projected self; when the meanings of self are distorted, and the interaction in relationships is based upon different perceptions of the self in relation to the other, and the other in relation to the self.

Our conceptions of ourselves are developed by taking the roles of the other and through the process of an independent selection of the properties to develop and convey. It is clear that the self is socially formed and in relationships the individual can change the image content and consequently, the concept of self. Each of us engages in interaction with himself. By interacting with himself, an individual is able to select from the range of social reality the things that will constitute his perceptual world. Therefore, human beings do not merely "react" to things; instead, they take note of them, or take them into account. In other words, human beings can control their own actions. Therefore, human behavior is not mere "reaction to stimuli." The self intervenes between the stimulus and the response, and determines the person's line of activity. For example, human beings can temporarily ignore hunger pains and make plans regarding when and where to eat lunch or dinner. This behavior would be impossible without the existence of the self.

By virtue of possessing a self, the human being is to some extent emancipated from the control exercised by others in relationships in which he or she is participating. Although the influences of culture and social structure are very strong in relationships, it is nevertheless important to note that, because he possesses a self, the individual can ward off some of the influences exerted by them in relationships. In interaction with his self, the individual "notes" and "takes account of" the expectations of others, and thus puts himself into the position of being able to act in ways other than the expected ways. His ability to communicate with himself and to respond to his own communications enables him to erect barriers between himself and others in relationships.

Self consciousness, within theoretical perspective, implies consciousness of others. In fact, self consciousness is usually at its height when one is in the company of strangers. In the company of strangers one is extremely aware, alert, guarded, and so forth. Under these conditions, barriers between oneself and others can be set up with greater ease than, say, in the bosom of one's family and close friends. In the company of friends and partners in relationships, the tendency is for one not to be as alert, aware, guarded and so forth. This tendency can lead to conflict, confusion, frustration, withdrawal, distraction, and disengagement in relationships. Human beings, then, are not mere bits of putty in the hands of others that surround them in relationships. By virtue of having a self, the individual can barricade himself against others, and upon occasion even rebel against them.

Self-Esteem and Personal Relationships

The importance of the self and the properties of the self are directly related to the esteem one has of oneself. Self-esteem has a lot to do with the way people respond to others. On a broader social level, persons with high self-esteem feel that they have less difficulty in making friends, are more apt to express their opinions, are less sensitive to criticism, and are generally less preoccupied with themselves. In personal relationships, people with very low self-esteem often experience a persistent and insatiable need for affection. When the individual is systematically developing the properties of the self, and concurrently developing styles to convey, in interaction, appropriate properties of the self, in various social situations, meanings of self are controlled by indications or designations, and interpretations by the individual and others, which allow for the devising of responses by those in relationships.

What is essential or the bottom line in understanding contemporary relationships, or being involved in same, is that we get a grasp of the nature and character of the group life within which relationships are expressed, and the properties of the self as they emerge in interaction. The understanding of contemporary relationships must be grounded in this theoretical perspective or orientation of the nature of human action in group life, the development of the self, and the social setting and situation of the relationship and its process.

Conclusions

Individuals are social selves and have the ability to be different selves in different situations and to different individuals. In this regard, the concept "self" is different from the concept "personality," which presented in the literature as rigid, fixed and deterministic in construct. The self is developed out of social situations and social interactions. Those who have written and spoken about the personality have done so in terms that suggest that the "personality" is a given, ascribed, structured, and assigned. S. Freud argued that the psychological structure of the human being consists of three parts: id, ego, and superego. These three parts interact with one another. But to say this is not the same as to say that interaction takes place between the individual and himself. Hence in the Freudian scheme, the individual does not have a self. When we posture individuals as not being able to make objects of themselves, or that they cannot act toward themselves as objects, we are arguing that they have no selves. Human beings can make objects of themselves and can deal with themselves as with any other objects. Every person can see himself as a certain kind of object, defines himself in a certain way, and can handle himself on the basis of his self definition. The self is socially generated or socially derived and results from diverse associations and from the viewpoints of different roles. The scope and variety of roles the individual can assume have greatly increased. Although the role of the parents is crucial, because the individual takes many roles during the course of his development, the cumulative effect of his taking all the varied roles can transcend the effect of his taking the role of the parents. There are many influences on the development of the "self-conception" of the individual and it might not be logical to assign importance to any one role or set of roles (Schultz, 1981).

It is crucial to human interaction and personal relationships that it is understood that people act toward objects on the basis of the meanings the objects have for them. Hence, a person's actions are based in part on the kind of object he is to himself. Because a person is an object to himself, he is able to act toward himself and to interact with himself. This means that he can makes gestures, or indications, to himself, respond to the indication, make further indications and so on. The mind, for example, is not merely a resurgence of images into the consciousness but a process of pointing out images to oneself. A person can interact with himself without making overt indications, and he can therefore create a private world. There is a tendency in social science to differentiate between the private world of the mind and the outer world of social interaction. But self interaction and social interaction are essentially the same processes; the fundamental difference between them is that the private world of the mind is not open to observation from the outside. Self interaction, therefore, is the basis for overt action. It is also an important means by which a person controls his actions in the external world. He confronts the world on the basis of his ability to make indications to himself. The only things in his environment he can deal with are those he can point out to himself. Therefore, individuals act on the basis of what they perceive to be the objects in their environment, and on the basis of what they define the meanings of those objects to be.

References

Berger, Peter L. and Thomas Luckmann
  1966 <u>The Social Construction of Reality. A Treatise in the Sociology of Knowledge</u>. New York: Doubleday.

Blumer, Herbert
  1966 <u>Symbolic Interactionism: Perspective and Method</u>. Englewood Cliff, N.J.: Prentice-Hall.

Swan, L. Alex
  1984 <u>The Practice of Clinical Sociology and Sociotherapy</u>. Cambridge, Massachusetts: Schenkman Publishing Co.

Shibutani, Tamotsu
  1968 <u>Society and Personality: An Interactionist Approach</u>. Englewood Cliff, N.J.: Prentice-Hall, Inc.

Schultz, D.
  1981 <u>Theories of Personality (2nd ed.)</u>. Monterey, Cali.: Brooks/Cole.

Basic Characteristics of Key Psychotherapies

Chapter 3

* * *

Basic Characteristics of Key Psychotherapies

Introduction of Psychotherapies

Because the psychoanalytic approach dominated the field of therapy for so many years, the view of many regarding therapy for emotional and social problems is the picture of a patient lying on a couch revealing his memories, thoughts, dreams, feelings, and fantasies to an analyst who listens attentively to understand and interpret the motivations that underlie the patient's actions. This approach, developed by S. Freud, employed diagnosis as a guide for the direction of therapy. The individual's past was explored and the relationship between the patient and the analyst studied to provide some clue as to the way the patient interacted with significant people from the past. This cure through talk approach dominates the field today, even though many psychiatrists are restoring to the cure through drugs approach. Most of the approaches today provide an opportunity for clients to talk and interact with others and the therapist about the social, emotional, and cognitive events and experiences in their lives and situations that are of concern to them. Because diagnosis was for the purpose of assigning clients to diagnostic categories and establishing the labeling process, therapists today tend to advocate description not labeling. Little or nothing is gained by labeling as well as giving consideration to the client's past, only in the context of how it affects the present. The time in which clients spend in the therapy has also changed considerably. The psychoanalytic patient spent three or more years in analysis; today, therapy ends after a matter of weeks or months, often less than a year. Nonetheless, caring, attentive listening, and the establishment of positive relationships between clients and therapists are essential ingredients in the sociadognostic and sociotherapeuitc processes.

We will present a brief overview of several therapeutic approaches in terms of their philosophy, their basic assumptions and their techniques. All of these therapeutic approaches are explanatory systems of problems that seek to explain the process whereby certain behavior and action on the part of the therapist produce change in the patient. The range of these explanatory systems is from the highly elaborated psychoanalytic therapy to reality therapy. These explanatory systems attempt to explain why clients have various types of problems and why certain interactions between client and therapist produce change and improvement. Our concerns should be: Are the explanatory systems reasonable and valid? And, is the therapy effective in producing change? An explanation offered by the explanatory systems, differs from an explanation that emerges from the process of scientific grounding. Theory or explanation that is scientifically grounded consists of descriptions of the situation and of the clients which are organized into a system of knowledge. Explanations must lead to understanding and enlightenment which enable us to place events, issues, ideas, feelings and desires in a broader context of interactions.

Explanations help us determine the relations that are available that relate behaviors or the problems in question to the situation, or context of the clients. This is the reason that scientific grounding is essential. Most of the failures in therapy result from the skewing of data related to the presenting and real problems to fit our preconceived or predetermined perspective of the problem. This is the case because no therapeutic approach and its explanatory systems address all problems of living; they are individualistic in nature and particularistic in character and application. The efficiency of specific techniques for problems must be directly deducible from the generalizations or constructs of the theories that emerge from the discoveries of the sociodiagnostic process. Techniques of therapy should be related to the theories of causation; the persons involved;

the goals of therapy, and the desired outcome. All of the modes of treating people with problems of living presented here have been verbal communication. There is thought to be a strong association between communication and relief of personal distress. Although verbal communication allows the client to experience a type of catharsis, it forms only a part of the treatment process. The principle mode of sociatherapeutic intervention is action.

Psychoanalytic Therapy

Since the psychoanalytic approach came first, we will present a brief view of the various approaches starting with the psychoanalytic. This therapeutic approach is a personality theory, a philosophy of human nature and a method of therapy. It argues that the human being is determined by psychic energy, unconscious and irrational forces, and repressed experiences. The individual is driven by aggressive and sexual instincts, and since later personality problems are rooted in repressed childhood conflicts, early development is of crucial importance.

The techniques employed in this approach are specifically related to its basic assumption and philosophy. In fact, the philosophy is intended to give direction and focus to the therapeutic activity. Consequently, all of the techniques employed in this approach are designed to help the client gain insight and surface repressed material so that it can be dealt with in a conscious and rational way. Life history data, diagnosis for labeling and assigning diagnostic category, testing and questioning are the ways often used. Other tools for making unconscious conscious are interpretation, dream analysis, free association, analysis of resistance, and analysis of transference.

This approach has been associated with long term individual therapy, but it can conceivably be adapted to ongoing group therapy. There is no question that this approach has had significant influences on all aspects of therapeutic activities. However, there has been a great deal of reaction to this approach as widened by several other approaches that challenge the basic assumptions and philosophy of the psychoanalytic approach. Those who use this approach feel that it provides a comprehensive and detailed system of personality; it emphasizes the legitimate place of the unconscious as a determinant of behavior, and it highlights the significance of the profound effect of early childhood development. Procedures for tapping the unconscious are also provided. Those who may have problems with this approach can argue that early childhood experiences, sexual impulses and drives, unconscious factors and relationship with one's parents are not determinants of the individual's present personality problems. The basic limitations seem to be that the approach is not based on healthy people, but on the study of neurotics, placing emphasis on instinctual forces, and ignores the social, cultural and interpersonal factors. There are problems of its applicability to crisis counseling and working with certain racial groups and to other fields of therapy. The aloof, detached and anonymous posture of the analyst so as to foster transference, or resurrect old feelings that the clients had toward their parents now directed toward the therapist, is also a role that is considered counterproductive to therapeutic value.

Person-Centered

Person-Centered or non-directive therapy places great emphasis upon the individual's own resources. The therapist attempts to generate a set of freeing conditions, warmth, openness, authenticity and facilitates the capacity of the individual to correct himself. The client is helped to think through problems by reflecting on his feelings. The therapist tries to avoid pushing, confronting, or suggesting in the process. Person-Centered therapy is a brand of existential psychology that stresses a phenomenological approach, both of which are reactions against psychoanalytic therapy. The client is placed at the center of therapy, not the therapist and the clients resources are used for becoming aware and for resolving blocks to personal growth. This approach is based on a subjective view of human experiences and is grounded in a positive of humanity that views the individual as innately striving toward becoming fully functioning.

The basic assumption of the client-centered approach is that the client experiences previously denied or distorted feelings and increases self awareness in the context of a personal relationship with a caring therapist. In the process, the client actualizes inner potential for growth, wholeness, spontaneity and inner directedness. This approach specifies few techniques since it stresses the client/ therapist relationship. Techniques are really secondary to the therapist attitudes, and the approach minimizes directive techniques, questioning, interpretation, probing, collecting history and diagnosis. Not that these are not used at times, but they are not seen as essential as active listening and hearing, reflection of feelings and clarification. A sense of support and just being there for clients is stressed. It is hoped, in this approach, that a climate of safety and trust in the therapeutic setting is established so that the client can become aware of blocks to growth by using the therapeutic relationship for self exploration.

This approach is useless with nonverbal clients, and gives little attention to the influence of the therapist's values and personhood. The real difficulty with this approach is that it is very problematic in attempting to grasp the subjective and inner world of the client. A discount of the significance of the past is extended to how that past may be affecting the person in the present. There must be an admission that people in crisis situations often need more directive intervention strategies.

Gestalt

The gestalt approach requires the therapist to be active in exposing problems and seeking solutions. This attempt often involves role playing, confrontation, the use of techniques to facilitate expression, such as fantasy games, etc. The therapist is required to be a strong and directive figure who emphasizes the present and avoids dealing with the past, "old tapes," and encourages the clients to live and think in the "here-and-now." Like client-centered therapy, gestalt is rooted in existential philosophy and psychology. The unity of the mind, body and feeling is emphasized. That individuals are responsible for their own behavior and experiences is the basic assumption of gestalt. Consequently, the approach is fashioned to assist individuals to more fully experience the present and to gain awareness of the "how" and "what," not "why" of their behavior. The focus of this approach is also on the role of unfinished business from the past and impasses in preventing an effective functioning in the present. In this sense, the approach is an experiential therapy that not only stresses here-and-now awareness, but also the integration of the fragmented parts of the personality. In gestalt, the client is taught the process of being aware of what he is doing and how he is doing it.

The focus is not on how he should be, or why he is the way he is. Clients learn to use their own senses to explore all aspects of their cognitions, emotions and actions and in the process, find their own solutions to their problems. It is not the objective of gestalt to teach the client how to adjust to a given situation; the client learns how to use his awareness in whatever situation emerges. Learning and using this awareness process is the essential objective of gestalt therapy. In gestalt, change is experienced by clearly knowing and accepting who you are and how you are; that is, accepting the given. The techniques and procedures used in gestalt are designed to intensify direct experiencing and to integrate conflicting feelings. The ways the client avoids responsibility for his feelings is stressed along with confrontation of discrepancies.

Role playing is an important technique in gestalt. The client gains greater awareness of the conflicts within himself as he plays out the various parts and polarities alone.

One of the problems with the gestalt approach is that it does not seem to be grounded in solid theory. The anti-intellectual posture of the approach is a limitation because cognitive factors are discounted. A sense of irresponsible towards others can easily be promoted by this approach in that it tends to stress a "do your own thing" philosophy. Gestalt lends itself to becoming a series of mechanical exercises, and the therapist, as a person, can hide behind them, and misuse them as a set of gimmicks. It is also possible for the therapist to manipulate clients with powerful techniques employed in the process of therapy.

Some may even argue that "pure" gestalt therapy tends to restrict group interaction.

Reality

Reality therapy was developed as an alternative to the other forms of therapy thought to be ineffective in many cases. This therapeutic approach utilizes intense personal involvement and having the client face reality to learn better ways of behaving. Through reality therapy, the client is assisted in gaining sufficient strength to handle the stresses and problems of life responsibly. Through this method the client comes to understand that he, not society, the environment, heredity, the past, or anything outside himself, is responsible for his behavior. The intent is to bring clients to the realization that their unhappiness is the product of their own decisions.

Clients are taught that they are not helpless victims of life, but that they can make better choices, and that their behavior is learned. Anything that is learned can be unlearned and relearned. Problem solving skills and autonomy tend to increase as clients learn to focus on the consequences of their actions and begin to feel they can control their behavior. As a reaction to the psychoanalytic approach, reality therapy is a didactic approach that stresses problem solving and coping with the demands of reality in society. The present is the focus and the client's strengths as a way of learning more realistic ways to behave. This approach rejects the medical model of mental illness and stresses moral and value judgments equating mental health with acceptance of personal responsibility. It also focuses on behavior change, not on insight, awareness of the unconscious, and attitude change.

The involvement with the client is essential in bringing about change. Together the client and the therapist examine and evaluate the client's ongoing behavior and devise a reasonable plan of action for change. This is an active, directive, cognitive behavior oriented therapy that is both supportive and confrontational. What and how questions are used, not why. The therapist seeks a commitment for action from the client and accepts no excuses for failure to carry out the commitment. Role playing, confrontation, modeling, humor, contracts and the formulation of specific plans for action are among the wide range of techniques used in this approach. Since the contract method is often used, when the contract is fulfilled, therapy is terminated. This approach is thought to be anti-deterministic and based on a growth motivation model. The individual is said to have a need for identity and can develop either a success identity or a failure identity. One of the real concerns with this approach is that there is no way to avoid or prevent the imposition of the therapist's values and views of reality on the client. Further, it tends to be symptom oriented, and imposes and encourages conformity rather than independent behavior.

Transactional Analysis

Transactional analysis focuses on cognitive behavioral aspects designed to assist a client to evaluate early decision and to make new and more appropriate decisions. The basic assumption of TA is that the individual has the potential for choice and for reshaping his own destiny. The individual is able to write a new script through awareness, even though past scripting may have molded him. Personality structure, for TA, consists of three ego states: parent, adult, and child. The client is taught which ego state is operant and thus learns to choose a given ego state. Because TA argues that human beings need stroking, the client is also taught to learn to ask for needed strokes.

The approach focuses on games played to avoid intimacy, rackets, early decisions, life scripts, parental injunctions, stroking and basic psychological positions. The therapist helps the client to achieve a degree of awareness that enables the client to redecide or make new decisions and become autonomous. For TA therapists this means becoming a script free and game free person with the capability of choosing for one's self. The contract is an essential technique in TA. Also important is the use of a script checklist and the questionnaire to detect injunctions, games, life positions, and early decisions.

Questioning is often employed along with other procedures such as structural analysis, role playing, analysis of games and rackets, analysis of rituals and positives, family modeling, the empty chair technique, didactic methods, and script analysis. TA provides the client with a framework within which to view his behavior. In learning how to recognize the parent-adult-child components of his personality, he develops the ability to analyze his interactions with others, which are called transactions, on the basis of these various PAC categories. The client can begin to change those transactions which make him feel "not ok" when he understands his typical transactions.

This approach tends to place clients in artificial categories and carries with it the potential of analyzing the self at a distance and making it a mechanical thing to be analyzed. Its emphasis on intellectual concepts can become a defense against feeling and experiencing that are so essential in gestalt. The approach can also become a game in itself, and its terminology can blur the therapist's creativity. Transference is not included in the model, and the therapist pays attention to mastering the technical style, leaving out himself as a person.

Rational Emotive Therapy

Rational emotive therapy focuses on having the client change his way of viewing his problem. The basic position of RET is that a person's negative emotional reactions do not result directly from experiences or events, but from beliefs about events and experiences. Irrational beliefs tend to cause the individual to catastrophize the event and give up hope. Rational beliefs, on the other hand, help the client to recognize the unpleasantness and inspire him to handle the situation better next time. In other words, RET seeks to teach and encourage rationality and attacks the client's irrational beliefs. The approach rejects the view that insights and awareness of early childhood events result in the reduction of the client's emotional disturbances. Instead, RET argues that individuals are born with the potential for rational thinking.

However, in the process, individuals fall victim to the uncritical acceptance of irrational beliefs that are perpetuated through self-reindoctrination. RET assumes that evaluating, questioning, thinking, doing, analyzing, practicing and redeciding are at the base of any behavior change. For RET, therapy is a process of reeducation through didactic/directive model. In other words, RET is a cognitive behavior oriented approach which stresses the role of thinking, and belief system as the roots of personal problems, and the role of action and practice in combating the problems which express themselves in irrational and self-indoctrinated ideas. RET is based on the ABC theory of personality where A represents the actual event; B, the belief system; and C, the consequence. RET therapists are trained to use scientific method of logical and rational thought to apply to irrational beliefs, the elimination of a self defeating outlook of life and the promotion of a more rational and tolerant way of life.

All of the techniques used are designed to get the client to critically examine his present beliefs and behavior. Various techniques are employed in this regard. The essential technique is active directive teaching. However, therapists confront, probe, challenge, model, explain, persuade, lecture, forcefully direct and teach rational thinking. Clients are required or forced to constantly use their cognitive skills and practice deconditioning role playing, do homework assignments, practice desensitization, counter-conditioning. Other techniques that are used include behavior research, assertion training, listening to tapes, contracts, hypnotherapy, and operant conditioning.

Why individuals tend to reindoctrinate themselves with irrational beliefs and cling to these beliefs is not clearly explained by RET. No rationale is provided for this position taken by RET therapists and no model for growth or for self actualization is presented, even though treatment is emphasized. Because RET is an over intellectualized approach, persons with limited intelligence might not do well with this approach. Further, the imposition of the therapist's philosophy on the client, and the force of the therapist's persuasion can be dangerous and psychologically harmful.

Behavior Therapy

Behavior therapy is based on the belief that all behavior is learned and shaped by sociocultural conditioning. Because all behavior is viewed as the product of conditioning, this approach is deterministic in its view of human behavior. Consequently, the principles of learning is applied to problem solving. Marked by an adherence to scientific methodology in evaluating specific results, behavior therapy is a reaction against both classical psychoanalysis and existentially oriented therapy. This approach stresses present behavior with little or no emphasis on the past. The focus is on overt behavior, clarifying treatment goals, developing specific treatment plans, and the objective evaluation of outcomes. Insight is deemphasized and behavior change, cognition, and action are the primary focus. The therapist in this approach helps make the goals, defined by the client, specific and concrete as they attempt to eliminate maladaptive behavior by learning more effective behavior patterns.

Many specific techniques are stressed by behavior therapy. All the techniques are based on learning principles and are geared to behavior change. Assertive training, modeling, self management, thought stopping, operant conditioning, systematic desensitization, implosive therapy, coaching, feedback, reinforcement and supportive measures, and challenging and changing conditions. All of these techniques are employed to achieve behavioral changes and cognitive restructuring. The degree to which behavior therapists can control environmental variables is the degree to which they can be assured of success. Those persons who function at high levels and desire growth oriented therapy, may not find this approach very powerful and helpful. The possibility for the therapist to manipulate the client and impose conforming on clients where there might be a need to challenge institutional policies and social practices.

Existential Therapy

Existential therapy's primary focus is on the human condition. As a reaction against behaviorism and psychoanalysis, it argues that the individual is basically alone when placed into a meaningless and absurd world. Consequently, he has to create his own meaning in life highlighted by the awareness of death. The individual is viewed as having the capacity for expanding self awareness, which provides the basis for freedom and responsibility and for shaping their destiny which leads to existential anxiety. Freedom, choice, purpose and self determination are stressed in its philosophy of human nature. Existential therapy argues that a sense of self develops from infancy and that the individual is a unique person. As an experimental approach, it stresses self awareness before action and that a faulty development is viewed as the failure to actualize the individual's potential, which leads to anxiety and guilt.

This approach seeks to maximize growth, awareness, spontaneity, and fulfillment and helps the individual exercise the personal freedom to decide what he wants to become. In this regard, the approach focus on the here and now and on what the individual is becoming. No specific set of techniques is prescribed since techniques are secondary to the importance of understanding. Existential therapists do borrow techniques from other therapies to achieve better understanding of the clients' world, and enhancing therapeutic activity. Techniques from other therapies can be easily incorporated into this approach because it is basically an attitude toward persons and an approach to therapy. The concepts used in this approach are rather abstract and lofty, which usually makes them difficult to grasp and apply in practice. The concepts are broad, often elusive, not readily testable by empirical methods and tend to complicate and confuse the therapeutic process. This approach seems suited only for clients who are desiring growth, not those who need assistance with social and emotional difficulties and problems, or clients in crisis states.

In concluding this section, let us look at the Eclectic approach which selects concepts and techniques from all of the other approaches as a basis for establishing and building one's own unique and Eclectic approach and counseling style. There are aspects of each of the approaches that are extracted to constitute the Eclectic approach. The unconscious and early childhood experiences and their influences on the client's present personality are taken from the psychoanalytic model, and the view that people are more than mere victims of their past and that they have the ability to assume responsibility for changing themselves and their situations is borrowed from the existential. From the person centered approach is taken the importance of the therapist in using himself and his relationship with the client as the major focus change. The action oriented techniques of the gestalt are borrowed. With them the client is challenged to relive unfinished situations from his past that might be cluttering up his ability to live fully in the present. Early in the process, the client and the therapist would work to formulate a clear contract to provide direction for the therapy. This position is provided by transactional analysis. It also provides for the exploration of injunctions and the early decisions that were made in relationship to the parental messages. From the behavior therapy perspective, the action oriented methods are also borrowed. The position that insights alone is not enough to cause behavior change, but that specific action must be taken in the real world is thought to be very significant. RET lends to the eclectic the notion that through the process of self-indoctrination of irrational ideas the individual keeps himself disturbed. The client is taught to understand this early in the session so that he can see that he is the only one who can uproot his faulty thinking and irrational beliefs. From the reality perspective, paying attention to what clients are saying by observing how they are actually behaving is valued and taught.

The assumption in developing the eclectic is that the significant elements that have compatibility from each approach can be drawn together to be effective in the therapeutic process. However, all of the elements of the characteristics of the various approaches are not compatible and can cause problems in diagnosis and therapeutic intervention. In attempting to avoid the limitations and drawbacks by pulling together or borrowing significant elements and concepts from other approaches weakens these elements when used outside of their context in isolation to the other elements of their therapeutic origin. Moreover, bringing these elements or concepts together has not eliminated the limitations in the concept, nor removed the limitations because of the coming together. It has not been shown that the elements and concepts once brought together form a consistent, coherent and effective approach for grounding theory and therapy for direct utility. All of the psychotherapeutic approaches are reactions to the psychoanalytic. Consequently, their concepts are in contrast to each other, and especially with psychoanalytic. The limitations and weaknesses of the various approaches are not avoided by employing an eclectic.

The limited applicability to crisis situations and the stress on the role of insight are not overcome in the psychoanalytic approach. The eclectic does little with the many lofty and abstract concepts that are often difficult to grasp and apply in practice in the existential approach. People in crisis situations often need more directive intervention strategies provided by the person centered approach. Neither does the eclectic counter for the difficulties which lie in grasping the subjective and inner world of clients presented by this approach. The "do your own thing" philosophy and the importance of self to the exclusion of others, which seem to characterize the gestalt approach, and the tendency to be anti-intellectual to the point of disconnecting cognitive factors are not challenged by eclectic.

The use of intellectual concepts in transactional analysis can become a defense against feeling and experiencing, and analyzing the self at a distance, thus making it a mechanical thing to be discussed is not adequately handled by the eclectic. Imposing conforming behavior, particularly in total institutional policies, of the behavior therapy approach; the danger of the imposition of the therapist's own philosophy on the client and the possible social psychological harm done to the client by the beat down persuasion techniques of the rational emotive approach, and the imposition of the therapist's values and views of reality are not accounted for in the eclectic approach. This brief presentation of eight of the various therapeutic approaches that dominate the field today and a brief treatment of the eclectic have encouraged several recent attempts to develop more complete and effective approaches. The limitations of these approaches are becoming more evident to an increasing number of professionals who have little or no time to challenge and construct their own approaches.

In the areas of theory and therapy today, we are not developing dramatically new theories and therapies. Instead, what seems to be the trend is the expansion and refinement of existing theories and therapies. GET argues that the action taken in therapy must flow from the theories or explanations about the social situation or context of the client's problem. The approach offers the clients the opportunity to talk, confront, disclose, interpret, discover and interact with themselves, others and the sociotherapist, and encounter their situations for understanding, clarity, direction and action. Reorganizing the weaknesses in all of the various approaches, several attempts have been made to develop an approach with no or with fewer limitations and weaknesses. The discussion and presentation of GET and problems of living provide direction in this regard. We have to allow the data collected in the particular case to tell us what is happening and what to do.

Summary and Conclusion

We will conclude this discussion by presenting a summary of four of the key characteristics of each of the therapeutic approaches: philosophy and basic assumptions; therapeutic goals; therapeutic relationship, and techniques and procedures. The main person of the psychoanalytic approach is S. Freud, who is credited with developing the first system of psychotherapy. It is considered to be a personality theory which includes a philosophy of human nature and a method of therapy.

Basic Assumptions and Philosophy

Human beings are assumed to be driven by sexual and aggressive instincts, and present personality problems are lodged in repressed childhood conflicts. This is the reason that early childhood development is of great significance. Irrational and unconscious forces, repressed experiences and psychic energy determine human beings and their behavior.

Therapeutic Goals

The therapeutic goal of the psychoanalytic approach is to make the unconscious conscious. The basic character and personality is restructured by surfacing unconscious conflicts, and working through them is a major goal.

Therapeutic Relationship

So that clients can project their feelings onto the therapist, anonymity is stressed. The focus is on working through transference feelings of the clients to the therapist and resistances in the therapeutic process. The therapist relies on insight, which occurs as a result of intensive regression to the past from which interpretations are made that are aimed at teaching clients the meaning of the present behavior relative to past experiences. Understanding casual factor for developmental problems is also a crucial focus.

Techniques and Procedures

Diagnosis, testing, questioning, and gathering life history data, interpretation, dream analysis, free association, analysis of resistance, and analysis of transference are basic tools used for making the unconscious conscious.

The main figure in the Person-Centered approach is Carl Rogers. This approach was developed in the 1940's and is based on a subjective view of the human being who is viewed as having the resources for becoming aware and for resolving blocks to personal growth.

Basic Assumptions and Philosophy

This approach assumes that the client can experience previously denied or distorted feelings and increase his self awareness with a caring therapist within the context of a personal relationship. In the process, the client actualizes inner potential for inner-directedness, wholeness, spontaneity and growth. The Person-Centered approach is grounded in a positive view of humanity which views human beings as innately good and striving toward becoming fully functioning.

Therapeutic Goals

The client is not encouraged to take cues for what he should or ought to become from the therapist. The primary goal is the creation of a climate of safety and trust in the therapeutic setting, using the therapeutic relationship, which allows the client to self explore and become aware of blocks to growth.

Therapeutic Relationship

Of major importance is the therapeutic relationship between the client and the therapist. The therapist attempts to convey to the client qualities that he possess such a genuineness, empathy, unconditional respect, non-possessive warmth, caring and the communication of the attitudes and qualities to the client. The hope is that the client will be able to translate his self learnings in therapy to outside relationships.

Techniques and Procedures

Very few techniques are stressed in this approach. In fact, the therapist's attitude and qualities are primary and techniques are secondary. Active listening and hearing, reflection of feelings, and clarification are maximized and interpretation, questioning, probing, collecting history and diagnosis are minimized.

Frederick (Fritz) Perls is the key figure in gestalt therapy. This approach is an experimental therapy that focuses on the what and how of behavior and the role of unfinished business from the past that might be interfering with the individual functioning affectively in the present. This approach also stresses the integration of the fragmented parts of personality and here and now awareness.

Basic Assumptions and Philosophy

Existential philosophy and psychology are the roots of the philosophy of this approach. Individuals are assumed to be responsible for their own behavior and experiencing.

Therapeutic Goals

The primary goal is to assist the client to more fully experience the present moment and to gain awareness of the how and what of his behavior. The client is challenged to more from environmental support to self support. Gaining awareness of moment to moment experiencing, the client is able to recognize denied aspects of self and proceed toward reintegration of all parts of the self. This process is believed to be curative.

Therapeutic Relationship

The client is helped by the therapist in experiencing fully all feelings and in making his own interpretations. The therapist focuses on the how and what of the clients' behavior but does not interpret for the client. The client also identifies his own unfinished business from the past that is interfering with his present functioning. This is done by reexperincing past situations again as if they were happening in the present.

Techniques and Procedures

Techniques that are designed to intensify direct experiencing and to integrate conflicting feelings are used. Confrontation of discrepancies and the ways the client avoids responsibility for his feelings are stressed by this approach. Through role playing, acting out all the various parts and polarities alone help the client to gain greater awareness of the conflicts within himself.

William Glasser is the founder and key figure in the development of reality therapy. The approach is didactic and stresses problem solving and coping with the demands of reality. The present is stressed along with the clients' strengths as a way of learning more realistic behavior.

Basic Assumptions and Philosophy

This approach argues that the individual, who has a need for identity, can develop either a "failure identity" or a "success identity." It is anti-deterministic and is based on a growth motivational model. The medical model of mental illness is rejected along with the stress on awareness of the unconscious.

Therapeutic Goals

The goals in therapy are to assist the client in deciding on a constructive plan of responsible action to implement behavior change which will lead to a "success identity," and to guide the client toward making value judgments about present behavior.

Therapeutic Relationship

The client is expected to decide specific changes, formulate plans and be committed to follow through and evaluate results. A personal relationship is established and the therapist gets involved with the client to encourage him to face reality and to make choices that will fulfill his needs in a socially acceptable way. The therapist does not accept blame or excuses from the client and punishment is avoided.

Techniques and Procedures

What and how questions are used, and why questions are avoided. The approach is directive, didactic, cognitive and active in its orientation, and the contract method is usually used. Therapy is terminated when the contract is fulfilled.

The founder and key figure in the area of Transactional Analysis is Eric Berne. The approach is designed to assist the client to evaluate early decision and to make new and more appropriate decisions.

Basic Assumptions and Philosophy

The belief that the client has the potential for choice and reshaping his own destiny is crucial to this approach. The client is thought to be able with awareness to write a new script even though past scripting may have molded him. The philosophical position is that human beings need stroking and must learn how to ask for it.

Therapeutic Goals

The goals are for the client to become autonomous and to achieve a degree of awareness that enables the client to make new decisions relative to future behavior and direction of life. The primary goal is to help the client become script free and game free capable of choosing for himself.

Therapeutic Relationship

An equal relationship between client and therapist is advocated by TA. This is expressed and characterized by a joint sharing of responsibility structured by a contract. When the contract, which the client makes with the therapist for specific desired changes, is fulfilled, therapy ends.

Techniques and Procedures

An important technique is the contract. Script checklist, questionnaire to detect injunctions, life positions, games, and early decisions are all techniques. Questioning, structural analysis, didactic methods, the empty chair, role playing, family modeling, analysis of games and rackets, analysis of rituals and pastimes, and script analysis are also employed in TA.

Albert Ellis who became disenchanted with the psychoanalytically oriented therapy, as so many others have, developed RET. Ellis discovered that emotional disturbances of clients were not reduced resulting from insight and awareness of early childhood events. Rational Emotive therapy focuses on the role of thinking and belief systems as the roots of personal problems and stresses the role of action and practice in combating irrational, self indoctrinated ideas. This is a highly didactic, cognitive and behavior oriented approach.

Basic Assumptions and Philosophy

In the process of growing up, RET argues that individuals become victims to the uncritical acceptance of irrational beliefs that are perpetuated through self reindoctrination, even though they are born with the potential for rational thinking.

Therapeutic Goals

The main goal is to help the client eliminate a self defeating outlook on life. Developing or acquiring a more rational and tolerant philosophy of life is also a significant goal.

Therapeutic Relationship

In RET, the therapist functions as a teacher and the client as a student. A personal relationship between the client and the therapist is not considered essential. Clients are expected to actively practice changing their self defeating behavior converting it into rational behavior, as they start to understand how they continue to contribute to their problems.

Techniques and Procedures

Techniques are diverse and borrowed from behavior approaches. Persuasion, suggestion, confrontation, direct attack, teaching reading, challenging, listening to tapes, contracts, homework assignments, questioning, probing, interpretations, role playing, desensitization, counterconditioning, behavior rehearsal, modeling, hypnotherapy, operant conditioning and assertion training are the many techniques employed to get the client to critically examine his present beliefs and behavior.

Several persons are responsible for the development of behavior therapy. As a reaction to classical psychoanalysis and existentially oriented therapy, this approach is marked by an adherence to scientific methodology in evaluating specific results.

Basic Assumptions and Philosophy

This approach argues that all behavior is learned, and is shaped by sociocultural conditioning. All behavior is seen as a product of conditioning and therefore the approach is an essentially deterministic view of behavior. The principles of learning is applied in solving problems.

Therapeutic Goals

The eliminating of maladaptive behaviors and learning more effective behavior patterns is a general goal. As an action oriented approach it stresses behavior change. The therapist helps make the goals specific and concrete that are defined by the client.

Therapeutic Relationship

A personal relationship between the therapist and the client is not advocated by this approach. However, a good working relationship is essential to implementing a treatment plan. The therapist functions as a teacher or trainer in assisting the client to learn more adaptive behaviors. The therapist is directive and active, and the client must develop a willingness to actively experiment with new behaviors.

Techniques and Procedures

Many specific techniques are stressed by this approach. All are based on learning principles and geared to behavior change. Techniques such as operant conditioning, systematic desensitization, assertive training, implosive therapy, modeling, thought stopping, cognitive restructuring, and self management are used in this approach.

Rollo May and Victor Frankl are the key figures in existential therapy. This approach also is a reaction against psychoanalysis and behaviorism.

Basic Assumptions and Philosophy

This approach argues that individuals have the capacity for expanding self awareness which leads to freedom and responsibility for shaping their destiny. Purpose, choice, freedom, and self determination are emphasized by the philosophy of this approach. The individual is viewed as being alone, for the most part, in an absurd meaningless world, and must create his own meaning of life.

Therapeutic Goals

Maximizing growth, awareness, spontaneity, fulfillment, and personal potential and to help clients exercise the personal freedom to decide what they want to become are the goals of this approach.

Therapeutic Relationship

The therapist tries to establish an authentic I/them relationship with the client by grasping the internal and subjective being in the world of the client. The client discovers his own uniqueness and is able to accept the freedom and responsibility of shaping his own future with awareness in the therapeutic relationship. Emphasis is placed on the authenticity of the therapist and on the human to human encounter.

Techniques and Procedures

Understanding is primary and technique is regarded as secondary. No techniques are clearly spelled out because it is basically an attitude toward persons and an approach to therapy. However, techniques from other models can be used.

References

Corey, G.
   1982 <u>Theory and Practice of Counseling and Psychotherapy</u>. Monterey, Calif.: Brooks/Cole.

Glasser, William
   1975 <u>Reality Therapy: A New Approach to Psychiatry</u>. New York: Harper and Row.

Rogers, Carl
   1970 <u>Carl Rogers on Encounter Groups</u>. New York: Harper and Row.

Kovel, Joel
   1976 <u>A Complete Guide to Therapy: From Psychoanalysis to Behavior Modification</u>. New York: Pantheon Books.

Ellis, A., & J. Whetely (eds.)
   1979 <u>Theoretical and Empirical Foundations of Rational Emotive Therapy</u>. Monterey, Cali.: Brooks/Cole.

Berne, E.
   1972 <u>What Do You Say After You Say Hello?</u> New York: Grove Press.

Parsons, W.
   1975 <u>Gestalt Approaches in Counseling</u>. New York: Holt, Rinehart & Winston.

Perls, F.
   1969 <u>Gestalt Approach Verbatim</u>. New York: Bantam.

Frankl, V.
   1963 <u>Man's Search for Meaning</u>. New York: Washington Square Press.

Brenner, C.
    1974 <u>An Elementary Textbook of Psychoanalysis</u>. Garden City, New York: Anchor Press.

Kaufer, F. N. & A. P. Goldstein (eds.)
    1980 <u>Helping People Change</u>. New York: Pergamon Press.

The Dilemma of Psychotherapy and the Challenge for Sociotherapy

Chapter 4

* * *

The Dilemma of Psychotherapy and the Challenge for Sociotherapy

Introduction

When Clinical Sociology reemerged in 1978, it found the treatment of problems of living legally and professionally dominated by the "trinity" of psychiatry, psychology, and social work, or more precisely, clinical social work. The practice of psychotherapy had experienced a transition from its traditional individualistic posture to a diagnostic and treatment posture which of necessity had to include the group, the family, the significant others within which the individual functioned, and with whom the individual, or the "identified patient", had relationships or interactions. In spite of this transition, the curriculum of psychology and especially that of psychiatry remained basically the same. There could be found no courses in the programs of psychology which prepared psychologists to understand problems of living from the perspective of the situation, or to include a method of discovery that allowed for the synthesis of scientific and ordinary, or common sense knowledge for understanding and application to problems grounded in a social/group context. The personality system was the continued focus, and instead of enhancing and even changing the programs to accommodate the transition, we see professionals who are legally and professional legitimized to address problems of living and issues of a social nature translate situational and contextual matters to individual matters in order to address them comfortably; thus, revealing their inadequacy and lack of preparation to understand and treat effectively

87

problems of living which are situational and contextual and not simply individual.

The individual is part of the whole; the context; the situation. To understand the context; the situation, is to understand and focus on the individual as a part of the context. However, to understand the individual or to focus on the individual is to understand only part of the whole. This is inadequate and insufficient for explanation, intervention and application. However, where there is a glaring lack of preparation is in the programs of psychiatry. The problems of living that psychologists, social workers and sociologists seek to understand and change are not medical; they are social and psychological in nature and character (Szasz, 1962). Consequently, the psychiatrist is not prepared by trainings in biology, chemistry, mathematics and medicine to understand and treat such problems. If the problems are medical, of a certainty they should be addressed by those trained in the field of medicine. To seek legitimation however, in spite of the fact that there is little training in psychology, and none in sociology, which is the scientific study of human behavior in group life and society; none in the family and family life; none in courtship, marriage and the family, these clinicians have created a variety of measures for understanding individual behavior in isolation to the behavior in social context, and have generated confusion as to the proper context for understanding and treating problems of a social nature. The majority of these clinicians do not have a theoretical perspective or a philosophical basis for a proper understanding of such problems. Consequently, there is an understanding, they believe, of the individual person to the exclusion of an understanding of the individual person as a social being. When this is not understood, there is evidence of the inadequacy in training, and a lack of appropriate academic and professional experience.

The Theoretical Perspective and Context

At the very outset, it should be clearly stated, that there is the individual, others, and objects with meanings that make up the social situation or the context for understanding problems of living. Human beings, as individuals, are social beings living group life. Because human beings live group life, their behavior must be understood within that context. The majority of therapists and counselors tend to lean on psychological perspectives and insights for understanding the behavior of the individual. Social workers, psychologists, psychiatrists, and family therapists all focus on psychological information for application and intervention in individual, couples and family matters which are social in nature. The limitations of the purely psychological perspective have been noted even by psychologists, yet, the addictive learning continues. However, some psychologists have created what they call community psychology, which is an attempt to fuse two traditions, the psychological and the sociological, to correct the problem created by the limitations of the psychological perspective (Bender, 1976). These two traditions have different philosophical bases. Psychology deals with the individual system, and sociology deals with the social system. Psychology is concerned with those determinants of behavior that arise from within individuals, and sociology is concerned with the effects of the environment or the social situation on individual's behavior. Psychology looks at the behavior of people by means of studying them as individuals, and sociology takes a look at behavior within the context of the society in situations which individuals find themselves, and especially if societal variables are far more difficult to specify than individual ones, and less amendable to studying in the laboratory.

Quite a few psychologists feel that their subject should have more to say about persons-to-societies and have become interested in utilizing more sociological and organizational concepts in their thinking. Psychology is designed to have us see the individual as an isolated case. Because we argue that the mental problems people face are primarily difficulties they are having in understanding and coping with the stresses of everyday life, or with the "problems of living", clinical sociologists advance a sociological social psychological perspective. The definition is a sociological definition of social psychology rather than a psychological definition. The sociological definition is concerned with "social experiences stemming from individuals' participation in social groups, interaction with others, and the emergence of social structure from these interactions, and the effects of the cultural environment on the social experiences and interactions with others" (Stephan and Stephan, pp. 5, 9). As clinical sociologists, we stress groups and group behavior rather than individual and individual behavior. The choice to behave is impacted and influenced by a variety of factors. Thus, social interactions are the primary focus along with the mutual influence of the situation on the individual and the individual on the situation. We argue that the individual and the social environment, or the social situation/context must be studied together for clinical and intervention purposes. The definition of clinical sociology as a scientific (process and discovery) study and treatment of group life and human behavior within the context of group life fits well in the sociological social psychological perspective. Sadly, however, in the process of seeking acceptance and legitimation, clinical sociologists are taking their scientific and clinical cues from professionals who have no academic and scientific training in the subject matter they seek to understand and treat. We have allowed them to define the nature of the problem and how best to deal with those problems which are social in nature. Consequently, to become legitimate or demonstrate an expert posture in an area for which they have no academic background and training, they label and define social problems, diseases, and illnesses. What a tragedy. The great contradiction, however, is that the cure they recommend and administer is not medical in nature, but social psychological. It has also been noted that psychologists, social workers, and psychiatrists, when asked social questions and questions that are sociological, they convert the questions to fit their perspective in order to answer with some sense of authority.

The several articles published to date demonstrate the lack of control regarding the focus and direction of clinical sociology. Clinical sociologists and sociology can be clinical at the macro and micro levels (Swan, 1994), and it is a mistake to allow psychologists, psychiatrists, and clinical social workers, to dictate explicitly or implicitly the clinical nature of sociology and sociologists. It must be remembered that clinical sociologists must be scientists as well as practitioners. If this fact is born in mind, we will not simply become reflectors of the assessment and intervention mistakes the "trinity" makes in dealing with individuals in group life. Psychologists and psychiatrists and the varying psychotherapy types have no academic background and training in the theoretical perspectives which ground sociology and the practice of clinical sociology. There are sociologists who think that they have to be trained by psychologists, psychiatrists, or by a member of the "trinity" in order to be clinical. This is a grave mistake because those who practice psychotherapy have bankrupted the therapeutic process and distorted the scientific process of discovery for intervention and application. The conceptual notion which is the basis of the science of sociology and must be the focus of clinical sociologists, for both discovery and intervention, is that human beings live group life which is the proper context for every problem that is of a social nature, or for every problem of living. Therefore, the presenting problem of the individual is not simply an individual problem, but one with a social context which must be discovered in order to properly and adequately understand and treat the real problem. Every problem has its own context in time and space. In an attempt to become visible, clinically legitimate, and to increase numbers, we have embraced perspectives and professionals who are creating confusion, distortions, ambiguity and producing the same old results—nothing of real value to clinical sociology. In the final analysis, we would not have made a difference because we would have done the same thing other clinicians are doing and in the same old useless way. This does not mean that we should be opposed to developing synthesis in perspectives, but it does mean that the sociological perspective must be present, or it must dominate because human beings live group life. Sociology is the study of individuals in groups, and it looks at behavior within the context of the society in situations in which the individuals find themselves. Increasingly, a great number of psychologists have come to embrace the need to say more about the social and are now utilizing more sociological and organizational concepts in their thinking and practice. Thus, social interactions are the primary focus along with the mutual influence of the society on the individual and the individual on the society.

Sociotherapists argue that the individual and the social environment or the social situation must be studied together for clinical and intervention purposes.

The psychological definition of social psychology attempts to understand and explain the thoughts, feelings, and behaviors of individuals and how they are influenced by the actual or imagined, or implied presence of others (Stephan and Stephan, 1985). The focus of clinical sociologists, sociotherapists, and more particularly, psychosociotherapists is concerned with or seeks to understand and explain the thoughts, feelings, attitudes, opinions, choices, behaviors, and social experiences stemming from individuals' participation in social groups influenced by the actual, imagined, or implied presence of others. Psychology does not provide this perspective because it studies the individual as an individual with a unique individual make-up. It deals with the effects of group life only in an incidental fashion. It further views the individual as operating within a field of stimuli to which he responds. The human group is part of the stimulus field to which the individual is exposed and to which he responds.

The sociological approach has a different emphasis. The sociologist treats the individual as a participant in group life. Participation is not simply responding to other people, to participate means to share activities of others and to interact with them. It even means incorporating into oneself the activities of others. Only in recent decades have students of human behavior come to regard the group as a basic influence on human development and individual behavior. There is independence exercised in choice, but the group life experience is the frame of reference or context for the individual. Copious observations of different forms of human behavior in various regions of the world previously outside the scope of traditional study placed such a great burden on introspective explanations of human behavior that these explanations tended to break down. There has been change from such tradition in which individuals were thought to be "self contained" in their behavioral motivations. The relatively new orientation stems from a recognition that human life is organized within groups, and that this organization has important effects upon human behavior. Clinical sociologists should not continue to support the dominance of the clinical and applied fields, especially that of sociology, by professionals who have little or no academic background in the areas for which they claim expertise. It is not enough that persons trained as medical doctors are trained in one or more of the current psychotherapeutic modalities, most or all whom have never taken a sociology, psychology, or social psychology course. It is not enough that psychologists take a course or two in personality or psychopathology.

When conducting marital and family seminars and workshops, I sometimes ask to introduce myself. I do so by saying, I have a B.S. in biology or chemistry and an M.D. I would continue by saying, I have never taken a course in sociology, psychology, or marriage and the family, but I am a psychiatrist, psychologist, or psychotherapist who specializes in marital and family relations. On every occasion, the participants would laugh in disbelief. I often inquire about their laughter as a response, and there would be shocking and surprising comments. Comments and questions such as: Where did you get your knowledge? Biology does not equip you with knowledge about relationships and interactions! How did you get a license? Are you licensed to practice? The fact that "human beings live group life" and that all problems of a social nature emerge out of the context, puts a death—nail to the authoritative and dominant posturing of all clinicians whose academic background and training are void of such perspective and content. This lack has created the dilemma in the practice of psychotherapy. The majority of the participants would be amazed that this is exactly the academic and training condition of the majority of the "professionals" the society relies upon to explain and treat problems that are lodged or grounded in social context. Behavior, issues, problems and difficulty must be explained within context and should also be treated in context. It is a mistake for the assumed role of traditional clinicians who pretend or purport to treat problems that are of a social nature to go unchallenged. The clinical role of sociologists must be developed and established. Presently, we have allowed the clinical experience of sociologists to be controlled by the definitions, theoretical perspectives, and philosophical assumptions of the traditional therapeutic community dominated by professionals who have no background in sociology; the subject matter of their treatment concerns. Group life is the subject matter and content which provides the context for understanding problems of a social nature. Such problems cannot be understood nor treated effectively without locating and understanding the context out of which they emerge.

Articles which are supposed to advance the clinical perspective of sociologists tend to confuse the issue instead of clarifying those issues which have to do with establishing the clinical role of clinical sociologists. Maybe clinical sociologists should close academic and professional ranks, establish an independent role and function for themselves, and establish legal and public legitimacy and validation for their claims for being clinical. If this does not happen, and they continue to posture themselves as psychotherapists, or as secondary clinicians, then there is no point to their existence as clinical sociologists. Presently, they have no such claim, but are trying to convince other (traditional) clinicians that their theoretical perspective and therapeutic potential are what is missing from the therapeutic community. This posture or positioning is a mistake. Acceptance of definitions and explanations of problems advanced by other clinicians places clinical sociologists in a dependency posture in the clinical community. As trained social scientists, sociologists should know that predefined and predetermined explanations of problems, especially for intervention and change are incorrect. We need experiences that can help us determine how by being clinical, sociologists can in the therapeutic community, define problems, distinguish between symptoms, the presenting and the real problems, the context out of which they emerge, and the devising, from discoveries, a plan for intervention, and the appropriate techniques for treatment. As clinical sociologists, we have to be able to determine how problems emerge, and the content and context out of which they emerge. Any role short of this renders clinical sociologists facilitating participants in the therapeutic community dominated and controlled by professionals who have no academic background and theoretical and therapeutic perspectives appropriate to the nature of human social problems.

The Dilemma of Psychotherapy

Most clinicians who label themselves in the therapeutic field today, do so by using psychotherapy. Social workers, psychologists, and even psychiatrists who are asked about a label use psychotherapy. Many psychologists have labeled themselves community psychologists, and many psychiatrists are using the label social psychiatrists in an attempt to capture the social nature of their theoretical and therapeutic concerns (Jones, 1962). Social workers who have come to believe that their academic background is akin to that of those trained in sociology, either because they were required to take sociological theory, methods and statistics, or because they were taught by trained sociologists, flirt with the psychotherapy label, but do not ground their activity in sociological context nor a sociological social psychological context. They all make the mistake of seeing or viewing human behavior in strictly individual terms. This mistake is the essence of the dilemma which has dire consequences for understanding and treating human social problems. The dilemma is theoretical, methodological and therapeutic.

When we address (assess and intervene) family relations and interactions, human relations in industry, school sociology, criminal justice systems, public and social policy (government), and community service systems, we are dealing with social settings created by individuals who have come together to relate and interact for various and specified reasons. These settings are therefore social in nature because of the coming together of the human beings. This coming together to relate and interact defines the context of their interactions, relationships, and the individuals' behavior. The settings are therefore sociological social psychological settings because the human beings must take each other into account as they behave, relate, and interact with and among each other within the settings.

L. Alex Swan

Philosophical Assumptions and Goals:
A More Critical Review

When we examine the basic assumptions explicit in the philosophical positions of the popular therapeutic modalities, it seems true that the theoretical perspectives of the clinician determines what he looks for, what he sees, and what he treats. Psychoanalytic therapy argues that human beings are determined by unconscious motivation, sexual and aggressive impulses, irrational forces and early childhood experiences. This means that the dynamics of human behavior is rooted in the unconscious. Therefore, the clinician has to engage in a long process of discovering and analyzing inner conflicts that are buried in the past or in childhood. Adlerian therapy argues that "people are primarily social beings, shaped and motivated by social forces." Deep feelings of inferiority are developed in childhood which we seek to overcome as we strive for superiority.

Existential therapy holds that our choices define us even though the range of our choice is restricted by various factors. The human being is viewed as the author of his life. Person-Centered therapy views individuals as having the capacity to understand their problems and that the resources are really with them to resolve their difficulties. Gestalt therapy argues that if people are to achieve maturity, they must accept personal responsibility and find their own way in life. A climate must be provided for individuals to experience their here and now awareness and recognize how they are blocking their living in the present. Transactional analysis argues that human beings have the potential for choice. However, because their early decisions were made when they were children, they were significantly influenced by the expectations and injunctions of those who were considered important to them. Nonetheless, human beings are not passively "scripted," and can make new decisions to change past scripting and self defeating aspects of their lives. Behavior therapy makes the point that people are shaped by socio-cultural conditioning and learning. Therefore, behavior is seen as the product of learning and conditioning. Rational-Emotive therapy argues that human problems are the result of their perception of life situations and their thoughts.

Human beings are seen as falling victims to irrational beliefs which they re-indoctrinate themselves with, even though they are born with potentials for rational thinking. Reality therapy holds that human beings have a great need for identity and will develop either a success or failure identity.

For the clinicians of these therapeutic systems, the goals of therapy are determined by the theoretical orientations and not by what is discovered through the scientific, diagnostic, and assessment process. Data are dictated and determined by the established assumptions expressed in the basic positions and philosophical perspectives underlying the therapeutic systems. Corey makes the point that practicing counseling and therapy "without at least a general theoretical perspective is somewhat like flying a plane without a map and without instruments" (p. 4). He then places the basic assumptions and philosophical positions underlying the major theoretical orientations under three categories of theory. The contemporary therapeutic systems are assigned accordingly. The first is "the psychodynamic approaches which stress insight in therapy" (psychoanalytic and Adlerian therapy); the second is the "the experimental and relationship oriented approaches, which stress feelings and subjective experiencing" (Existential, Person-Centered, and Gestalt therapy); and the third is the cognitive and behavioral "approaches which stress the role of thinking and doing and tend to be action oriented" (Transactional Analysis, Behavior therapy, Rational-Emotive and other cognitive therapies, reality therapy, p.4). It is the predetermined and predefined nature of clients' problems implicit in the philosophical positions of the approaches and the related goals that also present problems and create the dilemma in the field of psychotherapy.

All of the therapeutic approaches identified above have related goals. These goals are dictated by the basic assumption and philosophical position of the particular approach. The goals for the psychoanalytic are: to explore the unconscious, to assist clients to relive earlier experiences, and to work through repressed conflicts. For the Adlerian, the goals are: to help clients develop social interests, to provide encouragement to discouraged individuals, to facilitate insight into mistaken ideas, and to show how these ideas are related to one's unique style of life. The goals for existential are: to challenge clients to recognize and accept the freedom they have to become the author of their lives, and to show clients ways they are avoiding accepting their freedom and responsibility that accompanies it. For person-centered the goals are: to provide a climate of understanding and acceptance through the client/therapist relationship that will enable clients to non-defensively come to terms with aspects of themselves that they have denied or disowned, to enable clients to move toward greater openness, increased sense of trust in themselves, and willingness to be a process rather than a finished product, and an increased sense of spontaneity. Gestalt goals are: to challenge clients to move from environmental support to self support and to assist them in gaining awareness of moment-to-moment experiencing, and to encourage clients to experience directly in the present of their struggles with unfinished business from the past. For transactional analysis the goals are: to help clients to become script-free, game-free, autonomous people capable of choosing intimate relationships, and to assist clients to examine the basis on which early decisions were made in the making more appropriate decisions based on new evidence. The goals of behavior therapy are: to eliminate clients' maladaptive behavior patterns and help them learn constructive patterns, to teach clients specific skills that they can see in developing a self-directed and self-managed behavioral change program, and to help clients identify patterns of thinking that lead to behavioral problems, and to teach new ways of thinking that are designed to change the client's way of acting. For RET, the goals are: to eliminate clients' self-defeating outlook of life and to assist them in acquiring a more tolerant and rational view of life, to teach clients how they incorporate irrational beliefs, how they maintain this faulty thinking and what they can do to undermine such thinking, and to teach clients how they can teach themselves new ways of thinking that will lead to changes in their ways of behaving and feeling. For reality therapy the goals are: to challenge clients to make assessment of their current behavior to determine if such ways of acting are getting them what they want from life, and to assist clients to make plans to change specific behaviors that they determine are not working for them (Pinsof, 1983).

When a clinician embraces one of these therapeutic approaches, he confines himself to the theoretical limitations of its dictates and is forced to seek and achieve goals which might not be appropriate to the problems of the clients. Further, it stifles the grounding of the problems in the social context of the clients which makes adequate discovery virtually impossible. The context of the clients' problem must be located, determined, and understood if the treatment (therapy) is to be effective, or if real change is to take place. This is the reason that clinicians must assume a scientific posture before invoking the therapeutic stance. Therapists must be scientists because their initial task is to collect data, specific information and knowledge from their clients about their specific problems and the context of their problems. However, the scientific process must not be hampered by the predetermined explanations and predefined nature of the modalities regarding clients' problems. Every therapeutic modality in operation today allows this grave mistake to be realized. The collection of data must be carried out through the process of discovery to determine the real problem(s). This must be done because all too often the client is confused about the presenting problem of stress, depression, social conflict, racism, substance abuse, spousal abuse, crime, and the fear of crime, sexual problems, child abuse, etc., which might very well be symptoms, which so many therapists treat as the real problems, not understanding how to discover the real problems. Consequently, during the intake interview and beyond, they seek to make their clients fit into their approaches or predetermined and predefined systems. The struggle with the clients and the information they produce is to force them into seeing their problems from the perspective defined by the approaches. If the problem is not in the embraced modality, the clients cannot be helped unless the data they present are forced into the philosophical and therapeutic scheme of the therapist's modality. The outcome is tragic because the real problems will not be discovered nor will the context of the problem be determined.

A therapeutic approach should have the potential to allow for any value, attitude, perspective, disposition, ideology or cultural trait or characteristic to emerge in the process of encounter, disclosure, and discovery. It should also allow for the emergence of specific information and common-sense knowledge unique to the social situation of the clients. The modality must invoke a dynamic approach that provides a creative interplay between theory, research, education, and practice which produces knowledge and grounded explanations for the purpose of intervention and application at both the macro and micro levels of human social problems. How problems are discovered, identified, understood, explained and treated are crucial to the outcome (Swan, 1994).

Meeting the Challenge

To adequately and appropriately address the challenge, whether the client is the individual, the community, couples, family, industry, or the social order of the society, we must establish the proper contextual frame of reference for understanding human social problems. Human beings live group life and a sociological social psychological perspective is best suited for understanding the problems of humans within that context. The theoretical perspective of psychotherapy which focuses on the individual or personality system is alone too narrow. It is very clear that as clinicians we do not have prior specific and particular knowledge about clients' problems and the context of their emergence. Consequently, because of the therapeutic posture they embrace, the predetermined explanations of the psychotherapeutic modalities restrict proper and appropriate discovery. In fact, their stance is to tell the clients what their problems are and to assist them in viewing their problems from the established predetermined perspective of their modality.

Traditional clinicians see what they look for, and what they look for they see, and what they see is what their therapeutic modalities allow them to see; and what their therapeutic modalities allow them to see is what they treat. When we embrace a particular psychotherapeutic modality with predetermined explanations of clients' problems, we become bound by its vision of human problems. Traditional therapists are trapped by the expectations of clients because therapists have promoted the notion that they have the ability to tell clients why they are having the problems they present. The therapist's posture is that of an expert who can tell clients what their problems are. This is the reason that so many clients actually out rightly ask therapists, "Doc, what's my problem? What's wrong with me?" We must argue as sociological clinicians, who are scientists and practitioners that we must discover with our clients what must be known and understood about their problems and the contexts of their problems before they can be explained in order that intervention and application can be effective for change. No clinician should venture an explanation of human social problems until discovery of the explanation is achieved. When we posit in the minds a reason or an explanation, this becomes the reason and explanation. The power of the predetermined nature of the therapist's stance validates the reasons or the explanations. If there is disjuncture between the explanations and the beliefs of the clients, resistance results and the struggle begins to convince the clients that the explanations suggested by the modality are correct. Note that the explanations are not suggested by the context or situation of the clients and those implicated therein. Further, when we do not allow for the inclusion of all implicated in the social situation/context of the problem, the tendency is for the excluded to offer (especially family members) to our clients explanations and information which appear correct because they are closer than we are, as therapists, to the situation.

In order to truly advocate the sociological social psychological perspective, we must also challenge the perspective held about the personality, and present a proper understanding of the individual as a social self (Swan, 1994). An individual defines his self concept by taking the roles of other people and groups and looking at himself from the point of view of these roles. The group is the most important perspective from which the individual defines his self concept, particularly in the earliest stages of development of the self. An individual can interact with himself without making overt indications, and he can therefore create a private world of the mind. There is no differentiation between the private world of the individual and the outer world of social interaction. Self interaction and social interactions are essentially the same processes. The fundamental difference between them is that the private world of the mind is not open to observation from the outside, but the resulting behavior is a reflection of the private world of the mind. Self interaction is a basis for overt action. Self interaction is an important means by which a person controls his action in the external world. The individual confronts the world on the basis of his ability to make indications to himself. He acts on the basis of what he perceives to be the objects in his environment and on the basis of what he defines the meaning of those objects to be. Within this process, the individual develops an independence of self as he selects the properties and characteristics of the self to be developed.

The self eventually has a multiplicity of properties or characteristics developed at varying degrees over a period of time through interacting and relating with others. The social situation dictates which property to evoke in interaction. The individual has the ability to make adjustments so that a property of characteristic emerges consistent with an appropriate situation or occurrence. If a situation emerges which requires a particular property, the individual has the ability to posture that characteristics until, through many demonstrations, that characteristic is developed and becomes a permanent part of the social self.

Conclusion

How human social problems are discovered, identified, understood, and explained is crucial to how they are treated. Such problems should be treated within their context. They cannot be well understood outside of their context, neither can they be effectively treated outside of their context, neither can they be effectively treated outside of their context. Proper understanding and appropriate treatment are crucial to the outcome. Clinical sociologists who practice psychotherapy do so because clinical sociology and sociotherapy are not well known even though in practice, sociological knowledge and understanding have been used by other clinicians. Today, many psychologists are realizing that humans live group life, as such, they are making the necessary theoretical and methodological adjustments which will influence and change their therapeutic stance.

Clinical sociologists are also tempted to practice psychotherapy because it is legitimized and legalized and there are established treatment modalities and techniques for application. Clinical sociologists must develop their own therapeutic approaches if they are to become legitimate clinicians applying sociological knowledge. Very few attempts are being made in this direction. Instead, there is too much leaning and borrowing from the bankrupt approaches of psychology and psychotherapy whose flaw is that they do not allow for discovery of problems and related contexts. To lean on the medical, psychological or social work models is to misunderstand the nature of human social problems. We have to make conceptual attempts to identify the key characteristics of sociodiagnostic and sociotherapeutic models for clinical sociologists who apply sociological knowledge or those who deal with problems that are social in nature. This creative process will benefit other clinicians and their clients as well as sociological clinicians.

The psychological perspective which dominates the practice of psychotherapy has always overly influenced the way we have sought to develop the area of clinical sociology. Psychologists, social workers and others, even sociologists, are raising serious and rather damaging questions about our legitimacy when they see us using psychological concepts, terms, orientations, and approaches. Those of us trained in sociology who became counselors and therapists, especially before 1976, got in-service training from psychologists. We attend workshops conducted by psychiatrists, psychologists, and persons who called themselves clinical social workers. Some even think they had the good fortune of being trained or attended workshops conducted by Carl Rogers and Fritz Perls. Few, very few of us have tried to make a break, and there can be a real clean break from those perspectives if the effort is made. Various types of psychotherapists who review our published articles in the journal can see their ghosts running through each page.

Clinical sociology is being distorted and destroyed by the domination of theoretical, methodological and clinical perspectives that are not congruent with its theoretical grounding. There are no clinical populations and conceptual levels to which clinical sociology is not appropriate if the problems are social in nature or have a social context. We have to provide a scientific way for discovering the nature of the problems and their social context, and for explanations about the problems that emerge in the process of discovery, and the ways of making changes in the social situation or setting, views, and behavior of the clients.

The clinical role of clinical sociologists is not well developed and established, but it should not mean that the psychotherapeutic and psychiatric definitions, assumptions and perspectives should dictate how real problems are determined or how their contexts are located. In light of its bankrupt state, according to its own literature, clinical sociologists must not embrace traditional psychotherapeutic and psychiatric diagnosis and treatment to validate their clinical legitimacy.

Because we argue that the "mental" problems people face are primarily difficulties they are having in coping with stresses of everyday life, or with the problems of living, we advance a social psychological perspective. However, the depiction is a sociological definition of social psychology rather than a psychological definition of social psychology. This is the case because the individual's behavior is social in context, or group based—it emerges out of the context of a social setting. The social setting which is the concern of the sociological social psychological consist of social experiences resulting from the individuals coming together and the creation of and participation in the setting. The nature of the individuals' participation in group life, and the effects of the cultural environment on the social experiences and interactions with others in the setting, must be viewed in terms of the choices made to behave from the interpretations of the interactions and objects in the setting. Because of this perspective, clinical sociologists must close ranks which should have been done initially in order to avoid the distortions, confusions and misunderstanding within and outside sociology about their validity and legitimacy as clinicians.

We have allowed clinical social workers, psychologists and psychiatrists—the psychotherapy trio—to adversely influence what clinical sociology should be about and how it should go about being clinical. Its growth has been stifled by the imposition of traditional clinical types whose theoretical and methodological perspectives are not grounded in the sociological. It has been very clear from the re-emergence of clinical sociology that those already in the clinical field were not pleased with such a development. They had attempted to broaden their perspectives and approaches to include the sociological. However, the sociological is not peripheral; it is core in any attempt to understand and treat human problems that are lodged and grounded in a social context. The discipline of sociology and, especially the area of sociological social psychology, provide the basis for an appropriate, adequate, and effective approach to assisting human beings and their needs in group life.

The knowledge and understanding the discipline contains can serve clinical sociologists who wish to function as change agents, counselors, and therapists. The knowledge of social experiences allows clinical sociologists to understand the experiences and in doing something or taking action about the experiences. It must be understood that all individual behavior takes place in relation to or within the context of the group. Relating and interacting are properties of the group. Therefore, human group life consists of individuals interacting and relating with one another. In some cases, it is done well and satisfactory, and in others it is not done well and satisfactory, thus, creating situations and settings for understanding and change—individual and/or situational.

References

Bender, M. P.
  1976 <u>Community Psychology</u>. London: Methuen and Co.

Corey, Gerald
  1985 <u>Theory and Practice of Group Counseling.</u> Monterey, CA: Brooks/Cole Publishing Co.

Jones, Maxwell
  1962 <u>Social Psychiatry</u>. London: Tavistock.

Pinsof, William M.
  1983 "Integrative Problem-Centered Therapy," <u>Journal of Marriage and Family Therapy</u>, 9, 19-35.

Roberts, Lance W.
  1991 "Clinical Sociology with Individuals and Families." In Howard M. Rebach and John G. Bruhn (Eds.) <u>Handbook of Clinical Sociology</u>. New York: Plenum Press.

Stephan, Cookie White and Walter G. Stephan
  1985 <u>Two Psychologies.</u> Homewood, IL: Dorsey Press.

Swan, L. Alex
  1994 <u>The Practice of Clinical Sociology and Sociotherapy</u>. Rochester, VT: Schenkman Publishing Co.

Szasz, T. S.
  1962 <u>The Myth of Mental Illness</u>. London: Seeker and Warburg.

Grounded Encounter Therapy: A Sociadiagnostic and Sociotherapeutic Approach

Chapter 5

*   *   *

Grounded Encounter Therapy: A Sociadiagnostic and Sociotherapeutic Approach

Sociodiagnostic and Sociotherapeutic

Very few therapists practicing at the macro level or at the micro level understand, embrace, or practice sociotherapy. Many of those sociologists who define themselves as clinical sociologists tend to learn more toward the practice of psychotherapy than sociotherapy even though they advocate the application of sociological knowledge and information to problems lodged primarily in a social context.

Sociotherapy is concerned with the social situation and the interpretations and definitions of those implicated in the social system. On the other hand, psychotherapy is concerned with the personality system. In <u>Sociotherapy and Psychotherapy</u> (Eldeson, 1970), a detailed theoretical foundation for sociotherapy is established, and in another work, <u>The Practice of Sociotherapy </u>(Eldeson, 1970), case studies in sociotherapy, and the knowledge and skills required of the sociotherapist are set forth. As a new kind of a clinician, these works set forth the conceptual tools and skills required of the sociotherapist, and show how the sociotherapist's diagnosis, analysis, and interventions are oriented to the social situation and social context, rather than to the personality system and individual context. "The sociotherapist, then, is one trained in sociology who is capable of making social diagnosis and formal assessments of interactional patterns and social situations to arrive at clinical judgments, and to offer techniques, schemes and strategies for intervention to facilitate change" (Swan, 1980: 98). The sociotherapist approach, therefore, requires a scientific process for social diagnosis, and a therapeutic process for application and treatment. In this sense, sociotherapy might be defined as a process of social diagnosis "aimed at achieving constructive social and behavioral changes in social situations and in the interactional patterns among individuals, group(s), organizations and communities" (Swan, 1980: 98).

Therapeutic approaches do not mean very much, nor are they very effective if they do not convey the content and process of their dynamics. They are also weak and powerless if they do not have methodological procedures for social diagnosis, and for allowing theoretical insights to emerge from the content of the social situation discovered in the process of diagnosis. Most therapies in use today merely describe the structural relationship between the clients and therapists and are not grounded in methodological procedures and theoretical insights. Part of this criticism is not original; many therapists have voiced their recognition of this lack and weakness in many therapeutic techniques (Hurvitz, 1979; Olson, 1970; Nichols, 1974:32).

For example, concurrent family therapy, conjoint family therapy, collaborative marital therapy, multiple impact therapy (MIT), marital group therapy, and other such techniques are mere descriptions of structural relationships of various kinds (Greene & Solomon, 1963; Satir, 1964; Martin, 1965; MacGregor, 1952; Henderson, 1965). Treating people in social situations with interpersonal and relationship problems, or treating social situations, demands a scientific posture which relates method and theory for the collection of essential facts for diagnostic purposes, and the explanation of those facts bearing upon the problems and situations for therapeutic purposes. This is the way treatment gets grounded in the social context of the clients who are implicated in the situation and problems.

What is Grounded-Encounter Therapy?

Grounded encounter therapy (GET) is a process of encounter, interpretation, and situational analysis which allows for the discovery of essential facts and explanations that are grounded in the social situation (context) of the clients. It provides for the devising of strategies, plans, and approaches for change, growth, and development that are also grounded in the social context of the clients. As a sociotherapeutic approach, GET has as its focus the social health among individuals, groups, and other social settings of group life (industrial, community, organizational), and combines theoretical and methodological perspectives in the process of discovery and situational analysis so that the conclusions and explanations, as well as the prescriptions and plans for change are grounded in the particular social setting of the clients. Therefore, both the scientific and practical aspects of the therapeutic intervention are addressed by GET, and the process and content, and the structural matters are accounted for in the diagnostic and therapeutic approach. The diagnostic posture is a scientific function, and the therapeutic posture is a practical function and process. It is within this context that clinical applications of the discovered knowledge are complete and effective.

The social illness of the clients' situation, and the difficulties in their relationships, interactional and interpersonal life, as they are related to the clients' social situation, are discovered through encounter, and interpreted and explained for purposes of grounding the therapy. Encounter is for the purpose of diagnosis, and the data discovered through this process provides the basis for theoretical insights relative to the problem(s) and the social situation in which the difficulties faced are lodged. Through the process of encounter, therefore, therapeutic intervention for change, growth and development are grounded in the theoretical insights that are grounded in the data discovered in diagnosing the problem, and the social situation, or the social context of the difficulties. Grounding the therapy in the explanations produced through the discovery of information and knowledge through the process of encounter gives the assurance that the therapeutic intervention is related to the social context of the problems faced by the clients. GET, therefore is a sociatherapeutic technique for social diagnosis and treatment of problems faced by individuals, groups, families, couples, communities, organizations and industries that are lodged in social situations. It describes the process and content in the determination, interpretation and devising of plans and strategies for dealing with problems that are social in nature, or have a social context.

Grounded encounter therapy is process and content oriented because clients seek help in terms of gaining insight and understanding of the nature of their group life, and their participation therein. Others seek both insight, clarity and ways to bring about change in situations, interpersonal and relationship matters that are producing problems and difficulties for them. GET is therefore a dynamic diagnostic and therapeutic approach that provides a creative interplay between education, research and practice that produces grounded explanations (theories) for the purpose of applications by the therapist or the clients of their problems that are grounded primarily in group life, and a variety of skills, techniques and strategies for grounding the content of the clients, discovered through encounter and situational analysis, to what is, and what should and can be done. The creative interplay between methods and theory allows for the flow of information and knowledge from the real world of the clients during the diagnostic process. The sociotherapist gets a more accurate view, which is grounded in the social situation of the clients, during the creative exchange, of the subject matter which generated appropriate and useful information for decision making and therapeutic intervention.

This approach (GET) is different and appropriate for the clinical sociologist and sociotherapist because it is relevant to the nature, character and focus of sociology. It employs encounter as a methodological technique in the process of collecting essential facts (social diagnosis), for the discovery of information and knowledge about the situation and problems faced by clients. Theories and explanations are generated from the data collected through encounter, which grounds the explanations and interpretations of problems, and establishes the basis for grounding the treatment for change and growth (Glasner and Straus, 1967; Dean, 1976). In other words, therapeutic actions are grounded in the theoretical insights that emerge from the collection of information during the process of encounter.

The Diagnostic and Therapeutic Process and Content

Contact for intervention and assistance is usually made by one or both parties. If one person in a couple, or a family makes contact, it is sometimes important to determine the attitudes and dispositions of others relative to the contact. There are times when friends make the initial contact and they should be instructed to encourage the affected parties to call or visit the office of the sociotherapist. When the parties make contact with the sociotherapist, and an appointment is arranged, the clients should be made aware of the process of diagnosis and therapy. They should be clear as to what sociotherapy is; what is expected to be achieved; what posture clients and the sociotherapist are social context, or problems that are social in nature.

Essential to GET, as a diagnostic and therapeutic approach, is the personal encounter between the clients, and between and among the clients and the therapists. Through the dialogues and sharing of feelings and thinking, clients can communicate to each other their concerns and describe their situation so that the authentic picture comes through. It is when the clients are able to communicate and dialogue in each other's presence, and in the presence of the therapist, in an encountering posture, that the real experiences; the real sharing; the real learning happens. This is especially true in a sharing group with other clients, because it helps the clients that are dialoguing, in the case of a couple, and also causes insights and growth to be experienced by others. Because social diagnosis is a scientific process, the encounter strategy is employed to collect the essential facts from all persons implicated in the situation, the problems, difficulties, dysfunctions, etc. In the process, information and knowledge emerge as the encounter takes place. This process is essential to the treatment, which is a practical process, because what needs to be done becomes evident to both the clients and therapist from the data, and the situational analysis grounds the expectations of what the problems are for therapeutic action by the therapist who devises plans to achieve or experience change, growth and development. Therapy must be grounded in the social situation (context) of the clients, and in the interpretations, situational analysis, explanations and meanings that reveal themselves during the encounter among and between those who are implicated in the social situation.

GET does not allow for speculation. It engages the sociotherapists in a process using methods of science to gather accurate information that is relevant in helping create and develop theories that explain the events, processes, patterns of relating, and interpersonal matters occurring in the social context of the clients. Further, it allows the sociotherapist to use relevant methods of science to also test the plausibility of the explanations or theories that emerge from the encounter. The sociotherapist brings to the process, insights, understanding and knowledge about group life; human behavior to assume if the diagnostic and therapeutic processes are to be helpful and effective; the number of possible sessions, and the cost, which is followed by invited feedback from the clients.

Once the situation is designated or identified by the client(s), a determination should be made of all of the parties implicated in the social situation, and those who might be external to the situation, but have indirect influence on the situation. Couple and family members often come to the first session blaming each other or relatives and friends indirectly involved. It takes a couple of sessions for them to be convinced that this posture is unhealthy to resolving conflicts. Implicit in this stance is usually the belief that the other person should change, and if and when this happens, "things" would be different, or better.

Figure 1
Diagnostic and Therapeutic Process

Diagnosis	Interpretation and Analysis	Therapy and Treatment
(Collecting the essential facts; Identification and designation of problems)	(Theoretical insights, clarity of issues, and grounding explanations)	(Devising of plans, goals and strategies for change and growth)

The initial task of the sociotherapist is to accurately diagnose the client's social situation. To do this, a determination must be made of the essential facts; an understanding of their relationship to the social situation, and an assessment must be made of the relevant facts against the described pattern of interaction between the clients and the salient features of their social context. This process makes the diagnostic process reliable and guarantees that the sociotherapeutic planning and strategies are grounded in the explanations, or theoretical insights that emerged from the data collected from the social situation of the clients (Figure1). Adequate diagnosis, therefore, requires the determination of knowledge and information relative to the client's social situation and difficulties. This scientific process is the basis for fully understanding the client's problems in light of their social relationships and interactions so that practical plans can be formulated for social treatment. This process necessitates a methodological stance which is later complimented by a theoretical posture for explanation, and clarity. When this process is followed, clients can be assured that the treatment (therapy) is grounded and rooted in the social context (situation) of their difficulties and problems. The diagnostic and therapeutic process might be specifically identified as follows: 1) a description and discovery of the situation and related problems with methodological techniques to assist this task; 2) assessment of the situation and problems with theoretical insights; 3) implementation of strategies that are devised from the situational analysis for therapeutic intervention and change. It is important and enhancing when research support for the explanations can be located outside of the client's situation (Blumer, 1969; Burr, et., al., 1979).

During the first session, the sociotherapist should determine: 1) what is the problem and/or the situation from the clients' point of view; 2) the persons implicated in the situation, and 3) the clients' interpretation and meaning of the situation and problems in terms of their perceptions of themselves (Thomas, 1961; Rogers, 1970). This process is accomplished on an individual basis (concurrent) before everyone implicated in the situation comes together to encounter in group or collective (conjoint) sessions. Questions should be asked of each person in separate sessions, and the same or similar questions asked during the encounter in conjoint sessions. The goal is to collect data for situational analysis, and for the conversion of the hardcore data to theory and explanations of the situation of the clients. This is the key to effective and appropriate theory. Therapy must be grounded in theory which is grounded in data generated from the social situation of the clients, discovered through encounter. The sociotherapist engages himself in a scientific process in discovering explanations (theories) from data systematically obtained from social research with the clients. In this way the sociotherapist is arriving at the explanations that are suited to sociotherapeutic uses. This is a contrast to explanations of the client's situation and problems generated by logical deductions from prior assumptions.

Data collections might require several individual sessions, but each person must be given the opportunity to provide definitions, interpretations, and meanings of the relationship, interaction, and the social situation without intimidation and interruption from any other concerned party. The person is also encouraged to make individual designations of the problems and the social situation. In other words, the client is asked: What do you think the problem is?, and/ or What would you say is the situation? The data collected during the individual sessions are compared with data collected relative to the same or similar questions during encounter in collective sessions. It could be a grave mistake to start collective sessions without giving each person the opportunity and freedom to express views privately. All too often, therapists start to work collectively with clients without collecting adequate and sufficient data. There is the possibility that relevant data might never be discovered if not first revealed in individual sessions. In many cases, however, the therapist might not have the methodological skills and/or he might be tempted to give in to the pressure by clients to get the therapeutic process going. It is important that clients also know that effective and appropriate therapeutic intervention requires the generation of explanations that are discovered from the collection of essential facts about their social situation and difficulties. Clients tend to develop an attitude condusive to the collection of essential data, when they know the importance of this process to the effective treatment of their problems and situation.

Aside from the questions which speak to the situation and the relationship, responses should be sought relative to the goals, desires, anticipations, and commitments of each individual implicated in the social situation. Encounter is used only in the process of social diagnosis. To the sociotherapist, this is a most effective way to collect relevant facts about the clients and their social situation. No move should be made towards therapy until it is agreed that all related facts have been discovered and that the parties are ready to come together to work on what has been discovered about themselves and their situation, revealed and identified by them. When there is this agreement, the procedures, strategies and techniques should be explained to them and feedback should be encouraged.

Grounding the Therapy: Theoretical and Methodological Encounters

We agree that to be effective, therapy must be solidly anchored in the social context which constitutes the empirical world of the clients' situation, especially in marital and family relationships. This is the only way for the sociotherapist to determine their properties from evidence produced during encounter. The evidence from which the categories emerge is used to illustrate and explain the situation and problems. In this regard, the frame of reference of the clients; the content and process of their relationships; the nature of their interaction and their general social settings are subjects of the investigation.

<u>Figure 2</u>
Client's Social Context

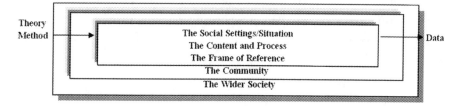

117

The clients' community and the influences, direct or indirect, of the wider society also provide information and knowledge regarding the clients' social context and their social process perspectives. To assist the clients manage, cope, change, rearrange, reestablish, and establish joint action; the individual and collective experiences and the interaction and relationship patterns must be assessed within the context in which they are lodged. If, for example, a young single parent who divorced her husband and returned, for a variety of reasons to live with her parents, are experiencing problems with her mother, and occasionally with her father in managing her son; when the sociotherapist works with the parent and diagnosis the case to be one of role conflict, the social context out of which the role conflict emerged must be addressed. The conflict might present itself in various forms and could be very stressful; causing other conflicts, or conflicts in other areas of family life. To deal with the role conflicts might not only require defining and redefining the roles of the parent and the grandparents relative to the son/grandson, but the social context, which includes economic and household support from the woman's parents, would have to be addressed along with the nature and perceptions of her presence in the household of her parents. Adequately dealing with the problem might require the removal of the single parent and her son from the home of her parents. This would require an assessment of the nature of her presence and position in the community as a single parent, and the impact or influence of the wider society on her community to allow her to survive and support her family independent of her parents. The social ties established between the son and his grandparents, and the emotional identification they share must also be assessed and investigated.

A more radical act would be able to leave the city, or state, or if she remains in the city, break communications with her parents for six months, or a year. When we ground the problem diagnosed in its proper social context, we are in a better position to suggest changes that get at the real matter. Once we ground the problem, we get a total picture of its roots and the various possible alternatives for management and change (Swan, 1981). The process of diagnosis and therapy is how we bring people, or how people come to understand, see and take note of what the problem actually is in their situation, interaction, and pattern of relationships, and the action taken in this regard. The method and process involved are the most important focus; otherwise we could arrive at distorted explanations, designations and interpretations that would lead to faulty knowledge and information for application to the problems and situation. The direction for change is therefore rooted and grounded in the discovery from the methods and process employed by the sociotherapist to collect the essential facts.

Some degree of preconception is inevitable. However, avoiding preconceptions is essential to grounding the therapy. The sociotherapist at times must immerse himself in the social setting, through role taking, and or participant observation. If there are no preconceptions to distort, and insights are keen, explanations will emerge as a consequence of the experience encountered. Encounter for the purpose of data collection is not confined only to encounter between and among clients, and between clients and the sociotherapist, but also between the sociotherapist and the social situation or setting of the clients. Coding and comparing incidents and actions of the participants in the situation will allow for a definition of what kind of a situation we are faced with. When theoretical properties of the setting are generated and categorized, they will provide the conditions under which the incidents and difficulties emerged. Interviewing individual members of the social situation is simply for purposes of further discovery and verification. Discovering explanations from the process of collecting the data through encounter, participation, role taking, and comparison, enhances the possibility to determine the dynamics of the problems and the ingredients of the social context of the clients, and establishes the uniqueness of each social situation. Grounding the therapy resulting from this social diagnostic process makes more reliable the diagnosis and more effective the treatment of the problems and the situation. As a trained sociologist, the sociotherapist should be capable, given this process of social diagnosis, to make applications of sociological knowledge and information to problems that are social in nature, or are grounded in a social context.

Employing Grounded Encounter Therapy

Using grounded encounter therapy with couples and families in collective sessions allows for the problems of interaction, relationship, and their situation to be identified as the individuals encounter each other in conversation facilitated by the sociotherapist. As specific problems are noted and identified, they are checked with the clients. Discussion is encouraged, monitored, and facilitated by the sociotherapist who provides clarity through analysis, and strategies are devised for establishing short term and long term goals, and assignments are made to effect change. At each point, commitment is obtained from clients to carry out the assignments to solve their problems and change their situation.

During the first individual session, questions are of a basic nature. A series of questions should be asked that are related to the basic questions. These questions should include those that speak to the clients' perceptions of each other's view of the situation, and what each thinks the other wants to do about the situation. What is disclosed during the individual sessions should be the basis for the encounter during collective sessions. Surprises, discrepancies, disagreements, and conflicts in perceptions and perspectives are discovered as the sociotherapist facilitates the process. Questions during the collective session should be specific and focused on aspects of the interaction, relationships and patterns of behavior and responses of the clients to each other. In the process of encounter, relative to the questions, they discover what the problems really are, and revelations of what needs to be done, and how to handle their problems emerge and are offered. New social skills are suggested and their home assignments are designed for the implementation of the devised strategies and skills.

Employing the grounded encounter therapeutic approach allows the couples or family members the opportunity to talk to each other on a face to face basis under controlled circumstances. This process is very important if problems persisted for a long period of time and were maintained by unknown factors, or factors that the parties were unwilling, or had an inability to openly discuss. As the process of encounter operates, understanding is achieved as to the pressures and factors that created the problems and those factors that maintain them. The schemes and strategies for change are grounded in this understanding. The diagnostic process is designed to allow each individual the opportunity to talk directly to each other and receive feedback from each other. If one of the problems discovered has to do with communication, the homework assigned would require the parties to note when the other allowed the other to speak, or when one person thought the other really listened. Other assignments might be to assess the strengths of each other, or identify and place emphasis on the positive aspects of each other. Another assignment might be for the individual to separately make note of their short and long term goals. It is also important during the diagnostic process to have each client identify those things they know about each other that they would not like to see changed. This attempt is to get the clients to focus on their strengths.

After the identification of their strengths, an assessment of the strengths should be made. Implicit in the analysis and assessment, emphasis should be on the potential for change in the relationship, or pattern of interaction that is presenting the difficulty, or in the social situation out of which the problems emerged. Those changes that are possible and productive should be noted relative to the difficulties discovered. Agreement should be sought from the clients that if these changes are made that growth, development and change would occur in their relationship, interaction and their situation. The sociotherapist should determine from the clients if they feel comfortable with the plans and strategies for change. This feedback is important because the exercises and plans for change are developed from the information so that, through practice by the clients of the assignments, changes occur, and the practice becomes the pattern of behavior for them in their marital and family situation. To finalize the diagnostic process, the sociotherapist should seek a contract (the meeting of the minds) for commitment for continuing and completing the tasks, and for follow through. In this regard, the long term goals are significant because they provide the basis for the clients to establish joint action, and complete short term goals.

In the treatment process (Figure 3), tasks are identified and planned in an added value manner. Task A establishes the basis for moving to task B, and so forth and so on until the termination of the therapy. The scale for rating progress allows the socitherapist and the clients to participate. If there is a discrepancy in rating, the clients and the clinician should analyze and discuss their interpretations and explanations of the tasks and activities to determine their differences. If there is no agreement, it is progressive to accept the clients' definition and designation of progress although the sociotherapist should make clear what the differences are and why there are such differences. There should be assigned a reasonable time for the task to be accomplished. In some cases the clients might be making satisfactory progress such that the clinician might take them to the other task without making maximum progress (5). In such a case, the activities of the latter part of the task of the present step are dove tailed into the beginning part of the next task of the next step.

Figure 3
The Treatment Process

Steps	1	2	3	4	5
	Task (A)	Task (B)	Task (C)	Task (D)	Task (E)
	|	|	|	|	|
	012345		012345		012345
		012345		012345	
	|	|	|	|	|
	Time	Time	Time	Time	Time
	|	|	|	|	|
	Assignment	Assignment	Assignment	Assignment	Assignment

Assignments should be related to the task, and it must be clear to the clients how they are related. During each session of the therapeutic phase, clients are expected to provide feedback on their assigned activities. The anticipation of feedback from clients means that the sociotherapist makes growth producing assignments. If the focus in the sessions is interpersonal and relationship problems, the tasks assignments might have to do with developing communication skills and patterns; redefining the situation; changing perceptions of self; changing patterns of interaction and of relationships; altering and modifying role performances; establishing joint action, and changing attitudes and dispositions.

If, for example, the clients are focusing on communications in their relationship as a problem, they might be facilitated in a discussion of the issue in such a way that allows each one to speak and listen so that the desired pattern is formed. The assignment to check the times each allows the other to speak without interruption, and noting the occasions when each really listens, reinforces the activities of the task during therapeutic sessions. Through this process, change in the manner in which they communicate with each other takes place, and the ability to see the situation from the other's point of view is developed. This posture is taken because the sociotherapist views communication as the ability of people to take one another's roles, and in this way to understand what others are thinking and planning to do. The clients should be encouraged to do their assignments faithfully, and to avoid discussing the related problem/issue on their own away from the sessions. A telephone call from the sociotherapist to the clients during the week serves this purpose well.

Grounded Encounter Therapy with Groups

By definition, sociology is well suited to the work of the sociotherapist with groups. Those who practice psychotherapy have focused on the internal state or personality system of an individual as a method of treatment. Those who practice sociotherapy as a method of treatment, applying sociological knowledge and information, focus on the social situation, particularly the social process in which the individual operates and creates (Edelson, 1970; Kovel, 1976; Parson, 1951). Since about 1950, professionals in the mental health field have gradually accepted the idea that group therapy is an effective technique for treating mental health patients. Group therapy techniques are rooted in group theory which argues that mental health problems are lodged in group relations and group life, and can be changed with new social relations, or by changing the nature of the current group relations. The fact that most problems faced by individuals are social in nature, suggests that the modification and/or change of individuals' problems cannot be dealt with in the same manner as the problems of persons infected by a social disease. The persons relations with social groups must be modified and/or changed if the problems are to be effectively dealt with. Group therapy has, therefore, become accepted, and in some cases has replaced individual therapy by professionals who have little or no body of theoretical knowledge and methods in which to group their practice. Consequently, they have had to borrow from the academic discipline of sociology for theoretical and methodological support for their practice because sociology is the study of human behavior in group life, and has created knowledge and information relevant to applications made in group therapy.

Mankind has always lived in groups, and traditional clinicians have seen man as standing alone. The sociotherapist use of sociological knowledge for applications is based upon the notion that the problems of individuals and groups are of a social nature, and are lodged primarily in a social context. Consequently, the group and group members who have social ailments need and deserve the care of a sociotherapist. This means that sociological knowledge and thinking (theory and methods) are used in a practical clinical way to assist human beings change their pattens of interaction, relationships, and their social situations.

The Group Experience Lab (GEL) is an appropriate strategy when working with groups. The members of the group can be taught to become concerned about the feelings and situations of each other through nonverbal and verbal exercises. The group might be used as a social meter to tell the members who they are in the eyes of each other, and how they are experienced by the group members. In the process, members of the group become aware of their own feelings and more sensitive to the feelings of other group members. The members should be encouraged to be themselves and not what others want them to be. Phoniness should be discouraged and involvement of everyone should be encouraged. In the group, there should be less concern with what the members were yesterday, but with what they are at the time, and what they want to become. The group operates, therefore, on the basis of the "here and now" (Perls, et. al., 1951).

Guidelines should be announced at the start of the group sessions. They should be: 1) Say how you feel in the here and now; 2) Own your own feelings; 3) Say whatever you feel and say it as and like you feel it; 4) Avoid value judgments and; 5) Be open and honest about what you say. The primary tool in the group process is the "feedback." Group members should tell each other, as honestly as possible, how they experience their presence, what they are really saying, whether they believe it or not, how they feel about them, not necessarily why, and the members should respond in the same manner. The members may not accept the feedback, but at least they will know. Knowing makes it easier to cope with the situation. In fact, knowing (through encounter and interaction) as the members will know in the group experience sessions, is the basis of change. This approach provides a step by step training experience which develops the insights necessary to overcome communication barriers. The group should be focused on such specific dynamic techniques as listening with increased awareness; role taking; sensitivity to one's own behavior and its effects on others; and alertness to the reactions that interfere with making accurate observations, interferences and decisions. The group experience lab should offer the participants an opportunity to acquire basic interpersonal skills relevant to all life situations.

The group experience labs are designed for those who wish to improve their relations and interactions with other people in social situations. The aim is to establish an informal group atmosphere in which individuals can communicate openly with a feeling of security. This process provides members of the group with a technique for the actualization of individual potential and effective functioning in group life (Ruitenbeck, 1970). A focus on the feelings of group members should also be a primary activity in the group. Feelings can be painful, and should be brought out in the open. We can change our feelings, deny, repress, and avoid the sources of our feelings. We can even shut out one kind of feelings or another. Because of this, life can become meaningless, flattened, and problematic. Group members should be encouraged to take risk of expressing their feelings whether they are anger, joy, warmth, tenderness, pain, affection, or love. In the process, members develop an ability to deal with the feelings of others as they take the risk (which has group support) of expressing their own feelings in an open and honest manner. The first group session should have some type of structure in that the members of the group should be led through a series of nonverbal and verbal experiences to allow for the expression of feelings in a relatively safe situation. Hopefully, the individuals will rediscover their sensitivity and awareness so that encounter can take place, and growth, development and change can be experienced.

Conclusion

Grounded encounter therapy is a process of diagnosis (for purposes of designation and indication), interpretation and situational analysis (for purposes of explanation), and treatment (for purposes of change and growth), that is grounded in data discovered by the clients and sociotherapist as they encounter and explore their experiences and the social situation (context) out of which client's problems emerged. The process includes the interpretations and meanings assigned to the situation by those implicated in the social situation. The defective elements that impeded growth and development in the interpersonal and relationship experiences of the clients are identified and clarified, and plans for change are developed and implemented. The interpretations and meanings provided by the client and those implicated in the social situation during the diagnosis and situational analysis, allow for the ethnic, racial, and gender differences to be noted and considered which must be accounted for in the explanations and treatment. These features are significant to the clients' situation, and should not be overlooked or ignored, but should be given serious consideration in the diagnostic and therapeutic process. Methodological and theoretical skills and knowledge are required in this process.

Ethnic and racial identity and differences have significant influences on group life and mental and social health. Various ethnic and racial groups perceive their situations in different ways. Their perceptions of themselves in relation to others in society are based upon what meanings others and society have for them, their perceptions of themselves by others and society, and their perceptions of themselves. This is the basis for interaction and the nature of their established relationships in group life. Through the encounter (between and among the sociotherapist and clients), data are collected, knowledge is gained, clarity is pursued, understanding is achieved, acceptance is promoted, commitment is encouraged, and plans for change are developed. Appropriate academic and clinical skills and insights are necessary at every level and stage in the process. The entire process is grounded in what is discovered to be the particular social context of the clients in the encounter. This is a dynamic strategy which allows for the content to emerge out of the context in the process of diagnosis and treatment. The essential social dynamics is that as the clients and sociotherapist encounter, they discover; the discovery is analyzed and clarified (situationally and interactionally), and strategies and plans are established for therapeutic intervention and change. Implicit in this posture is a scientific and professional stance which is dependent upon theoretical and methodological skills. Encounter establishes the dynamics for discovery, and the theoretical insights, explanations, and the therapeutic interventions are grounded in the essential facts discovered about the relationships, interactions, behaviors in the situation, and about the situation itself (Bagarozzi, et., al., 1982). The essential links between research, theory, evaluation, and practice are addressed by grounded encounter therapy as important aspects of the diagnostic and treatment process.

Grounded Encounter Therapy (GET) can be used and applied to many areas. All situations where there are individuals interacting with some degree of intensity; where there are interpersonal and relationship matters, this approach can function as a technique for discovery, intervention, and change. This approach can be used in the industry to assist workers with socio-psychological problems related to merger of companies, establishing task oriented activities, conflict resolution, etc. The same thing is true for those who are interested in problems related to the community.

This approach is also very useful and appropriate in churches and in other religious institutions with groups of religious leaders, church members, and the various church groups and community members that represent the community of which the church is a part. Even though governmental agencies have not included in their structural arrangements a need for the services of sociotherapists, the grounded encounter therapeutic approach is very vital in assisting in the enhancement of communications between ambassadors and their staff members, and the natives of host countries; improve and manage communications between staff members in various departments of government, and the clarity and understanding of social situations in which interactional and relationship problems emerge.

This approach has been very useful in handling interpersonal and intergroup conflicts and tensions. It has been used with a number of racial groups that have come together in the same room to talk and encounter each other, taking advantage of the opportunity to discover, understand, clarify and manage the tension and conflicts that existed between them. Often there was discovery of hostile and bitter feelings, but not a clear understanding of the social dynamics and context within which such experiences were grounded. Once this understanding was achieved, specific action steps were developed to change the patterns of interacting, and the situation. This approach has also been used in educational institutions where there was a great need for involving students in the educational programs that impact their lives. It is beneficial and progressive for establishing better communication between students, faculty, staff, and administrators. When GET is employed to deal with problems in academic settings, a greater sense of self and community is achieved, and it enhances the primary reason for the relationships and interpersonal and interactional context of the various participants.

The grounded encounter therapeutic approach is offered in the hope that those who are, and have been struggling to get a handle on how to practice sociotherapy and clinical sociology—what to do, and the dynamics involved might employ this approach for diagnosis, explanation, intervention and change. No doubt, the approach will be modified and changed as it is used, and that's the way it should be. However, when GET is understood and practiced, theoretical, methodological and facilitating skills and abilities will be developed that are appropriate to the problems and social situations that call them into action. It is very difficult for individuals to change their interpersonal and relationship behaviors in which they are stuck and are the essence of their social context, unless they can see or sense the possibility of getting them unstuck. The degree to which one sees oneself as a part of change, or that which is to be changed, it is to that degree one will assist or resist change. GET allows the participant to be involved in the discovery of self, others, the situation, the problems and a sense of reality and emergence of solutions which facilitate growth and change.

Therapy must be grounded in the social context of the clients, and in the interpretations, situational analysis, meanings and explanations that emerge during the encounter among and between those implicated in the social situation, GET, as a sociotherapeutic technique, is an effective approach in this regard, because it is a process of diagnosis, facilitated by encounter, which grounds the interpretations, situational analysis, discovery, and explanations of the essential facts, of the social context of the clients, for the purpose of grounding therapeutic intervention and change. Encounter establishes the methodological basis of the approach, and grounding establishes its theoretical and application basis. GET is dynamic because data is collected and theoretical insights occur in interaction and encounter. As a sociotherapeutic approach, it defines a process, establishes relevant content, generates theories and explanations, and provides for appropriate methods of intervention. GET is rooted in the theoretical premise that human beings live group life, and that their behavior and actions are the result of indications, interpretations and meanings assigned to persons and objects in their social world.

Human group life consists of people interacting with one another. Because they live within a group, people must necessarily fit their actions to the actions of others. It is the very nature of group life that the members are embedded in a social situation created by the actions of others. All effective therapeutic approaches must have the above characteristics and should be lodged in a particular theoretical perspective.

The basic philosophy of GET is that real change in the behavior and situations is a result of voluntary action. The assumption in this therapeutic posture is that the individual or client is entangled in a situation that is undesirable, not well understood and/or undetermined. Once determined and understood, ways to change the behavior and/or the situation will be sought and change made either voluntarily (individually) and/or with assistance (collectively). GET, therefore, has what all effective therapeutic techniques must have; a basic philosophy, key concepts, goals, specific techniques, applicability, and an established relationship between clients and therapists. Therapy or treatment must be grounded in the reality of the social situation of the client(s), discovered by the therapist and client(s) through the scientific process of diagnosis, facilitated by the techniques of encounter and interpretation. Everyone and everything that are implicated in the reality of the social situation are taken into account as explanations are sought. This is the essence of GET. GET is based on the findings of the empirical process of the diagnosis, and the emergence of explanations. Grounding the diagnosis is a way of arriving at theory suited to its supposed uses. The clients and the therapist encounter the social situation and each other, and the problems emerge along with explanations and solutions.

References

Bagarozzi, Dennis.
1982 <u>Marital and Family Therapy: New Perspectives in Theory, Research, and Practice</u>. New York: Human Sciences Press, Inc.

Blumer, Herbert
1969 <u>Symbolic Interactionalism: Perspective and Method</u>. Englewood Cliffs, N. J.: Prentice-Hall, Inc.

Burr, Wesley R. et. al.
1979 <u>Contemporary Theories About the Family</u>. Vol. II New York: Free Press.

Cohen, Harry
1981 <u>Connections: Understanding Social Relationships</u>. Ames: The Iowa State University Press.

Dean, Alfred, et. al.
1976 <u>The Social Setting of Mental Health</u>. New York: Basic Books.

Edelson, Marshall
1970 <u>The Practice of Sociotherapy</u>. New Haven, Conn.: Yale University Press.
1970 <u>Sociotherapy and Psychotherapy</u>. Chicago, IL: University of Chicago Press.

Glasner, Barney G., and Anselm L. Straus
1967 <u>The Discovery of Grounded Theory: Strategies for Qualitive Research</u>. Chicago: Aldine Publishing Co.

Greene, B. L., and A. P. Solomon
1963 "Marital Disharmony: Concurrent Psychoanalytic Therapy of Husband and Wife by the Same Psychiatrist." <u>American Journal of Psychotherapy, 17: 443-456</u>.

Henderson, N. B.
1965 Married Group Therapy: A Setting for Reducing Resistances."
Psychological Report, 16: 347-352.

Hurvitz, Nathan
1979 The Sociologist as a Marital and Family Therapist," American
Behavioral Scientist. Vol. 23, No. 3 (March-April) 557-576.

Kovel, Joel
1976 A Complete Guide to Therapy: From Psychoanalysis to
Behavior Modification. New York: Pantheon Books.

MacGregor, R.
1962 "Multiple Impact Psychotherapy with Family." Family
Process, 1: 15-29. New York: Pantheon Books.

Martin, P. A.
1965 "Treatment of Marital Disharmony by Collaborative
Therapy." In B. L. Greene (ed.), The Psychotherapies of Marital
Disharmony.

Nichols, William (ed.)
1974 Marriage and Family Therapy. Minneapolis, Minnesota:
National Council on Family Relations.

Olson, David H.
1970 "Marital and Family Therapy: Integrative Review and
Critique," Journal of Marriage and the Family, 32, 501-538.

Olson, David H.
1980 "Marital and Family Therapy: A Decade Review," Journal of
Marriage and the Family. Vol. 42, No. 4 (November), 973-993.

Parsons, Talcott
1951 Social System. Glencoe, IL: Free Press.

Perls, Frietz S., R. F. Hefferline, and P. Goodman
1951 Gestalt Therapy. New York: Julian Press.

Rogers, Carl
1970 On Encounter Groups. New York: Harper and Row.

Ruitenbeck, H. M.
1970 The New Group Therapies. New York: Avon Books.

Satir, V.
1964 Conjoint Family Therapy: A Guide to Therapy and Technique. Palo Alto: Science and Behavior Books.

Swan, L. Alex
1980 "Clinical Sociologists: Coming Out of the Closet." Mid-American Review of Sociology. Vol. 5, No. 1 (Spring), 87-98.
1981a "Clinical Sociology: Problems and Prospects." Mid-American Review of Sociology. Vol. 6, No. 2 (Winter), 111-127.
1981b Families of Black Prisoners. Boston: G. K. Hall and Co.
1981c Survival and Progress: The Afro-American Experience. Westport, Conn.: Greenwood Press.

Thomas, W. I.
1961 "The Four Wishes and the Definition of the Situation." In T. Parsons et. al. (eds.) Theories of Society. New York: Free Press.

Clinical Sociologists as Scientists-Practitioners: Using Grounded Encounter Therapy (GET)

Chapter 6

* * *

Clinical Sociologists as Scientists-Practitioners: Using Grounded Encounter Therapy (GET)

Abstract

What clinical sociologists and sociological practitioners require being clinical, doing discovery and making application is contained within the territory of the discipline of sociology. Clinical sociology and/or sociological practice does not rest on an assumption of relevance, rather, it is an attempt to demonstrate the relevance of the discipline of sociology. The creation of general knowledge via the complementary relationships between theory and methodology establishes territory and language of sociology and contributes to its growth. However, general knowledge is not contextually applicable, specific knowledge is. General knowledge is for knowing and specific knowledge is for doing and application. Historically, we have endeavored to explain and even treat specific problems using general knowledge. Therefore, the clinical sociologist must assume the role of scientist-practitioner to produce specific knowledge and embrace an understanding of human behavior resulting from the individual's interpretation of social situations, which leads to meaning and choice for action/behavior. This understanding must also capture the individual as a social self within the context of this process, and not as a fixed personality.

With its three dimensions, Grounded Encounter Therapy (GET) is most appropriate to facilitate the special and unique dual role of the clinical sociologist as scientist-practitioner since it does not allow for predefined and predetermined explanations of human social problems. Instead, it advocates the grounding of therapy in the explanations that result from scientific discovery of specific discovery of specific contextual knowledge from the data obtained from the social context of the clients. GET's attention to specific contextual knowledge for application is the distinction. Everything that is important and significant emerges and is considered during disclosure, discovery, and the process of situational or contextual analysis. Meanings are provided and assigned, and the relevance of ethnicity, race, and gender matters also emerges during the process. The continued development of the field of clinical sociology and/or sociological practice is most important to the discipline of sociology, otherwise, stagnation is inevitable.

Introduction

What clinical sociologists and sociological practitioners require being clinical, doing discovery, intervening and making application is contained within the territory of the discipline of sociology. Sociology is defined by its theoretical and methodological perspectives, and is embodied in the concepts, content, and knowledge created by the various relationships between its theories and methods. The territory created by the relationships has established freedom to explore human relations and interactions between and among human beings, and between human beings, structures, and objects. The relationships between theories and methods have also allowed for the freedom and latitude to create general and specific knowledge. While there are those who continue to create general knowledge which is valuable to the growth and significance of the discipline, clinical sociologists and sociological practitioners understand that knowing is the beginning of doing and doing is the completion of knowing. The fact is that mere knowing is not power, rather, knowledge put into action, or making application of knowledge is power, or empowers. The relationship of knowing to doing is unremitting and continual (Hillman, 2001).

The Scientist-Practitioner Role

The important thing about the clinical sociologist as well as the sociological practitioner is that because (s)he has to apply specific knowledge, (s)he must assume the role of the scientist who discovers that knowledge, and is in the same process the practitioner who intervenes and makes application of that knowledge. This posture is truly unique in clinical matters in that the clinician is a scientist-practitioner. Specific knowledge is knowledge that results from, is related to, provided by, discovered from and grounded in the data from context of the clients (Stehr, 1992). The discipline of sociology is limited only by the areas it has identified as its territory—human beings living group life seeking to establish social organizations, structures, objects, symbols and social arrangements within which they attempt to fit their actions to that of each other (Swan, 1988a). The result and consequence of such efforts call into play the role and function of clinical sociologists as scientists-practitioners. The need for these professionals is self evident since the issues and concerns come from within the territory of the discipline of sociology. The relationships between discovery of specific knowledge and its application are akin to the complementary relationships between theory and methodology discussed so well in a classic work by Robert K. Merton (1948).

The need for a clinical approach executed by a scientist-practitioner must be nurtured by the theoretical and methodological perspectives, and the various concepts that make up or constitute the language and territory of sociology. The perspectives, concepts, and language of the territory of any other discipline are inadequate and inappropriate for discovery and application in sociological practice. Again, the scope and limitations are territorial but inclusive, especially of history and social psychology. If there are any questions regarding this matter, then we need to review and examine more carefully the territory of the discipline of sociology. It is indeed safe to say that the territory contains most of the critical, perplexing and challenging problems of human interactions and relationships within the individual; the small group; the community; the industry; the society; and the world. It is believed that more money is spent and effort expanded to address nonsocial problems because, in fact, the harms and dangers of the social do not seem to be as evident or feared. Nonetheless, they are far-reaching and debilitating. Commissions have been established, reports written and knowledge created, general, that is, and that is the reason for the lack of intervention and application. General knowledge does not have contextual applicability, specific knowledge does. General knowledge is for knowing; it is for establishing territorial base, foundation and boundary. Specific knowledge is for doing and application. Traditionally, we have attempted to explain and even treat specific problems using general knowledge about the matter. In this regard, some practitioners prefer to cite cases in their works. One of the reasons for this practice is the belief that the cases demonstrate or represent what they perceive to be the importance of specific knowledge. In addition to other things, cases do represent specific knowledge. However, the problem with the presentation of cases is the tendency to reference them in a general sense to specific issues. Cases represent only the problems and contexts which they address. Consequently, the presentation of cases can be misleading if they are not understood in their individual context since every problem has its own context in time and space. We also tend to cite cases to explain other perceived similar cases. However, the findings in one case do not mean that they are applicable to other cases even if they have the same labels. One case does not explain any other but that case. Even if all of the indicators and variables are present in one case, it does not follow that similarity or comparability means applicability. No doubt, there are various reasons for the inclusion of cases; however the potential for distortion is too high in sociological practice.

Clinical sociology must be discovery free. Its scientific process has to be free of any content that comes from and/or leans on predispositions contained in or defined by prior cases. Each clinical effort must stand on its own and rely on the scientific and discovery abilities of the practitioner and the particular modality being employed. The best modality is one that allows for discovery instead of embracing and predefined and predetermined explanations and treatments represented in established and well documented cases. The use of the language of the discipline is also of concern. The uses of sociodrama instead of psychodrama, or resocilization rather than rehabilitation are appropriate examples. To be careless about this conceptual matter is to confuse the territorial boundaries and language of the discipline. The need for the territory of the discipline of sociology to be engaged by the sociological practitioner and the clinical sociologist in the discovery and application of specific knowledge is critical in addressing and resolving human social problems. The scientist-practitioner does not seek simply to build bridges over human troubled waters (s)he becomes involved in discovering why the waters are being troubled and resorts to intervention and application based upon the discovery (Larson, 1993; Deutscher, 1999).

Crime, delinquency, violence, family, abuse, failed social roles, social justice, drug abuse, alcoholism, suicide, oppression, sexism, racism, exploitation, riot behavior, discrimination, terrorism, capitalism, driving behavior, tokenism, social disorganization, hatred and anger are just a few examples of the territorial issues that sociology and sociologists seek to create general knowledge about. All of these issues are within the established legitimate territory of the discipline of sociology because they are issues of individuals living group life. The scientist-practitioner engages in the discovery of specific knowledge so that intervention and application can be grounded in the explanations represented by the data from the social situation of the clients and the territorial foundation of the discipline (Cole, 2001).

The Dilemma of Traditional Clinicians

Carl Rogers (Person-Centered), Fritz Perls (Gestalt), and Albert Ellis (RET) conducted individual sessions with the same client at different times, on video, demonstrating their approaches to psychotherapy. The sessions clearly demonstrated the attempts by three therapists, with three different approaches and philosophical assumptions, to fit the client into their modalities. Success was

139

accepted or acknowledged only when the client came to see things from the perspective of the therapeutic modality of the therapist conducting the session. This is not to suggest that clients may not have problems in the areas of each of the modalities mentioned. However, it is not true to the scientific process of discovery for data to be skewed by therapists and their therapeutic approaches which have predetermined and predefined explanations of clients' presenting problems. The scientific process of discovery allows for the emergence of the real problems and their contexts. The data discovered, dictate explanations, understanding and possible solutions or ways to change. To view clients and their situations from the particular therapeutic approach of the therapist with predetermined explanations and goals is to stifle the process of discovery and to exclude possibilities that might be beyond the dimensions of the particular approach. When we embrace a particular therapeutic modality with its predefined and predetermined perspective of human social problems, we are bound by its vision of those problems and locked into its goals, intervention and application strategies. It must be very clear that as sociological clinicians, sociotherapists, or as scientist-practitioners, we must discover specific knowledge with our clients, what we must understand about their problems, the explanations, and contexts out of which they emerge. This is the best chance we have for proper understanding, appropriate application, and effective intervention and change. Clinical sociologists should not get trapped in the dilemma of traditional psychotherapists who see what they look for, and what they look for they see, and what they see is what their therapeutic modalities allow them to see, and what their therapeutic modalities allow them to see is what they treat. Freedom from this dilemma is achieved and enhanced by a proper understanding of human behavior and individuals as social selves (Hillman & Ventura, 1992).

Understanding Human Social Behavior

It is a mistake to view and understand human behavior in strictly individual terms. This mistake is the essence of the dilemma which has dire consequences for understanding and treating human social problems. The dilemma is theoretical and methodological, with therapeutic consequences and implications. When we address (assess and intervene) family relations and interactions, human relations in industry, school sociology, criminal justice systems, public and social policy (government), and community service systems, we are dealing with social settings created by individuals who have come together to relate and interact for various and specific reasons (Bryant and Becker, 1990).

Contrary to the notion that a reacting organism produces a sequence of actions in a neuromuscular response to a set of stimuli, and that people act as they do because they have certain notions which initiate or drive the organism to action, the general and common sociological view is that social forces cause action. One view is that human beings behave as they do because they have internalized particular norms or values which are cultural prescriptions or rules about behavior. The other view in sociology is that external frameworks, or structures impose particular kinds of behavior on people. However, human beings can do much more than respond to stimuli (Reynolds, 2001).

Acts are constructed and reconstructed by the individual as s(he) observes or takes note of, thinks about, and acts upon stimuli. Consequently, an act is not an outgrowth or expression of a set of causes. An act begins with the awareness of an impulse and the formation of a goal. That is, the individual must decide what actions will satisfy his/her impulse and what actions are possible within the limitations of her/his situation. In the process of identifying the impulse and making an object of it in the form of a wish or a want, the individual plans for reaching his/her goal. S(he) can control, check, or even stop it. As s(he) acts, s(he) takes into account a variety of external objects, including the behavior of other people. Behavior need not be rational in the sense that it is wise. Many people make errors of interpretation and judgment as they plan and proceed with action. Many times they attempt to achieve goals by appropriate methods, not always seeing the real implications and consequences of their acts. Behavior can be stupid or wise, it can involve foresight and careful analysis of preconditions and consequences, or it can be rash and irrational. This describes and represents the sociological social psychological perspective of human behavior. There is no question that the social organization of the social order (society) constrains and pressures individuals into learning, believing and making choices to do and behave. Although the choices are the individual's, the focus of discovery, assessment, and intervention should not only be the individual's behavior, but also on the setting or context out of which the behavior emerged or is grounded. This theoretical perspective does not dominate the methodological and therapeutic activities of those presently dominating the clinical field.

Behavior is the result of choices made by individual interpretations of social situations and settings, which are influenced by the set of experiences and characteristics of the individual and the socio-cultural restraints and constraints relative to the possible, available and acceptable alternatives. Therefore, social settings/situations, plus individual interpretations equal choice, which results in action and behavior (Figure I). Choice is not biological, it's psychosocial.

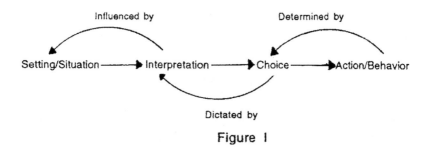

Figure I

We do not place emphasis on introspective explanations of human behavior. We have come to know that individuals are not self contained in their behavioral motivations. Instead, we recognize that human life is organized within groups and that this organization has important effects upon behavior. Human problems and difficulties must be explained, understood, and treated within their specifics contexts. To seek to understand the context of human social behavior is not to blame the context (setting/situation) for the behavior. To understand the context is to understand the socio-cultural and structural arrangements, restraints, and constraints out of which choice and behavior emerged. The context contains, in addition to individuals who have come together, certain potent forces (cultural prescriptions and social structure), which the individuals interpret, to which they assign the meaning and make decisions (choice) for action and behavior. Behavior, then, is always contextual. However, the behavior belongs to the individual, yet the behavior is social in nature because it emerges from a social context and finds expression in social settings by individuals who have come together in the settings. The individual nature of the behavior is that the individual makes the choice and executes it in the form of action and behavior. The process in figure one clearly demonstrates that:

- interpretation is <u>influenced</u> by a set of experiences in settings, situations, and conditions;
- choice is <u>dictated</u> by interpretation and assigned meanings of the situation;
- Action/behavior is <u>determined</u> by choice given the availability and acceptability of alternatives, and;
- desired outcomes are the result of action/behavior.

These notions are fundamental to the assumptions, characteristics, and principles of GET (Swan, 1986).

The Assumptions and Principles of GET

The statements which follow undergird Grounded Encounter Therapy. They establish the explanatory, methodological, and therapeutic boundaries of the approach.

- Human beings, as individuals, live group life.

- In group life, human beings, in attempts to relate and interact, seek to fit their actions to the actions of each other (some do it well and some do it poorly).
- Most human problems are problems of living, or social in nature.
- Human problems have their own social contexts and are best understood and treated within context.
- Specific knowledge and understanding about human social problems and their contexts must be obtained through the scientific process of disclosure and discovery. GET's attention to specific contextual knowledge for application is the distinction.
- To view clients and their situation from the particular therapeutic approach of the therapist with predetermined explanations and goals is to stifle the process of discovery and to exclude possibilities that might be beyond the dimensions of the particular approach.
- Ways to intervene, change, enhance and grow must emerge from the knowledge and understanding gained from the process of disclosure and discovery.
- The past is significant, in therapeutic matters only to the extent that it is affecting the present.

Within the context of these assumptions and principles, the task of the scientist-practitioner is defined. The essential role is to collect relevant, appropriate and contextual data that suggest explanation, provide understanding for the purpose of intervention and application. The need to know in a specific way comes first which establishes the foundation and basis for application. This position fits well the definition of clinical sociology and sociotherapy which is the "search for" (discovery) and the application (treatment) of sociological knowledge, understanding, analysis and principles aimed at, and for the purpose of reducing distress, managing and resolving conflict, achieving meaningful change and effective functioning, and enhancing interactional and relational patterns of behavior. The concept "search for" in the definition captures two types of methods: that of discovering fact through the description of the social reality of the clients, and the other type allows us to explain why things are the way they are. To be able to describe the social reality of the clients is the start or first step. When attempt are made to answer the question of what, who, or even why, we become engaged in the explanatory method, the second step.

The Dimensions of Grounded Encounter Therapy

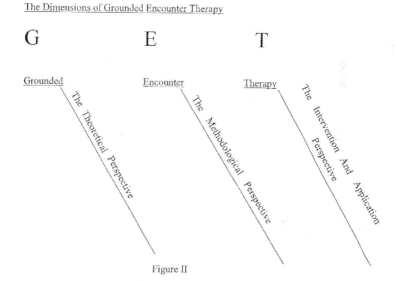

The Dimensions of Grounded Encounter Therapy

G   E   T

Grounded   Encounter   Therapy

The Theoretical Perspective

The Methodological Perspective

The Intervention And Application Perspective

Figure II

There are three dimensions of Grounded Encounter Therapy (Figure II). They represent the theoretical, methodological and therapeutic perspectives of GET. The first is the theoretical perspective that establishes the explanatory position of the approach. Theoretically, this position argues that therapy must be grounded in the theory (explanation) which is grounded or established in the data and knowledge gained from the social situation (context) of the clients. We have to always keep in mind that specific knowledge about the clients and their situation/setting is the appropriate knowledge for intervention and application, especially if the process is to be effective, and growth and change realized. For example, what we know about child abuse should not necessarily be the knowledge used in treating a case of child abuse. The knowledge to be applied comes from the process of discovery about the problem and the context of the presenting and real problems. The theoretical perspective is the foundation of the approach. This means that the encounter process and the intervention and application action must conform to and are dictated by the theoretical perspective. In turn, engaging the encounter process and the therapeutic action is assurance that the theoretical or grounding perspective is in place and followed.

The second dimension is the methodological perspective or the scientific position. The encounter process represents this dimension of GET that is responsible for the collection of data. The position of this perspective is that the social context of the clients along with explanations and therapeutic approaches are discovered as the sociotherapist and the clients confront and encounter themselves, each other, and the social situation of the clients. The parties engage in a process of dialogue, observation, disclosure, interpretation, and situational analysis for the purpose of discovering specific knowledge. The presenting problems are not usually the real problems; they provide the basis for exploring and probing for discovering the real problems and their contexts. During this process, we do not speak for the data, instead, we let the data speak, and we listen to what it has to say. We have to know what the discovered data is saying to us theoretically and therapeutically. The scientific posture of this dimension is a challenge to predetermined and predefined explanations and treatment of clients' problems. Scientific knowledge and common sense knowledge are combined to produce specific knowledge for understanding, intervention, and application. Everything that is important and significant emerges, and is considered during disclosure, discovery, and situational or contextual analysis. Meanings are provided and assigned, and the relevance of ethnicity, race, and gender matters also emerge during the process.

The third dimension of GET is its therapeutic (intervention and application) perspective. What is to be applied and the intervention strategies and application techniques employed are determined by the discovery made during the encounter (scientific) process by the clients and the sociotherapist. The problem and the social situation (context) are the clients' and they must be intimately involved in the discovery as well as the intervention and application process. What is discovered in the encounter process is used to determine and devise plans for therapeutic action. Any and all actions, at this point, are grounded in the theoretical insights which emerged from the collection of data, information, and knowledge during the methodological or scientific process. It is only as we allow the problems, their explanations, the strategies and techniques for intervention and treatment to emerge from the encounter with the therapist, the clients, and their social situation that therapy and theory are grounded. Engaging clients in the encounter and discovery process, defining their problems, determining the context and devising plans for therapeutic action, empowers the clients, and enhances the effectiveness and success of the process and outcome (Swan, 1988b).

Individuals as Social Selves

The nature and character of the social context of all human social problems are not known initially, but must be discovered and determined. The social context consists of human systems and the social milieu created by the coming together of the social selves. Since human beings live in group life, all individual behavior takes place in relation to, or within the context of the group. Relating and interacting are properties of the group that consist of individuals taking one another into account. The relating and interacting are experienced as social selves. We must, therefore, understand the individual as a social self and not as a fixed personality (Agger, 2000; Rebach and Bruhn, 1991). The social self eventually becomes a multiplicity of properties or characteristics developed at varying degrees over a period of time through interacting and relating with others in various situations. The individual develops the ability to define, interpret and assign meanings to situations so that a characteristic of the self emerges, consistent with the situation, to be employed in interacting and relating resulting in action and behavior.

This should be the essential focus for understanding and explanation for therapeutic purpose (Steele, Hauser and Hauser, 1998).

An understanding of the social self and the emergence of a variety of its characteristics from an interactional and relational context is properly lodged within the territory of sociology. Within the same theoretical context it is important to understand, when making discoveries, that individuals have the ability to make adjustments so that a characteristic of the self emerges and develops consistent with an occurrence or a particular situation. For example, a situation emerges, say the development of a relationship, and this occurrence requires a particular characteristic in the social self of one of the persons. The individual has the ability to posture that characteristic and indicate it to the other until, through many demonstrations, that characteristic is fully and satisfactorily developed and becomes a permanent part of the social self (Swan, 1994). Therefore, trying to understand the "personality system" and individual symptoms should not focus relative to the theoretical, discovery and application concerns of clinical sociologists.

Individuals define their concepts of the self by taking the roles of other people and groups, and by looking at themselves from the point of view of those roles. At the same time, individuals have the ability to indicate to others, via developed styles of conveyance, how they want others to see them. Even though there is some independence in the selection of characteristics that make up the social self, and the basis for interacting and relating, the group frame of reference from which individuals define the self, particularly during the earliest stages of development. Individuals interact with themselves without making overt indications and can therefore create a private world of the mind. There is no differentiation between the private world of the individual and the outer world of social interaction. Self interaction and social interaction are essentially the same process. The fundamental difference between them is that the private world of the mind is not open to observation from the outside, but resulting behavior is a reflection of the private world of the mind.

Self interaction and social interaction are essentially the same process. The fundamental difference between them is that the private world of the mind is not open to observation from the outside, but the resulting behavior is a reflection of the private world of the mind. Self interaction, therefore, is a basis for overt action and is an important means by which persons control their action in the external world. Individuals confront the world on the basis of their ability to make indications to themselves. They act on the basis of what they perceive to be objects in the environment or social setting and on the basis of what they define the meaning of these objects to be. It is within this process that individuals develop an independence of self as they select the values, properties, and characteristics of the self to be developed and become their unique social self. It is within the context of this understanding of group life and the development and existence of the social self, and how social problems are discovered, identified, understood, and explained that makes critical how such problems are treated. We are compelled to view the individual not as a personality, but as social self with the potential for development, growth, and change (Blumer, 1969; Mead, 1934).

Using GET as a Scientist-Practitioner

Clinical sociologists and sociological practitioners are concerned with scientific discovery and application of specific sociological social psychological knowledge and understanding to problems that are social in nature and character, that are lodged in the social situations of a variety of clients at different levels of social organization. The concern is with the social situation and the interpretations and definitions of those implicated therein. The clinician is trained to make discovery and engage in the clients in disclosures and in making formal assessments of interaction patterns and social settings to arrive at clinical judgments to offer explanations, strategies for intervention and application to facilitate change and growth. GET provides a scientific process of discovery, intervention and application for treatment. The aim is to achieve constructive social and behavior changes in social situations and settings and in the interactional patterns among and between individuals in groups, organizations, communities and societies. This process requires and demands a scientific posture for discovery which relates theories and methods for the collection of essential facts for assessment purposes, and the explanations of those facts bearing upon the problems and situations for therapeutic purposes. This is the way treatment gets grounded in the social context of the clients who are implicated in the situation and problems.

All three dimensions of GET combine the scientific and the practical, and are interrelated in terms of their importance to each other and the modality as a comprehensive approach. During the encounter process, which is the methodological process, when disclosures and discoveries are made, information and data are collected regarding the individuals (clients) and their particular setting (context). As we collect the data, certain theoretical perspectives and insights come to mind (social exchange, interaction, conflict, etc.), or some other theoretical perspective will emerge as the one most appropriate for explaining the problem indicated by the data. In all cases, a theoretical perspective will dominate, even though at times another or other perspectives might flicker or show themselves for a moment or two. This is the scientific or the discovery process of GET. As questions are asked and observations made, the data disclosed and discovered would indicate a theoretical bent or direction. This methodological process represented by the E of GET, is based on the theoretical position expressed in the G of GET. Therapy, the T in GET, must be grounded in the explanations which are grounded in the data discovered from the context of the real and presenting problems of the clients.

The entire process starts with the presenting problems, which are not always the real problems; the real problems must be discovered. Inquiring and probing will lead to the real problem and its context. The explanations, which are grounded in the data from the context of the problem and the clients, dictate the selection of the strategies and plans for intervention and application. Several things must constantly be remembered. The first is that every problem has its own context in time and space. The second is that we cannot understand nor effectively treat a problem outside of its context. The third is that therapy must be grounded in the explanations and specific knowledge that is grounded in the data from the social context of the problems of the clients. The fourth is that predetermined and predefined explanations of specific problems are inadequate and inappropriate for intervention and application. Next, what we know about the problem in general is not necessarily the knowledge used in treating a particular case. The knowledge and information to be applied come from the process of discovery and is specific to the particular problem and context of the clients. Finally, it is well to note that the past is significant, in the entire process, only to the extent that it is affecting the individuals and their situations in the present.

The utility of sociology as a discipline is enhanced by sociological practice. Clinical sociology and sociotherapy are legitimate practicing activities. Sociological knowledge and understanding pervades the social context of human social problems. Therefore, a mere injection of such knowledge and understanding is not appropriate or adequate. The acquisition of specific sociological knowledge suggests that this kind of knowledge is applicable. If it is sociological knowledge and is at the base of the discipline, it helps to define its content and will conform to the milieu or culture of the human social problems. Clinical sociology and/or sociological practice does not rest on an assumption of relevance, rather, it is an attempt to demonstrate the relevance of the discipline of sociology. The continued development of the field is most important to the discipline, otherwise, stagnation is inevitable.

Applying Sociology

The Department of Sociology at the University of Kansas, where the first sociology course in the United States is said to have been taught, offers the following as a definition of sociology: "Sociology is the study of social life, social change, and the social causes and consequences of human behavior. Since all human behavior is social, few fields have such broad scope and relevance for research, theory and the application of knowledge." This is clear. It has been argued that sociology and sociological endeavor began at the University of Chicago and that it was there the group focused on discovery for application. In recent years, the argument had been made that W.E.B. DuBois and his efforts at Atlanta University gave sociology, and especially sociological practice its beginning and foundation in the United States. Nonetheless, the founder of sociology, Auguste Compte, envisioned sociologists as practitioners using the discovered scientific truths to bring about positive and constructive change. Emile Durkheim, Karl Marx, W.E.B. DuBois, Anna Cooper, Ida Wells-Barnett, Jane Addams, and Max Weber also emphasized the practice (application) of sociology to address social problems. Lester Ward distinguished applied sociology from "pure" sociology and argued that the subject matter of "pure" sociology is achievement, that applied sociology is improvement. The former relates to the past and the present, and the latter to the future.

The pioneers of the history and development of sociology anticipated a duality in the discipline. However, the practice component never really developed as the academic and scientific component did, mainly because of the competition (self imposed) with other social science disciplines to prove that sociology can be scientific; using the scientific method. To continue to perceive and even discuss the discipline as having a superior and therefore an inferior aspect is to continue the schism. Sociological practice is directly tied to the academic and scientific. It validates the academic, and the scientific provides the contextual data, information, and specific knowledge for intervention and application. In other words, knowing is the beginning of doing, and doing (application) is the completion of knowing. The "either or" positioning that seems to be emerging or is being maintained does not help the discipline to advance. However, it is indeed comforting to know that the debate of sociology, as a discipline, is defined by its content, and we can pursue its duality or in combination.

Sociological Knowledge and Application

Application is the most important aspect of sociological knowledge. However, there is very little written about sociological application. There are several works on critical analysis and interpretation but little devoted to principles of application. I have often argued that knowing is the beginning of doing, but/and doing is the completion of knowing. Another saying I often employ is that mere knowledge is not power, but knowledge put into action is power, or knowledge applied is power. Sociologists, for the most part, have over the years missed the most important aspect of the discipline of sociology. Sociology is a discipline that is complete as a continuum from discovering knowledge to applying that knowledge. The relevance, viability and usefulness of sociology is not simply in the scientific and empirical approach to the collection of data and the discovery of knowledge, but equally to the application of sociological knowledge.

Sociology must be real, relevant, useful, and applicable. Its knowledge must connect and many teachers of sociology and even some sociologists do a good job, in most cases, in helping us to understand the sociological world; their discussions and analysis provide somewhat clear explanations of the various problems faced by individuals, groups, industries, communities, organizations and the society, but all too often, they make no attempt to relate their information and knowledge to the real world. One of the reasons that W.E.B DuBois got so frustrated and even angry, and eventually disillusioned by the academic world was that after completing such a masterful study of the African American conditions in Philadelphia, and even offering specific recommendations for application and change, those in positions to do something about the matter paid little or no attention to the work—<u>The Philadelphia Negro</u>—and those who gave it some attention treated it simply as a great piece of sociological research completed by an abled sociologist/social historian who obtained/earned a doctorate from Harvard. The ultimate goal of sociology ought to be application.

No doubt, sociology and sociologists have done a good job in helping the public and those in various positions in the social order to understand the society and the social world. In many cases, there are clear explanations of the problems faced by the various segments and entities in society. It is regrettable that no effort is made for application. Perhaps, it was assumed that application is best done by those not thought of as academic or scientific. This has turned out to be the most dangerous posture to assume because as we can see, that the territorial content of sociology can be misrepresented, distorted, and even adopted to be the property of other disciplines that have practice components, and professions that are exclusive application in nature with no empirical or scientific base to create knowledge. We must assume that application of sociology knowledge is best made by the sociologist who created or discovered that knowledge and that the knowledge is sociological in nature and social in context. Sociologists are determined to expound sociological knowledge in terms of findings, but they fail to build a bridge or get into the water to stop the waters from troubling. Instead, they join others who continue to build bridges to cross or cope with the troubled waters. The reason for this could be that sociologists tend to create general knowledge when specific knowledge is required for application. Nonetheless, a move on the continuum is required to go from the creation of sociological knowledge to sociological application. We must be about the business of applying sociological knowledge to the realities of human life.

There are sociologists who do not apply sociological knowledge to their own lives and situations. Our students, our associates, sociologists and other professionals should hear us using the concepts of sociology in our conversations, and using sociological knowledge in our social situations. The use of the concepts of other disciplines, and the application of knowledge of other disciplines, no matter how close, does not promote the value and significance of sociology or sociological knowledge. No matter how common or popular the concepts and knowledge, if it is not sociological then we should replace the concepts and knowledge with appropriated sociological concepts and knowledge. Rehabilitation, personality, reinforcement, etc. are not truly, fundamentally, and authentic sociological. This is the reason that even professionals are not making the distinction between sociology and closely related areas such as social work and psychology. The lay person thinks sociology is a common sense discipline. We need to take the same care in applying sociological information that we do to interpret and explain social phenomenon. We need sound principles for application as we use for collecting and interpreting data. Of course, it is impossible to discuss application without talking about interpretation. Therefore, we will touch on aspects of interpretation before we discuss aspects of application. The rest of this effort will focus on the theory and practice applying sociological knowledge.

Although, since sociology is a social science, it is ludicrous to assume that sociology can somehow become a precise science with all guesswork removed. Applying sociological knowledge to specific problems of living is an art, which at times cannot fully be reduced to rules and principles. Yet, we believe that most of the guesswork can and should be eliminated by scientific and empirical principles and methods. By focusing on some rules and principles which are essential or helpful in the application of sociological knowledge, we do not have to become overly analytical or intellectual. Because it comes out of the social, or that sociological knowledge is social in nature, we do not have to reduce sociology and scientific and empirical principles for sociological knowledge to have an impact on the lives of human beings who live in group life. Common sense knowledge, ordinary knowledge and scientific knowledge must wed in the process of application. The very essence of life and living reaches far deeper than our intellect and cannot be analyzed or quantified. Therefore, we will focus on aspects of application which can be discussed and evaluated. We do realize that this is only part of the story. Sociologists tend to write for scholars because they believe they are dealing with complex subject matter pertaining to complex beings. Nonetheless, we have to present complex matter of a social human nature as clearly as possible. Application is possible and successful when we do just that, even if we come down on the side of simplicity; once we arrived to that point using sound principles and methods. For me, this is a beginning at attempting to understand and explain, at the same time, the nature of applying sociological knowledge.

The Goal of Application

Sociologists must learn and accept the notion that knowledge cannot be divorced from commitment and action. It started with our being told that we must remain detached, aloof, objective if we truly want to know something. Such detachment in acquiring sociological knowledge is nonsense. True knowledge is impossible apart from commitment, involvement, and action. We must immerse ourselves in our subject if we want to know it. Objectivity is the degree to which we are subjective-immersed. There is no doubt about the relationship between knowledge and action. Sociologists cannot continue to look in the mirror, as it were, and observe that our faces are dirty and do nothing, or take no action to rid them of the dirt. We should, in our writings and actions, be emphatic about the relationship between sociological knowledge and action/application. If we want sociology to mature and grow up, we must act on what we know.

As we immerse ourselves in the creation and understanding of sociological knowledge, because it is contextually social, we have to learn, think and respond to every situation as closely as possible, the way the subject herself/himself would. Is this an impossible goal? We know and understand that everyone is different; think differently and interpret situations differently. If we are close to the situation of the individuals and if we immerse ourselves in their situations we can put on, conform to, take on, and be recreated or reestablished in their understanding of the situations and understand the matter from their point of view. This rebirth, so to speak, is essential to application. This is somewhat like role taking not role playing. At the mental level, we take, or assume the role of the other, and in so doing, come to view, perceive and understand the situation from their perspective. We have to start this process by thoroughly studying the situation. A number of things will be revealed to us through close study (study close up). Share and check our discovery with that of the clients (micro, meso, macro). Any discrepancy must be checked, clarified, verified, and rectified. We cannot move forward until this process is exhausted. Each common experience between clients and the sociologist should be internalized by the sociologist who is technically distant or not truly/really a part of the situation personally, yet is personally a part of the situation. It becomes a mind-heart experience for recall and empathy. This means that our innermost professional and personal being takes on the character or essence of the situation. As we rehearse in our minds the shared common elements of the situation, we carefully put into operation the process of discovery so that together we and the clients come to view the situation similarly. This goal achieved empowers the clients to develop faith and trust in the sociological process of discovery and the creation of specific knowledge for application.

Learning to Apply Sociological Knowledge

Among some students and faculty, sociology is hopeless and irrelevant. Many do not really know the value of sociological knowledge because no representation of its value and importance had been demonstrated either in the classroom or with community projects that require sociological understanding. Even some sociology majors often voice their dismay because sociology and the study of sociology did not bring value to them. Some students have stopped telling what their major is and in some deviant frivolous way they avoid identifying with a discipline that does not add value to them. I tend to blame sociologists for the low in value perception others have of the discipline. Much of what sociologist do today seems irrelevant because it seems to have no utility.

Sociology and sociologists are not bragging about anything today, and other disciplines which have an application or practice component have incorporated sociological knowledge into their practice. Consequently, since the knowledge is not represented as sociological, sociologists do not get the credit for the knowledge.

The problem is also in the academic culture where sociologists are so unsure of their explanations of human social behavior that they have not closed ranks, but have allowed other more popular explanations, although extremely defective to their thinking. They have allowed social workers, psychologists, and even psychiatrists, with no social contextual academic content to influence, and in some cases, dominate their conferences, in seminars and workshops. Seemingly, sociologists have no confidence in their theoretical perspectives. There is no need to aspire to become a sociological practitioner if you have to be trained and even supervised by one of the above practitioners. The general society has greater acceptance of the above mentioned practitioners, especially because they have been legalized, certified and put before the public as those who are legitimate in areas where the content is clearly sociological. Sociology is a discipline that has the potential to speak directly to the needs of human beings in ways that are appropriate to their situation. Sociologists, therefore, do not have to offer instead, pious platitudes that simply sound good. Sociologists cannot continue to give abstract analysis; they need to provide examples which are concrete.

The tendency is to provide analytical treatise on the problem of poverty and crime, they have to provide examples of poverty and crime and let us see sociology and sociologists at work in the lives of the people. Students can identify with the human involvement and with their struggles. They will grow a confidence and trust in the discoveries and see implicit in the discoveries and disclosures ways to make application for change, growth and development. Increasing more and more students are showing up in all classes all over this country and around the world with issues that sociology and sociologists are suppose to address. The students are, in quiet and silent ways, saying we need some answers and we expect to find them in and through this experience. Therefore, no longer can sociologists wait and put off the challenges the "new" student brings to the classroom and their expectations. They want to understand the problems, but they also want to help solve them because they are directly affected, or their sister, brother, father, mother or some close friend or relative is being affected, and they are quietly demanding answers and ways to apply their knowledge and understanding.

Every individual may not have the same issue, but, whatever the issue, they want it understood and appropriately addressed. Whenever there are human beings interacting and relating, at times high levels of intensity, in families, on the highways and freeways, in organizations and industries, in companies and community agencies, and in churches there will inevitably be tension, friction, conflict, disappointment, and a general and specific breakdown, needing the services of sociologists. No doubt, sociology and sociologists must be relevant, and it is within the context of their relevancy that application is imperative. Even when situations and issues are dissimilar from our own we can learn applicable remedies. If you were instructed not to muzzle your ox while it is treading out the grain, you would probably think that's irrelevant information since you're not a farmer living in Iowa. However, if you are a farmer who uses oxen, this would be an exciting time since it never dawned on him how unfairly he had been treating his oxen. He prevented the ox from eating while working, even though the ox is out there in the heat working for him. If you are not a farmer, and if you use a mechanical thresher, the assumption would be to assume that did not apply to him. Most of us do not own an ox or muzzles, so the example of a situation that is dissimilar from our own might not do. So this suggestion about muzzling the ox while it is treading the grain is relevant to our needs. Is this example irrelevant? Answering this question and finding a way to apply the suggestion we will come away excited by what we would discover.

In order to make appropriate and adequate application we must remember the essence; the core; the ethos of the presenting problem and the original situation. The practitioner who functions initially as a scientist to do discovery must remember and understand the original situation in the present. This is the reason that during the discovery process the sociotherapist must seek to share in the experiences so as to come close to the situation and realize it as personal. This is when objectivity is realized or captured through subjectivity. Identifying and sharing in the experience of the situation/condition/circumstance is crucial to discovery and application. Disclosure, for one, is made easier. When the sociotherapist inquires and the clients discloses they do so in the hope of sharing in the experience of the event; the situation; the condition. No better understanding can be provided and obtained but by and through this process and posture.

The process of disclosure and discovery has a greater and broader principle of specific application, that is that human beings have a right to understand their situations and a right to address them with the intent to grow, develop, and change. Therefore, the professional should be excited about the journey and the privilege of sharing in the experience. A greater insight is that when the professional takes the journey of sharing, she/he would have sown healings or growth needs into the live situation of the client and the benefits are also shared although hopefully different in nature and maybe in extent. In attempting to apply sociology, we must seek to first understand the original situation as revealed in the data presented and described in the information disclosed and discovered and the role and position of each individual involved and implicated. Our application must be faithful to the original situation and to the data therefrom. We must next determine whether the data from the situation reflects a specific application of a broader theoretical principle—like a person's rights. Then, finally, we are ready to apply the general principle to the situation(s) we face in life.

There are life troublesome things that seek to torment us. Many times we wonder whether such intensely personal and specific problems can adequately and successfully be addressed within the context of the discipline of sociology. However, if we follow the steps outlined above, we will see that we can clearly succeed. There are sociological clinicians who also allow for divine intervention. They simply allow their sociological knowledge to be informed by divine insight. This process is empowering because it allows the clients to understand and embrace a process that goes beyond the present or particular situation so that in the future any such situation can be addressed successfully by making a specific application of a broader principle. The answer to solution to a particular issue goes beyond the clients' immediate situation and beyond the person or persons, organization or agency, industry or community. The formula will work in all situations under all circumstances—human effort plus divine intervention equal success. The more situations that require the use of the formula, the more the client will be empowered, and the more of a guarantee for success. These situations that might not require the use of the formula, but there are those moments when the hook-up is the only sure deal. The paradox is that when the clinician feels powerless that's when s/he is powerful; for divine insight and intervention is sufficient for all situations.

Conclusion

Our success in applying sociology is dependent on the steps discussed above. No doubt we have to develop the skills to accomplish that. Yet, knowing what to do is not the same as knowing how to do it. How do we get to and understand the original situation from the data presented? How do we engage the clients in a process of disclosure and discovery? How do we develop and discover general principles implicit and explicit in the data and conversations we have with each other within the data base? We will know whether a general principle will legitimately apply to the situation today when we bring in the past and the original situation to the now. In the long run, if what happened in the past is affecting the now, then, the only way to address "it" is in the now. Moreover, that is the only way the past is significant, if "it" is affecting the now.

References

Blumer, Herbert
  1969 Symbolic Interactionalism: Perspective and Method. Englewood Cliffs, N. J.: Prentice-Hall, Inc.

Mead, George Herbert
  1934 Mind, Self, and Society. Chicago, IL: University Press.

Merton, Robert K.
  1948 "The Bearing of Empirical Research Upon the Development of Social Theory." American Sociological Research. 5:505-515.

Swan, L. Alex
  1994 The Practice of Clinical Sociology and Sociotherapy. Rochester, VT: Schenkman Publishing Co.
  1985 "Grounded Encounter Therapy: A Sociodiagnostic and Sociotherapeutic Approach." Mid-American Review of Sociology. 2:93-109.
  1988a "The Social Psychology of Driving Behavior: Communicative Aspects of Joint-Action." Mid-American Review of Sociology. 1:59-67.
  1988b "Grounded Encounter Therapy: Its Characteristics and Process." Clinical Sociology Review. 6:76-87.

Deutscher, Irwin
  1999 Making a Difference: The Practice of Sociology. New Brunswick, NJ: Transaction Publishers.

Cole, Stephen (ed.)
  2001 What's Wrong with Sociology?. New Brunswick, NJ: Transaction Publishers.

Agger, Ben
  2000 Public Sociology. New York: Rowman and Littlefield.

Bryant, C. G. A., and H. A. Becker.
1990 <u>What Has Sociology Achieved</u>. London: MacMillian.

Steele, S.F., A. Scaribrick-Hauser, and W. J. Hauser
1998 <u>Solution-Centered Sociology: Addressing Problems Through Applied Sociology</u>. Thousand Oaks, CA: Sage.

Stehr, Nico
1992 <u>Practical Knowledge: Applying The Social Sciences</u>. Newbury Park, CA: Sage.

Larson, Calvin J.
1993 <u>Pure and Applied Sociological Theory: Problems and Issues</u>. Fort Worth: Harcourt Brace Jevanovich College Publishers.

Reynolds, Larry T.
2001 <u>Reflective Sociology: Working Papers in Self-Critical Analysis</u>. Rockport, TX: Magner Publishing.

Rebach, H. M., and J. G. Bruhn (eds)
1991 <u>Handbook of Clinical Sociology</u>. New York: Plenum Press.

Hillman, J., and M. Ventura
1992 <u>We've Had a Hundred Years of Psychotherapy and the World's Getting Worse</u>. New York: Harper Collins.

Family Types by Member Relationships and Interactions

Chapter 7

* * *

Family Types by Member Relationships and Interactions

Introduction

A wide variety of professionals have attempted to explain family relationships whether they have studied, researched or assumed intellectual and academic expertise on the family. Many of these persons have had no academic training nor have they had a course in their becoming "expert" professionals on the family. Many have simply resorted to common sense knowledge in writing and talking about the family and family relationships. For these reasons, there is confusion in the field. There are those who argue that we must insist on the importance of family context in the understanding of individual behavior, especially at a time when clinical psychology and psychiatry continue to wed the view that the person or personality system is the basic unit of therapeutic meaning. Others argue that just as family processes illuminate individual behavior, so the behavior of families is best understood within the larger context of culture. In the clinical and therapeutic community, the society has licensed and sought the views of psychiatrists for understanding a subject for which they have no academic background. This fact has not been adequately addressed in the clinical and therapeutic community by those with the academic background most appropriate for understanding and diagnosing family relationships.

Explanatory Position

Attempts at explaining marital and family relationships have focused on family structure and very rarely on family interaction. The nuclear, the extended and the augmented family structures have provided insights and understanding regarding the nature and function of family systems. The nuclear family system is composed of a married pair and their dependent children living together, and is considered a closely linked unit. The extended family system is composed of the nuclear family plus relatives, and is considered to have several advantages over the nuclear family system. Shared resources, including wealth and power, protection of property rights, education and care of the young are tasks that the extended family assumed for the survival of the kinship group. The augmented family which is composed of the nuclear members, and the extended family members also include non-relatives. This family system is not very popular in modern industrial societies. However, in nonindustrial societies and in the rural sectors of modern societies both the extended and augmented family systems are more evident. For some families, their structure has been the result of economic conditions and cultural traditions. Consequently, most societies have elements of all patterns of family systems. Numerous exchanges and mutually supportive relations with each other and with other kin exist in extended and augmented family systems. However, what makes a family strong and functional is not its structural system but the nature and character of the relationship and interaction between its members, whether they are joined together by marriage, ancestry, or adoption. This focus on member relationship and interaction is crucial in understanding the internal dynamics of the family and marriage, and for intervention and change (Cox, 1981).

There are a variety of elements that have been identified as family strengths or elements which when present in a family have the potential for establishing strong families. If the choice of a marriage partner is satisfactory and sound, and the essential marital and family schemes or mechanisms are in place to deal with conflict and potential conflict, the other significant matter that must receive attention is the joint-action in the family. Fitting the actions of each member to the actions of each other defines the types of families in terms of member relationship and interaction. It might be important to understand families in terms of nuclear, extended, and augmented, but a more dynamic approach is to understand the family from the view of member relationship and interaction. In order to build the kind of family you want, you have to know the kind of family you have become, and how members relate and interact with each other most of the time.

Another way we have tried to understand the family, is to look at its structure in terms of whether the father or mother dominates the family system. The matriarchal family system is that form of family organization in which power and authority are vested in the hands of the females, with the eldest female usually wielding the greatest power. The majority of societies, however, have organized around the male lineage and the patriarchal family system. The authority and power are vested in the hands of the males, with the oldest male having the greatest power. There are those family systems that are equalitarian in that members in the family are regarded as equal. The husband, in particular, is not regarded as having more privileges or authority than the wife (Allan, 1986).

We define the family as a number of persons related to each other by blood, marriage, or adoption to constitute a social system. Sociologists argue that membership of a family is determined by a combination of biological and cultural criteria, which may vary considerably from culture to culture. Further, the structure of the family is specified by positions and roles of family members and is culturally determined. The functions performed by families also vary from culture to culture, and include procreation, care, socialization of children and the provision of affection for family members. It is within this context that member relationship and interaction become important. The organization and structure of the family are significant, but the kinds of relationships and the nature of the interactions between and among members have greater potential for understanding, clarifying and intervening in family situations. This position allows us to focus not only on family problem areas, but also on family development issues, which enhances our explanatory power.

There are various explanations regarding family relationships and interactions. There are those family members who have come together to maximize their chances for a happy relationship. They looked for a good deal, a bargain, if possible, in which their assets and liabilities were compared with those of the potential relationship. They continue the relationship on the assumption that they will get more out of it than it will cost. Those different from and especially below their own level of exchange are likely to be out of luck. Complementary needs theory suggests that people select others for relationships who make up for, balance, or supply needs that they themselves do not have. Thus the talker looks for a listener, the eater for a cook, etc. Another notion suggests that people who share common values and common definitions about roles are more likely to enter into relationships with each other. If they have different values and differing role expectations they will not establish a relationship.

Process theory argues that establishing relationships involves a number of social and psychological processes. After employing factors as physical attraction, religious and racial differences, role and vale similarities, and psychological influences, relationships are established. In many cases, however, individuals tend to just settle for partners and the relationship they have with them. These explanations are applicable to families and the coming together of their members. However, all families are not alike (Henslin, 1985; Swan, et al, 1983; Burr, 1979).

Types of Marriage Relationships

Marriages and families need intimacy, trust, emotional support, acceptance and companionship in order to endure satisfying and fulfilling relationships. Economic reasons, sexual regulation and reproduction, and the socialization of children, played a significant role in the past in holding marriages together, but seem now to be declining in importance for continuing the relationships. As a result, there are various types of relationships among marriages.

Cuber and Harroff (1965) studied a couple of hundred couples who had been married for over ten years and had not considered divorce. They discovered five types of marriage relationships: the conflict-habituated, the devitalized, the passive-congenial, the vital, and the total.

The conflict-habituated relationship is one in which the partners fight about anything. The relationship is tense and dominated by conflict. As much as possible, they try to control and conceal the conflict from others. The little emotion that exists in the relationship is negative. The couple nag, quarrel and bring up the past to each other frequently. If there are children, they are very aware of the conflict nature of their parents' relationship and interaction.

The devitalized relationship is one characterized by its lack of emotions. Partners who admit that they were once filled with positive emotions and love for each other were now drained of such emotions and lacking of love. Once deeply in love they enjoyed spending much of their time together and being intimate. Now, they have disengaged emotionally and are not enjoying their intimate involvement as they once did. Their interests and activities are no longer common, but share a genuine concern for the development and well-being of their children.

The passive-congenial relationship is like the devitalized relationship in that it lacks emotional ferver. However, this condition of passivity existed since the beginning of the relationship. No time in this relationship was there a more exciting partnership. Their emotional involvements are not intense and they behave towards each other in a practical and sensible manner. They are prudent, responsible and plan ahead carefully. Marriage is viewed as a convenient institution and the proper way to live and solve many problems. Partners expect to perform certain tasks and are satisfied with the relationship being orderly.

The vital marriage sharply contrasts all three types of marriage relationships. They are alike in their concern for their children, jobs, homes, and communities. For the vital marriage relationship the partners have an intense psychological intimacy which is the essence of life for them. They enjoy and receive great satisfaction in sharing time and activities together. After many years of being together in the relationship, couples in vital marriage relationships "find their central satisfaction in the life they live with and through each other" (Cuber and Harroff, 1965, p. 283). Conflict does emerge sometimes in this type of marriage relationship, but it is resolved quickly and the disposition is to avoid conflict where possible, and not let it dominate their relationship.

The total relationship is the most complete because the couples share more parts of their lives with each other. They may travel together whenever either has to travel. They may be collaborator, business partners or share some other important activity and they have a lot of emotional content and contact. All conflict was approached in a manner that would not damage their relationship.

All of these types of marriage relationships are found among marriages today. Divorce as conflict is found among all types, but for the total and vital types these matters are rare and dealt with differently. The relationship for the vital and total must be meaningful, fulfilling and satisfying to endure. Their primary goal is to maintain a high quality in their relationships and interaction. They could not endure a devitalized, conflict-habituated or passive congenial relationship. Conflicts and divorces are more frequent among these types and they never seem to achieve vital and total relationships without much collective effort and professional help. Among these types of relationships it is very difficult to achieve emotional intimacy, yet, not impossible.

Classifications of Family Types

Classifying families by types enhances the way we view the family. The family has its own organization and structure which define its uniqueness. How the family is structured according to its various parts is significant to its functioning. Gerda L. Schulman (1982: 37062) has discussed several types of families in his work. "The Intact Family" is a bio-social unit which consist of two generations living together. They are a parental pair and their offspring." There is the

Single Parent type. "The SP family is either a transitory or permanent family arrangement. There are two types of SP families; the one which starts as a SP family and the other which starts as an intact family, but due to circumstances loses a parent." Then there is the Reconstructed Family. According to Schulman, this type of a family allows us to "see how various systems influence each other."

There are any number of variations in this kind of family from the most complex is one in which both spouses have children not only from an earlier union, but both have their children living with them in the same household while at the same time a child is born to both of them. The "his" "hers" and "ours" refer to the three subgroups comprising this family in which only one subgroup shares both parents. Each parent forms a natural alliance with his/her children, an alliance which is based on blood, heredity and shared history (p. 43). The Intergenerational Family has been the prototype of family structure in the past and is still quite prevalent in some cultures. In the intergenerational family, three generations live together in the same house.

Schulman also presents another way to view families. The developmental stages of individuals are suggested which leans on the views of Erickson. "Families move from one stage to another requiring different adaptations for the whole unit, not just for the individuals who also are experiencing changes in developmental stages." Another way of classifying families is related to family climate. There is the Autocratic Rigidified Family. This family has clear boundaries which separate and differentiate the parents from the children and each child from each other. The line between the generations is firmly drawn, as are the boundaries between the family and the outside world. This type of family is hierarchically oriented and power and status is invested according to age and gender (p. 52).

The Chaotic, Acting-out Family is characterized by "weak boundaries toward the outside world—little distinction between parents and children in terms of position; roles are easily interchanged and the system and its members are in perpetual motion. The marital-parental axis is weak; one would need a movie camera to capture it." The other type is the Enmeshed Family. This type of family is one "where the intergenerational boundaries between the nuclear family and the family of origin are blurred and where the major emotionally meaningful transactions take place between at least one spouse and his (her) parents and other related kin." The final type of family identified is the depressed-Isolated Family. In the depressed family every family member seems separate and few transactions occur among its members. This family is too isolated from the outside world not because it perceives the outside world as dangerous (enmeshed family), nor because it is afraid of bad influence (autocratic family), but because there is little energy left and it therefore can but experience few remarks in interchange with the outside world (p. 61).

Family Types by Member Relationship and Interaction

The family exists in some form in all societies. Since this is the case, it is argued that the family must serve a purpose; fill basic needs, and perform essential tasks. The family controls reproduction, controls sexual expression, care for and socialize children, provide close affectional and emotional ties for the individual, and placement or status ascription. With regards to these functions families are alike. They carry out these functions even though they may do so in a variety of ways. Families may also be alike in terms of structure, but where they differ is in the way members relate and interact with each other, and among each other within the different structures. When family members come together, they anticipate and hope for intimate relationships where there are social bonds and strong emotional ties. Often a process of interaction is established to achieve this goal. Some families achieve it, some are always in the process of achieving it, some start and fail, repeating the process several times, and some quit trying and redefine their goals and restructure their relationships and patterns of interaction to facilitate their new goals.

The way they start relating and interacting is not the way they are after three, five, or ten years. Members might have assumed a variety of relationships with each other, and established various patterns of interaction in an attempt to establish joint-action. It is very essential that members attempt to fit their actions to the actions of each other in family setting. The distance or closeness is determined by a number of factors and assigned meaning by the members in interaction. There are those members who want some distance in relationships; those who want mush distance, and those who want closeness. Consequently, within the family setting, there might be either or all of these levels of distances and closeness operating. There are four family types that seem to represent these levels in relationships and patterns of interaction. The focus on member relationship and interaction seems crucial in understanding the internal dynamics of these family types for intervention, application and change. Strong, functional, weak, dysfunctional, stable or unstable families are not related necessarily to its structural system, but more so to the nature and character of the relationships and interactions between its members, whether they are joined together by marriage, ancestry or adoption, or whether the male or female dominates.

The first type of family in terms of member relationship and interaction is one in which the members are in peripheral or boundary relationships and interaction. Independence is primary in this type of family and individualism is the basis for functioning. Some degree of social and emotional contact is established and maintained. There is an attempt to avoid knowledge of self resulting from the feedback of other members; and there is the avoidance of knowing others, the situation of the family and no one takes the initiative on behalf of the collective, and no one assumes responsibility for the matters in the family setting. Consequently, conflict is intentionally avoided. In this type of family, growth is limited and encounter is shunned. Members in this family type are not really distant, but they are not emotionally connected nor are they socially bounded. They have surface relationships and roles are not clearly defined and assumed. There is constant avoidance in establishing real intimate, emotional and social bonds. It is not safe to suggest that this type of family is dysfunctional or unsuccessful. There are needs of family members that are served best by establishing peripheral and boundary relationships and interactions. If this type is fulfilling the needs and achieving the goals, and expectations of the members, then they are succeeding. If the needs, goals and expectations change, then that type of family by member relationship will emerge to accommodate their needs.

The second type of family is characterized by intimate interaction and close relationships which make conflict inevitable and pronounced. This does not mean, however, that the family is in trouble because of the conflicts. This means that this family type must have in place various mechanisms for dealing with the inevitability of conflicts. These mechanisms provide ways in which the family can manage their relationships and interactions so that the conflicts do not destroy their relationships. Conflicts only destroys family relationships when there are no mechanisms in place available to deal with the conflicts, or when they are in place but are not employed or are employed ineffectively.

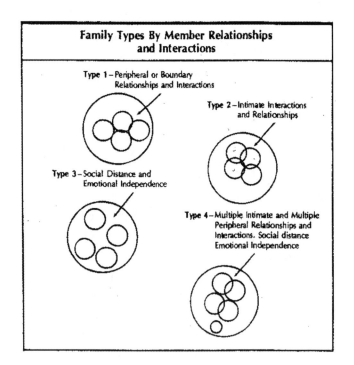

Figure 1

The members in this family type are emotionally and socially connected. Their association with each other is intense and their identification is internal to significant persons within the family kin. Joint-action is very crucial in this family type and disclosures and discoveries provide knowledge about and of each other for the purpose of fitting each action to the action of each other. In joint-action, the concern is not necessarily who does what, but what needs to be done, and who is available at the time to do what needs to be done, providing the person best suited to do that is occupied at the time. So if the cook is sick, or is otherwise occupied, another takes or assumes the responsibility. This is the essence of joint-action. The members are socially bounded; encounter is intense and growth is progressive. This is the reason that mechanisms should be in place early and activated as situations determine their need.

Social distance defines the relationship between the members of the household of family type three. There is no intimate contact and emotionally they tend to function independently. This family type does not provide the emotional and social support for each other that the individuals must have in understanding themselves, others and the security that is necessary for emotional releases, self expression, disclosure, growth and change as a result. Everything in the household is individualized and the various problems that each encounters outside the household and those that emerge inside the household are dealt with individually. Identification of members is external to the family, and the values, norms and mores are individualized and multiple, which means that they are not shared among the members. Their reference group is external to their family, usually other families, especially their families of origin, or other families they wish they were a part of. There are no strong social and emotional bonds among and between the members of this family. In such cases, conflict is avoided, but the lives of the members are dull and unfulfilled. Everyone does his/her own thing in this family type, and no joint-action is established. Nonetheless, the members need closeness but a number of things get in the way of their achieving close ties.

The fourth family type has elements of each of the other three types. Because of this, ambivalence, confusion, conflict, misunderstanding, emotional pain, and social distance tend to dominate this family. Growth is possible among other members. In multiple intimate multiple peripheral, and distant relationships and interactions, joint-interaction is difficult to achieve, and in some cases is not deisred. For some individuals in the family, the distance they experience in the family allows them to avoid being open, or having to express their feelings or declaring their needs, or making demands on others. Some members cannot function very well in this family in the same way as other members, to the same degree, or to the same degree of intensity, therefore they try to establish an optimum distance with each member to avoid conflict and emotional pain. Some members are also in constant conflict acting and reacting to what other members do relative to the distance and nature of the interactions and relationships. Those who have close and intimate ties are usually objects of the open and subtle hostility of other members, and at times they attempt to monitor reactionary behavior and the frequent "wars" that emerge among some members.

These family types suggest that our understanding and actions when dealing with family problems must be related to the type of member relationships and interactions that characterize the particular family. For example, because of the nature and character of these family types, it is not true that in every family what happens to one member affects the other or other members as systems experts suggest. This situation depends on whether the relationship or interaction is peripheral, distant, or intimate among and between the members of the family. It is also not the number of persons in the family, in terms of structure, that determine the character of the family. The interactions, the relationships, or the nature of the interactions and relationships determine the character of the family. The type of family, in terms of member relationships and interactions, defines the internal dynamics and process of the family. This should be the focus of social scientists and sociotherapists who seek to explain family functioning and process, and those who engage family clients in encounter for disclosure, discovery, and assessment for treatment.

Disengagement in Member Relationships

There are very few families where there are multiple intimacy and strong emotional and social bonds. In a large number of families there are members who enjoy this kind of relationship and interaction, and there are members who within the same families have boundary relationships or experience distance in interactions and relationships. Consequently, there are members of families who live in the same household who have withdrawn from intimate activity with each other; who have no close relationships with other members, and have a weak, or poor emotional identification with each other. This experience may be identified as disengagement. Disengagement is the adjustment to persistent problems and difficulties in member relationships, where one or all members withdraw from the intimate activity and interaction and emotional identification with each other to the point of social distance. Often when members reach this point in their relationships, we can assume that one or all of the members have already experienced emotional separation.

It is often that members, soon after they come together, begin to take each other for granted. This posture in relating often leads to dispositions and attitudes that stifle sharing, openness, disclosures and increased emotional attachment. These members are not usually actively engaged in their relationships, and soon find themselves stuck with unresolved problems and conflicts and no way of understanding each other and the social setting in which they find themselves. This pattern of relating results in members disengaging from each other in intimate and intense ways. Members who are not actively engaged in their relationships; when they begin to drift, and disengagement sets in, relaxing their intimate exchanges and interactions, allow for other interests to find entrance into their lives and causes distractions.

Distractions are things, persons, events, challenges, and activities that significantly interfere with intimate, emotional and intense relationships of family members to the extent that the individuals experience disengagement from each other in intimate and emotional contact. Distractions usually cause family members to raise questions, doubts, reservations, and even be reluctant in establishing or utilizing mechanisms for growth, development and change. They also reduce members' ability to establish and maintain joint-action. There often emerges a reduction in the desire to grow, improve upon what they have together, correct a conflict pattern, and establish short term and long term goals. Distractions will vary depending upon the needs and desires of the members, and what is available at the time of disengagement. Whatever the distractions, however, they will play a significant role in the relationship of the members. A definite sign that a member is disengaging, or has disengaged from intense, intimate and growing relationships with another or other members is when the member begins to establish or maintain social and emotional distance from other family members and is still living in the same household.

Reasons for Disengagement

There are a number of reasons for members becoming disengaged with other family members. One is that they have come to a realization that they made the wrong choice; their hopes and dreams may not be realized, or that they may never establish a satisfactory relationship with another or other family members. This is a most distracting realization for members to arrive at in the course of their relationship in the family. If they are not growing as a result of their coming together as a family unit, the relationship can become stagnant and distractions will be attractive and appropriate alternatives to intimate, emotional, and social involvement with the family members will present themselves, or become evident and accepted. In this process, the member who is about to disengage will establish, at the mental level, a variety of arguments to embrace the distractions in order to neutralize the guilt feelings, and to justify the disengagement, or disengaging posture.

Another reason for disengagement is the lack of joint-action in the relationship. In families, members must seek to fit their actions to the actions and behaviors to those of each other if their relationships are to be successful and progressive. The process of joint-action is facilitated by sharing, companionship, love, common goals, decisions, disappointments; developing an attitude of understanding; an ability for being adaptable to inevitable changes, flexible but committed to the relationship, and forgiving. If these dispositions and behaviors are present and in place, decisions can be made without distractive conflicts; power struggles can be overcome, problems can be solved, conflicts resolved, crisis managed, and situations changed. Even if the relationships are floundering, they can become better when joint-action dominates the pattern of interaction.

It is true that skills, insights, confidence, desires and willingness to make the relationship work are the ingredients necessary for joint-action to be effective and the relationships rewarding. However, these qualities can be developed as the members interact with each other in an open and trusting context. Further, implicit in the development of these ingredients, is the basis, the process and nature of growth. In the absence of joint-action, emotional detachment sets in and becomes very hard to change, especially if the distractions have become meaningful not merely as substitutes, but as permanent, independent, and real parts of the social setting of the members.

There are members who disengage also because they think they have problems and difficulties with other members that are long standing that they do not want to deal with, or that they have not been able to solve, or that no one has helped them manage or change. In many cases, they have especially excluded the member or members as persons who can help. More often than not, the excluded members are the very ones that can assist in making the necessary correction and change in the interactional matter. If the problem is a long standing one, often the member is defined as the problem and therefore not thought to be a source to a solution.

Members who desire viable and growing relationships in their families usually determine that nothing nor anyone will distract them from primary responsibility being actively engaged in their relationships with each other. Being actively involved with each member is an excellent way to protect or guard against distractions which lead to disengagements and transference of love and affection from member or members to the distractions. It is very difficult for members to become distracted when they are actively engaged and committed in their relationship with each other. When disengagement sets in, however, anyone and anything can distract members from each other causing major difficulties, challenges and problems.

A more recent cause for distractions and disengagement is the growing belief that association and identification with family members only cannot satisfy all of the basic social and emotional needs of each other. Therefore, members tend to seek other social relations in order to be complete and fulfilled. While human beings are social beings and must interact with others outside the family setting, that association and identification should be enhancing and enriching to member relationships and interactions. If such external interactions are distracting causing disengagement, then they should be terminated, altered and changed. All distractions should be avoided, and one can be aware of a distraction when the actively, interest, or even causes a reduction in social and emotional identification with other family members, and stifles growth and development in relationships. Distractions that serve a need in the life of a member, however, are hard to break away from, especially when there is no alternative forthcoming from the situation, or from other family members.

All distractions do not have the same effect, or the same strength. Some distractions are initially not as powerful as others and provide members with the excuse of embarrassing them because they appear harmless, relatively safe and satisfying. Gradually, however, this importance becomes more significant and members tend to rely on them as a matter of course. In the process, they begin to disengage from each other in intimate and emotional interaction, and joint-action becomes difficult, and establishing and employing mechanisms for solving family problems and managing conflicts become monumental.

Both individuals and things can be distractions. Neither of these areas of distractions is easy for members to deal with, and one is not easier than the other. In fact, even though there are those who believe they can handle, or manage one better than the other, both areas are very difficult to relate to, especially if they are significant in relation to the social situation of the relationship of members. Things are usually the first source of distractions and areas for disengagement. After a while, they may be replaced by individuals. In some cases, both things and individuals are embraced by family members, and the distractions and disengagement are doubled in strength.

There are family members who use distractions occasionally in order to cope with, or deal with a breakdown, discrepancy, or difficulty in their relationships. If these occasional and temporary distractions are effective in helping, or easing their defined problem, even if they are a bit uncomfortable, or occasionally uncomfortable, the likelihood is that the distractions will become permanent. This posture becomes the standard way in which the members will relate to discrepancies, conflicts, and difficulties in their relationships, even if the objects and sources of the distractions shift from time to time, or are changed as they present themselves, or as they are sought out.

What Can Be Done

If members of a family sense that there are distractions in their relationships and interactions, they should first determine, individually or collectively, their nature, character and the exact form in which they present themselves. The next step is to determine the most effective way to deal with them once their source and strength are determined and clarified. Individual and collective commitment is essential to the task. Members who are experiencing disengagement need to be assisted in transferring their attention to each other so that engagement can be resumed. Once engagement is restored, specific strategies and plans must be developed for growth and development. First, restructuring of patterns of interaction is a must so that the members are forced to confront and encounter the challenges and bring about understanding and change. Second, there must be a redefinition of each other and the situation in the direction of the restructuring and the engagement. Sociograms which employ nonverbal strategies for depicting each member's experience of self in relation to others in the relationship can be most helpful in this regard.

Since disengagement is related to distractions, if disengagement is to be changed, several things must take place. First, the nature and purpose served by the distractions must be diagnosed. It must be acknowledged that the disengagement is real. Secondly, there must be acceptance of the members as a present reality from whom the member is disengaging. If perceptions and dispositions are changed, there must be a realization that redefinition of the situation and the member is possible. Thirdly, the members should establish guidelines for fitting their actions to the actions of each other. In this regard, they may need professional assistance. Lastly, the members should establish and put in place appropriate and viable family mechanisms or strategies (plans) for dealing with difficulties and problems when they surface.

Conclusion

It is much easier to understand and treat families when we focus on member relationship and interaction. The internal dynamics of the family are exposed to close scrutiny for grounding theory and therapy. Finally members can behave individually or singly when there are distractions which cause disengagement from intense, intimate, social and emotional relationships, even when they are living in the same household. All members in families will have challenges, problems, conflicts and difficulties that are invitations to distractions and disengagement. However, these challenges, problems, conflicts and difficulties do not have to destroy the relationships of the family members. In the absence of joint-action and family schemes, or the lack of utilization of established schemes for dealing with matters in the family, relationships can get stuck and no growth is possible.

Through the process of disclosure and discovery between and among family members, an understanding can be achieved relative to the presenting and real difficulties. Family meetings are excellent times for dealing with these matters. During the meetings, members become a part of the process of discovery of their setting, the problems, and how they can be solved. A plan of action may also be devised for changing the pattern of interaction to allow for growth and development. All of this is possible, especially when we seek to understand the family by looking at the internal dynamics of the family in terms of member relationships and interactions. Within this context, the various types of families can be established; the various kinds of relationships and interactions determined, along with their related problems, and specific ways for intervention can be devised.

Families may start their coming together with close social and emotional bonds, relating and interacting at a high level of intensity. However, for a variety of reasons, one, two or all of the members may want to be released from the intensity of the interaction and relationship and establish an optimum distance of closeness with other members. It is this shift and movement that tend to create problems for family members. It is also at this point that their focus is adjusted by distractions, and disengagement is experienced. It is only as we assess the internal dynamics of the family by member relationship and interaction that we can hope to be effective in understanding family matters and intervening in the family situation.

References

Allan, Graham
   1986 Family Life: <u>Domestic Roles and Social Organization</u>. New York: Basil Blackwell, Inc.

Burr, Wesley R. et. al.
   1979 <u>Contemporary Theories About the Family</u>. New York: MacMillian.

Cox, Frank D.
   1981 <u>Human Intimacy: Marriage, the Family and Its Meaning</u>. St. Paul, Minnesota: West Publishing Co.

Cuber, John F., and Peggy B. Haroff
   1972 <u>The Significant Americans: A Study of Sexual Behavior Among the Affluent.</u> New York: Appleton-Century-Crofts.

Henslin, James M.
   1985 <u>Marriage and Family in a Changing Society.</u> New York: Free Press.

Schulman, Gerda L.
   1982 <u>Family Therapy: Teaching, Learning and Doing.</u> Lanbam, MD: University Press of America.

Swan, L. Alex, et. al., eds.
   1983 <u>Issues in Marriage, Family and Therapy.</u> Lexington, Mass.: GinnPublishing Co.

Institutional Treatment

Chapter 8

* * *

Institutional Treatment

Institutional Treatment

Modern trends toward corrections continue the objective of punishment as a strategy to treatment for the purpose of rehabilitation. Prisons are thought of as therapeutic units for the management and change of inmates for successful reintegration into society. Extension of the model allows for the definition of society as a therapeutic environment within which many inmates can be treated and changed. However, neither the prisons as therapeutic units nor society as a therapeutic environment have been responsible for successful reentry of the inmate. Prisons are good at confining and punishing inmates. They have never had a true rehabilitative function. Moreover, it is almost impossible or highly improbably for professional workers and prison authorities, under the present conditions of prison life to determine when an inmate is successfully rehabilitated. As a means of rehabilitation, institutional treatment (imprisonment) has had little success. It has not been effective primarily because treatment programs within the prison tend to be dehumanizing.

There is the argument that rehabilitation will work, and the consequences would be the reduction in recidivism if treatment programs are individualized. However, most of the treatment programs in prisons, whether designed to meet individual needs or not, operate on the basic assumption that the individual is a criminal. This is not true for a large number of persons imprisoned. They are convicts but are not criminals. In spite of the institutional treatment, many inmates do not return to prison. The reason for this is that in many cases, inmates do not internalized the negative concept held of them by prison officials. Another reason for this trend is the particular circumstances the inmate faces upon release and the legitimate opportunities acceptable and available to him/ her during the first four to six weeks after release. The facilitating circumstances must be created by the inmate or others. She/he must develop the ability to void the power of others to define him/her in criminal terms and must be convinced that it is no longer necessary to participate in criminally defined activity.

During the mid-60's an increase in coercive behavior-modification techniques for managing and controlling those inmates who threatened the social order of prisons became rampant. Such techniques as electronic surveillance, electrical and chemical stimulation, and psychosurgery were the techniques employed. There are suggestions and recommendations today that the brainwashing techniques used on American prisoners of war by North Koreans could be employed to rehabilitate and change inmates' behavior (Schein, 1962). Several tactics are identified in the brainwashing techniques, which prisoner groups have referred to as the Manifesto of Dehumanization (Federal Prisoner's Coalition, 1972). The conclusion is that prisons do not rehabilitate and inmates are not successfully treated in the prison environment. One reason for this is that confinement is the dominant mode of business in prison. Jessica Mitford notes that:

In prison parlance, "treatment" is an umbrella term meaning diagnosis, classification, various forms of therapy, punishment as deemed necessary, and prognosis, or the prediction of the malfeasant's future behavior: Will/won't he err again? While the correction crowd everywhere talk a good line of "treatment"—phrases like "inadequate personalities," borderline sociopaths," "weak superegos" come treppingly off the tongue of the latter-day prison warden, having long since replaced the sin-stained soul and fallen men or women with whom his predecessors had to cope—very few prison systems have actually done much about implementing it in practice. Nationwide, only 5 percent of the prison budget goes for services labeled "rehabilitation," and in many states there is not even the pretense of making "therapy" available to the adult offender (Mitford, 1973: 97).

Another reason for this failure in prison is the conflicting objectives and different priorities in dealing with inmates. The members of society assume and expect inmates to be reformed during their prison experience. The professionals and prison authorities also expect them to change during confinement. Custodial workers are concerned with maintaining control and this concern is reflected in their priorities of action in a given situation as well as in the considerations they express in planning and supervising inmates' activities. On the other hand, treatment personnel tend to be concerned with mitigating the psychological and interpersonal problems of inmates. Conflict engendered by these different priorities is exacerbated because custodial and treatment workers, by virtue of their different responsibilities, are also frequently confronted in a different manner by inmates. These workers thus develop different conceptions of the inmates and each staff group becomes convinced of the correctness of its view and decides that of the other (Piliavin, 1966: 125-34).

Inmates recognize the conflict and also perceive the treatment programs to be nothing more than a cover-up for control, inmate domination, and repression in prison. One ex-inmate disclosed: I'd go into a room and be treated like a human being and the possibilities seemed unlimited. Then I'd leave the room and my reality was the prison. Then some hack would holler "line-up, bend over and spread your cheeks. Stand up, move out . . . ." and I would be angry and resentful—as much against the people with the programs as I was against the hack. I began to resent the outsiders because they teased me. They let me think I was a human being with dignity. I stopped going to the meetings (Rothenberg, 1976: 10).

A modification of the custodial setting of institutional treatment are work-release programs outside the prison, halfway houses where offenders receive residential treatment while they attend school or work. These techniques and measures are employed because professionals and prison reformers have come to believe that prisons do not rehabilitate and that inmates are not successfully treated in the prison environment. Saleem A. Shah has argued that: During the past many years there has been considerable evidence justifying the increasing disillusionment with the rehabilitative and treatment effectiveness of traditional correctional institutions. It has become glaringly evident that such institutions have been designed primarily to meet the societal objectives of restraint and containment, rather than the stated concerns with treatment of rehabilitation. Indeed not only are correctional institutions generally ineffective in regard to attaining their rehabilitative objectives (which objectives they cannot be expected to meet without considerable efforts in and by the larger community), but the deleterious and destructive effects of such, incarceration appear further to add to the problems of correctional clients (Shah, 1972: 111).

Community-based treatment and correctional programs for adult offenders got strong support from the U.S. Bureau of Prisons. We in corrections know that offenders can change—can be reintegrated into the community—if provided the proper assistance, support and supervision. The focus of this effort is, of course, the community-based programs. We must continue and expand these programs and develop new ones of promise. All of us at every level of government, in public and private agencies, must share in this work (Nelson, 1967: 82-91).

Reentry

Given the failure of the prison process to assist the inmate in avoiding the criminal justice system, and the failure of community-based programs, for a variety of reasons, to effectively assist ex-inmates to stay in the society, how is successful reentry achieved? There are those who seek a set of circumstances created by relatives, friends and those who care to assist that would enhance their successful reentry. For some a job establishes the basis for the set of circumstances. For others interested in pursuing an education, the college establishes the basis. There are, however, a significant number of inmates who have embraced a religious experience, which accounts for a high rate of success among those who reenter society from prisons. When these factors are brought to bear on the person reentering, along with certain positive decisions and choices made by them, a network of support systems interact to assure success.

Environment for Success

The network of support systems that provides the basis for successful reentry constitutes an environment into which the ex-inmates enters. The environment consists of four subsystems (the family, work, school, church) that interact with each other to produce conditions conductive to reentry. Consequently, the subsystems must be prepared for the reentry of the ex-inmate. If they are not prepared, there is rejection and alienation, conditions sufficient to produce high rates of recidivism.

The Family

In those cases where the ex-inmate has been in prison for long periods of time, the family makes adjustments necessary to continue its scheme of life. The adjustments often exclude the physical presence as well as economic and emotional input of the individual. Consequently, reentry requires readjustments for the inclusion of the individual if he is to enter the family and receive assistance for a successful reentry. It is not very easy to change people or help them adjust constructively. The problem is often in controlling the direction of the change or adjustment so that the individual's life becomes more successful and more self-enriching, rather than less so. If the family decides to admit the person and attempts readjustment, the role of the person must be clearly defined. In the process of establishing effective family relationships, the members must focus upon and reemphasize what was and is positive in their relationship. Complaining and focusing on the negative aspects of their relationships can be seriously disruptive to successful reentry of the person. When family members switch their own emotional focus, family members allow these people to let down their built-up ego defenses and begin to appreciate themselves more positively. This is usually a gradual process, but adjustments and changes are achieved and experienced by all members. It becomes easier for the family members to establish joint-action in the fitting together of their lines of action to the actions of others in the family. Further, family members must seek to reinforce what they like about their relatives' behavior and not reinforce what they do not like. Dislikes and likes must be carefully ascertained, and members must take note of those situations that produce or stimulate positive reactions. There are times when certain actions of the person will be ignored, especially when they remind family members of behavior prior to imprisonment. A step-by-step upward rebuilding of relationships can provide the strength necessary and sufficient to make the relationship even better than before the separation. Most people who reenter are inclined to be silent about their feelings and experiences. The family context is a very safe place to assist them improve their communications. Communication is the only way to understand what they are feeling. Understanding is a first step to acceptance and assistance in making the adjustments crucial to successful reentry.

The Job/Work

The prison experience is perceived by ex-inmates and the general public as a handicap. Consequently, ex-inmates feel severely restricted in terms of social, political and economic activities. Even though the definition and the effect depend largely on the individual ex-inmate, the self-concept of the individual labeled as handicapped by his prison experience determines in a large number of cases his relationship with others. It is the perception of others, or adjusting to others, especially in the job environment, that most ex-inmates have problems dealing with. In the majority of cases, the family is prepared or assisted by family members, relatives, friends, and sometimes social agencies in preparation for the reentry of the ex-inmate. However, very rarely is the job environment prepared for the inclusion of the ex-inmate as a legitimate partner and worker. Often the disposition is that he will always be a "criminal" and that the assistance given by the company, in the rehabilitation effort, is a waste of time.

In all cases investigated the ex-inmates discerned the negative attitudes and quickly removed themselves from the environment.

Whispering about their status as ex-convicts and the care with which the workers interact with them, removing valuable items from their immediate presence, suggest that they are not really welcomed and not to be trusted. For this reason, probation and parole officers are persuaded that it is not always the best gesture to find employment for ex-inmates until and unless the total environment is thoroughly prepared for their inclusion. It is not enough to inform the foreman or the supervisor of the convict status of the individual. The attitudes of the appropriate associates should be determined. If there are negative attitudes they should be expressed and dealt with in the open prior to the inclusion of the ex-inmate into the work environment. It must be very clear to the workers that the company is not just engaging in public service.

Often when certain skills and abilities are demonstrated and promoted by supervisors (posing no threat to the workers) there tends to be greater acceptance of the person entering the work environment. In the majority of cases, inmates do not have special skills demanded by their jobs and the companies employing them. Consequently, they are not defined as being significant to the job situation or very important to the outcome of the product (goods and/or services). In such cases the ex-convict occupies a peripheral role in the work environment and is not taken seriously as a significant or dependable worker, or one who need be depended upon.

This situation is easily and quickly perceived by the ex-con. What is especially frustrating for ex-convicts is the perception of them, by those who found them jobs, that they are unable to hold a job. The emphasis placed on the ability to hold a job is oppressive. Emphasis should be placed upon the hostile work environment and its preparation to include an ex-convict and the preparation of the ex-con's coping skills to adjust to the work environment as it presents itself. It is the breakdown in this preparation for joint-action that allows the interpretation of ex-cons to exclude themselves from the job environment.

The majority of the jobs secured by ex-convicts are dead-end jobs with wages inadequate to restore them as primary breadwinners.

In many cases they are unable to take care of the basic necessities of food, shelter, and clothing. If they are married, the survival strategy employed by spouses and family members to continue their "scheme of life," coupled with the satisfactory participation of people in the work environment, helps them to be able to achieve and maintain a successful reentry experience. In other cases, where the responsibility are not great, requiring significant financial attention, single and married persons, especially if they have started an interest in academic (educational) matters in prison should pursue their interest in college either in the technical, professional or academic fields.

The School

The school environment is not usually so hostile as the work environment. Many students, especially those representing oppressed and exploited groups, or those participating in acts that are private but are clear violations of the law, realize that the ex-con could have been any one of them; he was merely the one adjudicated. College students tend to perceive the ex-con as one who has certain kinds of information regarding the nature and character of the criminal justice system. In the classroom, especially in courses in criminology, deviance, and various courses in criminal justice, he is treated as an expert with inside information as a participant. Most ex-cons who enter the college environment tend to disclose their status as ex-cons to fellow students either inside or outside the classroom. Seemingly, the college environment is more tolerant and accepting of the ex-con and little or no prior preparation for his inclusion is necessary. The perception of the ex-con as an expert on matters pertaining to crime and the criminal justice system enhances his acceptance in the college environment and is therapeutic in the sense that the ex-con accepts the expert status, which means that he does not need to repeat the experience. Even though students may tend to be cautious in establishing intimate relationships with ex-cons on the college campus, they do not alienate them from social gatherings. If they attend they are never denied participation.

The classroom and the college environments provide a network of support for the ex-con that are not yet clearly defined nor adequately identified. It is within the context of this environment that the ex-cons feel free to discuss their experiences frankly, openly, honestly and freely. Ex-cons take pride in disclosing how tough the prison system is and how rough they have had it on the inside. Their disclosure is usually a warning to students to suggest that they not participate in criminal acts and that they not get caught. Such disclosure might not scare many to conform, but it causes many to become cautious about their deviant activities. The emphasis placed on the difficult experiences encountered in the criminal justice system by the ex-cons allows fellow students and teachers to perceive them as survivors and persons who can endure hardship and even oppression. In this sense, ex-cons come to see themselves as superior to their fellow students and even their teachers who might not have had such experiences.

The Church

Many people assume that the church would be filled with born-again ex-convicts, and there are those who worship in churches who have been changed by conversion experiences. The fact of the matter however, is that very few ex-cons participate in the environment of the church as members in good and regular standing. This is not to suggest that churches are not engaged in prison ministry or that a good number of inmates have not been influenced by the efforts of the church. Data tend to indicate that the membership of the church does not contain many persons who have had very extensive public deviant careers. This fact suggests that the church has not been very interested in attracting such persons to membership, even though they are not actively discouraged from church participation. For some reason not many such persons are found to be members. It could also suggest that the church shares the common definition of the general public that "once a criminal always a criminal," negating the very essence of what they preach and teach that Jesus can save from the "guttermost to the uttermost." Consequently, their interaction with ex-convicts is not attractive or inviting. Many church members feel safe working with inmates who are safely behind bars, but once they are released, even when there is testimony of conversion experience, the members are usually afraid to associate freely with ex-cons. In the case of male ex-convicts, the experience has been that mothers with daughters in the church discourage any form of association that would suggest an interest.

Several churches today are being encouraged to establish prison ministry programs to increase their influence in the lives of prisoners and ex-convicts. Despite some reluctance to develop such programs, discussion continues. Some individual members of churches work with prisoners as a commitment to their religious faith. In several cases in Nashville, Tennessee and Huntsville, Alabama, the membership of a few churches had to be worked with to allow the inclusion of professed converted ex-cons. Some who professed conversion but were still serving time did not receive an open-armed welcome from the churches. In fact, one pastor wanted the matter to be kept a secret for fear the members would be scared away. This condition suggests that the definition of criminality and the deviant label attached to ex-convicts and their behavior are significant in the minds of individuals and come to bear their dispositions, attitudes and beliefs as they interact with those representing such definitions and subjected to such labels. It is ironic that church members have such attitudes and dispositions when it is their declared mission to introduce "salvation to sinners." With the exception of the Nation of Islam, one or two others, there are few organized religious groups that are systematically focusing upon the prison population with the expressed intent to reduce recidivism through conversion. The Nation has an impressive record of resocializing prisoners through the internalization of religious values. It is possible, given the nature of human behavior and the ability of individuals to develop in the process of interaction, for church organizations to create environments and establish a set of circumstances for the successfully reentry of the ex-convict.

Conclusion

The family, the college, the job and the church have the potential to create environments that act together or separately to produce a conducive set of circumstances and conditions for successful reentry of ex-convicts. Given the exploitative and oppressive nature of the social order, reentry success requires a restructuring of the economic, political, legal, and educational arrangements of the society. However, the family, the college, the church and the job have developed coping strategies for survival and progress that can be transferred to the inmate who is attempting to develop coping skills for successful reentry. Handling the problem of crime and criminal behavior might come only as the nature and character of the social, economic, legal, and political character of the social order is changed. In the absence of a restructuring of the arrangements of the social order, the therapeutic environments made possible by the efforts of the family, the college, the church and the job create imperative circumstances for the successful reentry of ex-convicts. The history of struggle and survival of these support social systems speak to their ability to transfer or bestow survival qualities to those ex-convicts needing assistance and protection from deviant labels and criminal definitions.

Institutional treatment has varying effects on inmates. Some inmates do not return to prison in spite of the treatment; some because of circumstances encountered upon release. Some do not return because of the realization that it is no longer necessary or wise to engage in criminal activity. Other ex-convicts do not return to prison because they are able to avoid the criminal definitions and labels of those in positions of power to make such definitions and labels stick. Institutional treatment has made some inmates angry, frustrated, passive, and radical. It has caused some inmates to internalize definitions of themselves that are negative and destructive to their growth and development. This fact is unfortunate and oppressive. A significant number of the persons in prison are there convicted for survival crimes and are not career criminals. However, they can easily become career criminals if they are not significantly impacted by the environments of the network of support systems mentioned above. Consequently, to identify, label and treat ex-convicts as criminals through the process of adjudication has serious consequences for their further participation in criminal activity. The support to ex-convicts found in the community within the context of the family, the church, the work experience, and the college can allow for success conditions that can challenge the negative circumstances created by the prison experience, the need of the state for prison labor, and the need of the police and the other subsystems of the criminal justice system to be legitimate (Swan, 1974, 1982).

In order for ex-cons to reenter society successfully, apart from the above considerations, the following conditions must prevail:

1. They must want to reenter the outside society more than their wanting to leave the prison society.
2. They must decide and make a commitment to making positive choices to create a different scheme-of-life.
3. They must realize and understand the status they occupy in the minds of others and the interactional consequences of their perception of their status.
4. They must allow for the possible discrepancy between their perceptions of themselves and others' perceptions of their projected selves.
5. They must sense that their communities welcome them as fully participating members with all the rights and privileges of such membership.
6. They must understand their limitations, weaknesses and strength.
7. All important persons and institutions in the community must be prepared for the reentry.
8. Group sessions, including those who are making the transition, those who made the transition, and those who did not have to make the transition officially, should be established to deal with the problems of status passage. The group process can provide sociopsychoreligious basis and the formal and informal support systems necessary to the transition.

9. The community must demonstrate in tangible ways its willingness to aid in the process of transition.

10. All facilitating programs must be functional to the extent that they allow for the rise and development of the ex-con's self-image. Within this context, there must be individual involvement, independence, and acceptance and responsibility for their own personal decisions and behavior.

11. The oppressive (racist and colonial) nature of the relationship between the wider society and the ex-con and their communities must change.

12. Ex-convicts must be assisted by the parole system, community agencies, friends and family in managing their images in interacting with significant others.

13. Inmates reentry programs must be established in the prisons that address the issues of reentry to enhance the ability of inmates to negotiate the various forces and make the transition successful.

When these conditions are properly and adequately addressed, successful reentry can be assured and recidivism significantly reduced, especially when the network of support systems are prepared for and do support their reentry.

References

Federal Prison Coalition
  1972 "The Mind Police," <u>Penal Digest International</u> 2 (August): 8-10.
Mitford, Jessica
  1973 <u>"Kind and Unusual Punishment</u>. New York: Alfred A. Knopf.

Pilivian, Irving
  1966 "The Reduction of Custodian-Professional Conflict in Correctional Institutions," <u>Crime and Delinquency</u> 12 (April): 125-34.

Rottenberg, David
  1976 "Failure of Rehabilitation: A Smokescreen," National <u>Catholic Reporter</u> 12 (April 16)): 10

Schein, Edgar H.
  1962 "Man Against Man: Brainwashing, "<u>Correctional Psychiatry and Journal of Social Therapy</u> 8, No. 2: 91-91.

Shah, Saleem M.
  1972 Foreword to Marquerite O. Warren, <u>Correctional Treatment in Community Settings: A Report of Current Research.</u> Rockville, MA. National Institute of Mental Health.

Swan, L. Alex (ed.)
  1974 Blacks and the U.S. Criminal Justice System. <u>The Journal of Afro-American Issues</u> (May).
  1982 "Incarceration Rates: Blacker Than White." <u>The National Association of Black in Criminal Justice.</u> Silver Springs, Md.

The Social-Psychology of Driving Behavior: Communicative Aspects of Joint-Action

Chapter 9

* * *

The Social-Psychology of Driving Behavior: Communicative Aspects of Joint-Action

Introduction

Social scientists have paid little or no attention to driving behavior as a social phenomenon even though it has been the cause of thousands of deaths and injuries. Driving is one of the most intense forms of communication and interaction where joint-action, interpretation, observation and social participation take place. Driving behavior is said to account for over 50,000 deaths each year. It is also argued that there have been more deaths by accidents than all of the deaths resulting from the wars in which the United States participated. In Houston, Texas approximately 250 accidents are reported each day by the police to the Records Division of the police department. It is also estimated that between 260 and 530 accidents occur each day in the city of Houston. This suggests that there is a serious breakdown in joint-action in the driving environment in the city. Fitting lines of action together or establishing joint-action in the driving environment requires taking note of the action of others as indications are made. The assumption is that the meaning of the indications are shared by the actors in the environment.

Eighty-five percent of the accidents in the city occur when drivers are not taking note of what is occurring in their driving world. This means that they are not able to fit their action to the actions of others or form joint-action in driving. Because most accidents occur in Houston between 7 and 8 a.m., and between 5 and 6 p.m., does not mean that hostility is a powerful enough variable to explain accidents as psychoanalysts might be tempted to suggest. Other person trying to explain accidents on the freeways cite rampant aggressiveness, high speeds, and the crowded freeways and highways as explanations. These are not distractions to establishing joint-action on highways and freeways. Some of the distractions in driving are the attitudes of drivers, their dispositions in driving, combing hair, eating, feeding babies, husbands and wives, applying make-up, lighting of cigarettes, attempting to kill an insect, picking up an object on the floor of the car, meditating or reflective thinking, talking, etc. The other fifteen percent of the accidents result from inadequate interpretations of acts and symbols, inappropriate designations, confused meanings, and wrong selection of alternative responses.

Given the number of people coming into the city of Houston daily, it is not surprising that the National Safety Council figures confirm a grim fact that Houston's traffic is the deadliest of the nation's big cities. Houston out distances Los Angeles by nine percent, and the death rate per 100,000 population is twice as bad as Detroit; more than three times that of Philadelphia and more than double New York's and Chicago. The figures suggest that the traffic situation in Houston is out of control and that it will get worse. Over 300 new vehicles are reported to be added to the driving environment in Houston each day. Most explanations for most of the accidents in Houston are merely conditions and symptoms of the problems. All accidents result from the failure or inability of drivers to establish joint-action with objects in the driving environment. In other words, when there is a breakdown in joint-action in the driving environment accidents will occur. Preventing this breakdown requires taking note of significant acts and actors in the driving environment; understanding and interpreting gestures, symbols and indications adequately, and sharing appropriate meanings of the driving world in the process of establishing joint-action.

Driving is learned behavior and the learning is primarily self-initiated. A significant number of individuals are taught the basics in high school or by relatives, friends or private firms established to offer services in driver education. Experience is gained in the process of learning, and although the driving classes are not usually conducted over a long period of time, the majority of drivers complete their learning on the crowded streets and freeways gaining additional experience after the formal test are passed. The social context of the driving behavior includes a varied number of experienced participants with varying styles, meanings, anticipations and attitudes toward driving. There are also a variety of driving cultures in the driving environment, the context of which provides the basis for understanding driving in the American Social Order and for offering solutions to the problems of driving which causes the deaths of a very substantial number of American citizens. The analysis for this work is based upon extensive interviews, participant observation and investigation of accident reports.

Driving as a Source of Revenue

Driving behavior provides the cities and states with a substantial amount of revenue. In addition to the fee each driver pays for the license to participant in the behavior, there is the fee for license plates and registration. There are rules and restrictions which when violated also provide another source of revenue to the cities and states. Police are made to believe that they must demonstrate through the insurance of tickets that they have been functional. However, their function is after the fact to the alleged violations. Consequently, they do not really render a service to the driving citizens if they do not prevent the occurrence of violations. Their services are primarily rendered to legitimize themselves and bring additional revenue to the cities and states. There could be a significant reduction in traffic accidents if police services were before the fact of violations, attempting to prevent the occurrence of traffic violations. If this approach to policing were taken, the revenues to the cities and states through this source would decrease. Driving, therefore, is functional to the economy of cities and states. The rules and regulations are legal constructs that attempt to regulate driving behavior in general, and have come to be measures of significant revenues to the cities and states. Because driving is functional to the economy of cities and states, crowding on the freeway and streets of cities and states is one indication of how profitable driving behavior is to cities and states.

The rules and procedures for driving are not usually based on the cultures found in each town, city, state, or village. Neither do they address the cultural and interactional context of driving. Very few drivers remember, give attention to, or assist others in following the rules and regulations that constitute the legal codes of driving. There are also driving suggestions posted on streets and freeways that are given little attention by drivers. Most drivers abandon the teaching, instructions and warnings received during their classes because they feel restricted and inhibited by such instructions. For example, instructions that drivers keep both hands on the wheel; look out for the other driver; get into the exit lane at a safe distance prior to making the exit, or giving proper signal before shifting lanes are usually ignored. Most drivers do not give any signals, and a significant number of the others give such signals only immediately upon shifting lanes or after they have made the initial move to shift. In most cases, the attitude is that once indication is made, in spite of its lateness, the driver has the right to make the shift and others should yield to such right. Anticipatory behavior, which is essential to participation in driving, is also absent in most of the cases.

The Nature of Driving Behavior

Driving behavior consist of people interaction with one another. Because they drive within the context of a group, drivers must necessarily fit their actions to the actions of each other. It is the very nature of driving behavior that the members of the driving public are embedded in a social situation created by the action of others. Interaction in driving is the presentation of action, which at the same time is a request for a reaction. The clerk and customers, the student and the teacher, each fits his actions to the actions of the other. Orderly social interaction takes place when the different lines of activity of different actors mesh smoothly. In trying to understand the causes of so many accidents which cause thousands (50,000) of deaths each year, we cannot ignore the process of driving interaction itself. To concentrate on the causes which precede interaction or the structural and legal context of the interaction will not provide as powerful a casual explanation. Because the interaction process of driving operates in its own right to lead to the formation of behavior, many so called causes of behavior do not have the importance for driving behavior that most social scientists believe they have.

There are two basic classes of interaction on which people fit their actions to the actions of one another in driving-symbolic and nonsymbolic. Symbolic interaction takes place when the participants interpret one another's acts and formulate their own actions on the basis of the meaning they derive from the interpretation. Nonsymbolic interaction takes place spontaneously, without reflection. This form of interaction takes place primarily among animals, but also among human beings. People tend to be unaware of their involvement in nonsymbolic interaction because it is by definition spontaneous and unreflective (Blumer, 1961). Most important interaction takes place on the symbolic level, primarily by means of gestures. A gesture is a part of an action which stands for the rest of the action for what is to come. Both words and movements are gestures. Gestures are very important in driving behavior. In fact, they are basic to driving interaction because people respond to what they expect others to do, as well as to what others have already done.

There are three identifiable parts of symbolic interaction: 1) the designation or indication (an act or gesture); 2) the interpretation of the designation; and 3) the devising of a response on the basis of the interpretation. Driving behavior which consists of actions by various individuals, necessitates constant interpretation of the actions of others so that responses on the basis of the interpretation might be devised. In a robbery, for example, the robber indicates to the victim how he should act by telling him to raise his arms or to lie on the floor. The victim, on the basis of her interpretation of the gesture (the request) and the intent of the robber will decide whether to comply. If the robber is pointing his finger instead of a gun, or if water is dripping from the gun will make a difference to the victim's interpretation of the intent and seriousness of the request (Blumer,

1969). A gesture implies two things: 1) what will be the remainder of the action of the person who makes it, and is in this sense a prelude to further action; 2) that there will be a particular response to it by the person to whom it was made. A gesture is therefore, intrinsically, joint-action because it cannot take place in the absence of another person (Blumer, 1969).

In order for drivers, in interaction, to fit their actions together, and smoothly interact and reduce accidents, drivers must understand the meaning of one another's gestures and must interpret the gestures similarly. The whole process of driving interaction depends upon the ability of the driver to take one another's roles, and in this way to understand what other drivers are thinking and planning to do. Communication is not interstimulation and response, it is the use of the significant symbol. Consequently, drivers who communicate to other drivers must recognize what they are doing and must have the ability to take the role of the other drivers in anticipation of how they will respond.

Driving and the Driver

Driving behavior takes the form of acts, and may be analyzed in contemporary social science in three ways: 1) the stimulus response theory argues that a reacting organism produces a sequence of action in a series of neuromuscular responses to a set of stimuli. This perspective cannot easily be applied to complex acts involved in driving behavior; 2) motivational theory suggests that people act as they do because they have certain motives. Motive is defined as an initiating agent that drives the organism to action. This view implies that to learn the motives of someone is to learn what she will do; 3) sociological theories suggest that social forces cause action. One sociological view is that human beings behave as they do because they have internalized particular norms or values, which are cultural prescriptions, or rules, about behavior. Another sociological view is that external frameworks or structures impose particular kinds of behavior on people. Roles, for instance, impose standards of conduct on the people who adopt them (Skidmore, 1979).

Driving as conduct which takes the form of acts is not an outgrowth or expression of a set of causes; instead, it is constructed by the actor (the driver). The driver as the actor can do much more than respond to stimuli—she can observe, think about and act upon the stimuli. Drivers build up their conduct in relation to stimuli rather than respond to them. Drivers can view their conduct in progress. Because they are able to take note of their action; they can act back upon their act—they can guide, control, check or even stop it. Drivers can "stand over against" their act as it develops. They can identify their impulse, make an object of it in the form of a want or wish, and set up their goal and their plans for reaching it. As they act they can take into account a variety of external objects, including the behavior of other drivers, fitting their own action to the actions of others. They can continue to make their plans—to map out their act—as they proceed with the overt phase of their act. Driving acts need not be rational in the sense of being wise. Some drivers make errors of interpretation and judgment as they plan and proceed with action. At times they attempt to achieve goals by inappropriate methods. Often they do not see the real implications and consequences of their acts. Consequently, acts can be stupid or wise, they can involve foresight and careful analysis of preconditions and consequences, or they can be rash and irrational.

Driving acts, once begun, need not be completed. Drivers often transfer or divert acts, and they terminate acts before they are completed. Drivers must decide whether they want to seek the goal toward which they are directing their efforts, and whether their efforts will achieve the goal. Their judgment about their action can change as they proceed and they can modify or halt their action.

It is possible for drivers to interact with themselves without making the self an object of the interaction. For example, drivers who are deeply engrossed in driving can interact with themselves as they figure out their motives, but they are thinking about the driving rather than about themselves. However, as drivers construct their acts, they may find it necessary to make an object of themselves, and consider what impact their acts will have on them. They might ask themselves for instance, "What will these drivers think of us if we do what we are planning to do?"(Charon, 1979).

Drivers who are prepared to begin the overt act (to make a move to switch lanes, over-take, etc.) who have their goals defined and identified and their plans laid still have to take into account the acts of other drivers as they begin to carry out their overt action. If they wish to complete their act, they must avoid being prevented from doing so by the acts of other drivers. They must fit their action into the actions of other drivers. Sometimes the drivers must change the direction of their acts in order to do so. Objects not immediately involved in an act under formation can have a profound effect on driving behavior. For example, a driver about to succumb to a temptation to pull from the left lane, across to the right lane to avoid missing his exit, may resist and change his course of action if he thinks of an accident or a death resulting from an accident.

Objects in the driving environment come to be involved in the driving act as it proceeds, and must be identified and analyzed. Driving must often be modified as the relations of objects to the ongoing driving act changes. In constructing a driving act, the drivers do not note everything involved in their action. They make notation only at scattered points in their action, usually when they must make a plan or a choice. For example, at the end of a lecture, a student may note to herself that she has made plans to meet a friend at the student union. The notation to self, however, is just one narrow phase of the entire act of going to the student union. The student may walk all the way to the union without making any further indication to herself. For example, she will not consider each step she takes. Only under unusual circumstances does one have to examine and take into account the nature of the ground on which she is walking. The self does not constantly direct the act, but intercedes in the act only occasionally. When the self intercedes in the driving act, drivers must become conscious of every part of their act. They are conscious only when they take note of something. All actions have unconscious aspects. For instance, someone may not be aware of the impulse to which he is responding, or even that he is responding. Not only is it possible for someone to be stirred into action by an impulse that he cannot identify; it is also possible for someone to make an object of his impulse to define it incorrectly. If someone misrepresents his impulse to himself, his response to it will be constructed on the basis of the misrepresentation. A person can deal with an impulse only on the basis of the kind of object he makes of it. If he makes a fictitious or distorted object of an impulse, he can act only on the basis of the distortion. Drivers often act on the basis of misjudged definitions of a situation, without taking into account all that might properly be taken into account that is, without making a careful, probing examination of the impulse they make into objects. This is very important in driving behavior because in the formation of driving conduct, there is a constant interplay between impulse and image. Impulses initiate acts; images give direction to impulses. For example, before someone can satisfy her hunger, she must indicate to herself where she can obtain food, and what kinds of food are available. This means that she must present to herself images of where she can obtain food, and of what food is available. The image gives the impulse form and organization it gives structure and direction to the developing act.

Driving behavior consist of interaction between drivers. It is not simply an aggregation of separate organisms acting independently. The actions of an individual member of the driving society are necessarily connected with the actions of other members of the driving society. Every individual act must be adapted to the actions of others who are involved in the driving act. The essence of driving behavior is that the individual, as he constructs his act, must take into account the behavior of other drivers who are implicated in the driving act. Hence, driving behavior is an ongoing process in which all participants take one another into account, and fit their lines of action together.

Driving is a social act, and as such is joint-action, or collective action, made up by the fitting together of the lines of action of the separate participants. Like individual acts, a social act is constructed in a process in which people know what other people are doing and what they intend to do, and build up their own acts on the basis of the actions of others. Driving behavior is social action which consist of people acting together to achieve a goal (Charon, 1979). Driving, then, as a social act requires reciprocity. If a participant withdraws from the act, does not respond in a way consistent with the kind of act engaged in or indicated, or changes his line of action, the social act breaks down or changes to a different kind of act, usually an unanticipated act. It is within the context of this breakdown that accidents occur.

In cities, communities or towns where there are various forms of driving cultures, dominating or interacting with some degree of intensity, it is difficult for drivers to form joint-action, and conflict in driving is inevitable because drivers do not always fit their line of actions to the actions of other drivers. This is the case especially when drivers do not understand the meaning of one another's gestures or do not interpret them similarly. The entire process of driving interaction depends upon the ability of drivers to take the role of the other in the process of driving. This is how joint-action is achieved on the highway.

Most accidents occur when drivers interact at the nonsymbolic level, not properly and effectively indicating and interpreting the gestures of other drivers at the symbolic level to establish joint-action in driving. Driving behavior, therefore, is constructed and embedded in a socio-cultural context within which drivers interact and provide the basis for meanings, expectations, anticipations, interpretations and demands on drivers in the driving area or space. The driving space is the area of visual observation of about a hundred yards in circumference from which drivers might make important driving observation, accurate interpretations and sound judgments about the driving behavior of others in relation to their own driving action. This area is the significant driving space for drivers to take note of in an attempt to establish joint-action. The socio-cultural context of driving might be simple, say in rural areas but rather complex in large urban areas especially where there are various ethnic and international groups occupying the driving environment. In more complex socio-cultural driving situations, establishing joint-action is more difficult to achieve in driving.

Types of Drivers and Driving Behavior in a Growing City

Houston is considered the fastest growing city in America. It is estimated that approximately 1,000 persons come to the city each week. Of this number, approximately two thirds are active drivers. These new residents to the city of Houston come primarily from Mexico, India and Asia, Canada, Africa, the Caribbean and from other parts of the United States. They bring with them various diverse norms, values, belief systems and modes of driving. What results on the highways and freeways is a driving process that includes a number of driving cultures interacting at a high level of intensity to produce conflicts in gestures, interpretation, anticipation and communication. The large number of accidents in Houston, and in any other large city with multiple driving cultures interacting at a high degree of intensity, could be attributed to this conflict in driving cultures.

In Houston there are three distinct driving cultures interacting at a high degree of intensity in the driving environment. A significant number of the pocket traffic jams are due in part to the negative interacting of these cultures. Pocket traffic jams are those that occur when all lanes on the freeway are impassible because drivers representing these cultures are usually occupying these lanes. The shot gun nature of the driving, where drivers are scattered all over the lanes, impeding easy access and safe passing, does not help the situation.

The casual-cautious drivers represent one of the three cultures. These drivers operate in the middle lane driving at or below the speed limit. The social-occasion drivers represent the second culture. They operate in the left or the extreme right lane whichever is free for visual observation and casual conversation among the participants in the car. Indians and Asians dominate the first culture and Mexicans represent the second. The majority of Americans (black and white) represent the third culture that dominates the freeways and highways of Houston. Americans are destiny drivers who operate usually in the left lane, if clear, but also out of any other lane that is free. Destiny drivers usually exceed the speed limit and shift from lane to lane in an attempt to avoid being boxed in by cautious-casual and social-occasion drivers. What makes it most difficult for the destiny driver to make progress on the freeway of Houston is the position the social-occasion and casual-cautious drivers take in the left lane and in other lanes impeding the progress of the destiny drivers. The problem is made more complex in Houston because there is no fast lane concept operating in the city. A significant number of drivers may be classified as leftlaners who cause additional problems or compound the problems related to joint-action.

Leftlaners

Leftlaners are drivers who have a sense of safety and security in driving in the left lane. Leftlaners come from all three of the driving cultures. Their driving behavior is conflicting and contradictory to that of most drivers and conforms to that of islands and countries where drivers drive on the left hand side of the road, and overtake on the right. In such islands and countries, the steering wheels of most of the cars are positioned on the right hand side of the cars which makes for easy observation of passing cars.

The drivers of the left lane, or leftlaners, are dangerous because in order for other drivers to establish joint-action with them they have to interpret, redefine and role play contrary to the context for driving and the meanings established within the environment of driving on the freeways of America where driving is done on the right side of the road and overtaking or passing is expected to take place on the left. Leftlaners assume that they have a right to occupy the left lane without any interference from other drivers whether they are going the speed limit or not. Any attempt to overtake is forced to occur to the right contrary to driving practices in a society where drivers drive on the right hand side of the road.

There are three types of leftlaners—the chronic, the occasional, and the convenient. All three types are dangerous in the driving environment because of the position others assume in relation to them, and the difficulty in establishing joint-action with them. However, because of the mobility, the type that is most dangerous and is most likely to cause accidents is the convenient leftlaner. Usually, the convenient leftlaner will shift positions in lanes to assume the most convenient lane, and for most of them the left lane is the most convenient. The chronic leftlaner and the occasional leftlaner are more likely to get trapped in the left lane than the convenient leftlaner. It is within this trapped experience of the chronic and occasional leftlaners, in their attempt to exist, that provides the most danger for accidents to occur. These drivers increase the possibility of accidents when they anxiously cut across three or four lanes of active traffic to achieve their goal to exit. The convenient leftlaner does not allow himself to be so trapped and creates no real danger in this aspect. However, it is the mobility in the concept of convenience that renders the convenient leftlaner dangerous. Chronic leftlaners usually drive the posted speed limit and have the tendency to believe that if they are obeying the law in this regard, they have the legal right to stay in the left lane unmolested by anyone making indication for them to move over. This attitude is also evident even when the police, ambulance, and fire truck make such indications to pass.

Driving behavior by the causal-cautious driver and the social-occasion driver is due in part to the fact that the driving environments of America's large cities where these drivers live are intimidating to them as foreigners or strangers to such environments, but more so to the nature and character of driving in their respective countries. Second and third generations who were born in America conform more to destiny driving of Americans. The leftlaners of the social-occasion and casual-cautious drivers tend to move to the left lane for no obvious reasons; reasons that cannot be anticipated by others in the driving environment. After listening to a large number of persons to testify in accident cases and analyzing the data from the records of the accident division of the police department, it is evident that a significant number of accidents that occur are usually between the destiny driver and the social-occasion or casual-cautious driver. It is also evident that those Americans who conform to the casual-cautious and social-occasion driving are the elderly, the handicap and those who have been driving for less than six months. Pocket traffic jams on the freeway are usually caused by leftlaners, casual-cautious and social-occasion drivers who occupy the front lanes not allowing destiny drivers access to pass.

Pocket traffic jams are instances when three drivers are at the front of the traffic on the freeway driving at a low rate of speed or diving at the speed limit in close proximity to each other not leaving enough space between them for others to pass. In such cases the leftlaner does not move over for passing to take place and is sometimes boxed in the left lane by the bearing down of traffic on the front three drivers. Drivers who are immediately behind the front of the drivers are open space while behind them in traffic almost at a standstill. Leftlaners do not fully know or recognize the primary use of the left lane, and often come into conflict with those who do, who seek to form joint-action on the basis of such knowledge.

Pocket traffic jams on the main streets, other than on the freeway, occur when leftlaners pair with slow trucks and other slow drivers in the right lane to impede access to passing. Again traffic gets backed up because of such behavior causing the destiny drivers to maneuver in traffic from lane to lane hoping for a breakthrough. The aggressiveness of the destiny driver is encouraged by the view that in front of the leftlaner and the social-occasion or the casual-cautious right lane driver is open space. Any encouragement by the destiny driver to force the leftlaner to use the left lane poorly or correctly by blowing the horn or blinking the lights, indicating a desire to pass, is reacted to negatively. They either stay in the lane ignoring the indication, or they put on brakes if the destiny driver is driving too close attempting to force them into compliance. There are leftlaners, however, who, upon a gesture to pass from destiny drivers move over to the right lane to allow passing, but immediately thereafter move over to assume their leftlane position.

Leftlaners are also dangerous drivers because they will pull in front of a car in the left lane from the right lane simply to be in the left lane. This behavior makes anticipatory behavior difficult because there is usually no apparent reason for the move except that the drivers are leftlaners. In many cases, leftlaners tend to make right turns from the left lane because they do not plan their turns in time or because they are forced to stay in the left lane until they are at their turns by destiny drivers and others who are forced to use the right lane to pass them. There are leftlaners who in such an event would slow down or even stop for an opportunity to make the turn.

There is a new group of potentially dangerous drivers in Houston. This group I have labeled meditators or dreamers who think contemplatively as they drive. As the economy worsens and the steady increase in the Houston population is realized, this kind of driving behavior will be more evident and problematic. What is dangerous about these drivers is that they are not locked into the rules, signals, and actions of the driving process, and are unaware, during those moments of meditation and contemplation, of the realities in their driving environment. Their control of the social situation in this environment of intense and ongoing interaction is lost and they become an ineffective partner in a social situation which they are a part and are participants.

The meditators, in a posture of contemplation away from the driving environment, cannot respond to the gestures being made by others for joint-action which is necessary if conflicts in driving are to be minimized and avoided. Even when there are indications made to the meditators in anticipation of their interpretation for the purpose of a specific response, no response is forthcoming because they are locked into their contemplation and are not receiving the designations made by other drivers. There are some indications however, that are capable of getting them unlocked. At such time as they rejoin the ongoing social reality of the driving environment, by the blowing of the horn, or by some potential mishap caused by their erratic or staggering driving, they assume the capability to form joint-action in the driving environment and continue to fit their actions to the actions of others in the process of driving.

Many meditators are leftlaners and are not aware of their exits on the freeway until they are at them and are unable to plan or negotiate a successful exit. Dreamers or meditators are not safe drivers in any lane on the highways and freeways because they have the potential of moving into part of another lane temporarily. Nonetheless, they are safer in the extreme right lane on the freeways and in the right lane on double lane highways. What makes meditators dangerous is that while meditating they are incapable of interpreting the indications of other drivers in the driving world and devising responses that are anticipated in order for joint-action to occur. When there is a breakdown in joint-action in the driving environment, accidents and other conflicts in driving are inevitable.

Conclusion

There are several things that must be done if accidents are to be reduced and the lives of drivers saved. First, drivers must come to realize that driving is conflict-free when drivers attempt to interact with each other by fitting their actions with that of other drivers in the driving world, not by following or obeying primarily legal rules for driving. Being right is not the essential consideration in the driving environment. Joint-action requires reciprocity to avoid total breakdown in social action. It also requires adequate indication by gestures of what is intended. Driving is a social process and drivers must know what other drivers in the driving area are doing and planning to do. This knowledge allows them to build up their own acts on the basis of the actions and anticipated action of others.

The driving environment is not simply an aggregation of separate drivers acting independently. The actions of an individual driver within the environment, regardless of how wrong, foolish, illegal, or inconsiderate, are necessarily connected with the action of other drivers of the driving area. Every driver's act must be adapted to the actions of other drivers who are especially implicated in the act. Hence, the driving environment, especially the driving area, or space, is an ongoing social process in which all the participants must take one another into account, and fit their lives of action together. When drivers fail to accomplish joint-action and do not fit their lines of actions to the actions of other drivers, accidents will occur, especially in driving environments where there are various driving cultures interacting at a high degree of intensity.

Increasingly, there are other drivers who are emerging in the driving environment who can be classified or categorized, even though they are not in abundance and are not dominating the driving situations. For example, there is the dining-room driver who has a number of food items on the passenger's seat and is eating as she drives. There are ice cream eaters, chicken, hamburger and taco eaters who make it a regular habit to eat and drink while driving. Then, there is the powder-room driver who has a number of make-up items on the dashboard of the car, or in the passenger's seat, even in her lap, administering these items to the face and hair, initially during stops at the light and stop signs, but the activity continues as she moves along in traffic. Both drivers make it rather difficult to establish joint-action with other drivers, and for other drivers to respond in appropriate ways. They are just as dangerous as the others identified above. This behavior is observed when these persons are going to work in the mornings and when they are leaving work. One such person informed us that this is done when one has a date after work, or when one is going to happy hour after work.

There is also the indicator-driver who believes that once indication is made, designating intent to shift from one lane to another, he has the right to do so regardless of how close, fast, safe or dangerous the move might be. Emerging also in the driving environment is the library driver who carries newspapers, pamphlets, and even books to read at every time he has an opportunity. Again, the activity does not stop at the light, or when traffic is slow, or at a stop sign, or on the freeway or highway, but it continues as the traffic moves faster making it more difficult for the driver to establish joint-action with others in the driving environment. The same thing is true for cell phone drivers who text and make calls while driving.

Drivers tend to drive differently in different neighborhoods and do not change their driving posture and attitudes when they move into different neighborhoods. In such cases, joint-action is also difficult causing frustration, anger, confusion and hostility to be expressed between drivers. Often the responses are, "Why don't you go back to the country, or the city, you country driver, or you city driving fool?" This difference is also observed in drivers coming into the city from out of town. It becomes very difficult, at times, for them to make the necessary adjustment and establish joint-action with those of the various drivers from the city who are functioning in the driving environment according to the driving milieu of the city.

The various conflicts which lead to accidents and death in the driving world result from the absence or breakdown in joint-action between and among various drivers. Any attempt to reduce accidents and prevent deaths must understand the nature of joint-action in the driving environment. Any attempt must also be grounded in the view that driving takes place within the context of a group of drivers attempting to fit their actions to the actions of each other. Anything that is done to distract drivers will diminish their ability to establish joint-action. Drivers are therefore embedded in a social situation created by the actions and responses of each other. It is within this context that data is collected for application to problems in the driving environment for the establishment of better driving relationships between and among drivers.

References

Blumer, Herbert
  1969 <u>Symbolic Interactionalism: Perspective and Method</u>. Englewood Cliffs, N. J.: Prentice-Hall, Inc.

Charon, Joel M.
  1979 <u>Symbolic Interactionalism: Perspective and Method</u>. Englewood Cliffs, N. J.: Prentice-Hall, Inc.

Skidmore, William
  1979 <u>Theoretical Thinking in Sociology.</u> New York: Cambridge University Press.

Application and Intervention Examples of GET

Chapter 10

* * *

Application and Intervention Examples of GET

Problems of Living and GET

Sociology is not the only academic discipline that studies human behavior and societies. Several other disciplines share an interest in various aspects of the social world. Economics, anthropology, history, political science, criminology and psychology are neighboring disciplines to sociology. They share the characteristic of a coherent base of knowledge which is grounded in theory and research and one or more distinctive methods of obtaining knowledge. Law, social medicine, social work, clinical psychology, public administration, education, industrial sociology, and business administration are closely related professional areas that draw upon the social sciences to deal with practical problems or problems of living. These professional areas have also added to our knowledge of social life through systematic studies.

Professional differences of opinion and differences in origins have prevented and interfered with academic and professional relationships among these fields. Each discipline separates out certain behaviors as its particular focus of study, but all of the social sciences study human activity and communication. Sociology has focused its study of the core aspects of social life: societies, and social structure; culture; socialization; groups and organizations; deviance and crime—social inequality: social stratification, social class; oppressed groups; the elderly and inequality; gender roles and inequalitysocial institutions: the family; the economy and work; power and politics; education;

religion; science and technology—social change: collective behavior and social movements; population and health; urbanization and suburbanization. Sex and sexuality, the sociology of driving, sports and leisure are additional areas that sociology has attempted to study on a systematic basis.

The many problems of living can be identified among the various areas listed above that sociology has sought to create knowledge. Sociology recognizes that humans are social beings and has sought to explore the social contexts and social processes that determine social activity and influence human lives. It is important and significant to understand the patterns that occur in the interactions of individuals with each other and with various social groups if we are to be free and achieve our human potential. Therefore, sociology has practical value as we try to understand how the social world affects us and as we attempt to make personal decisions and behave or take action in those directions.

Sociology tries to understand some of the most trying problems of society. We have to recognize that personal problems and macro social problems are affected by community factors, national factors and even international factors. Consequently, some problems are shared by people in all parts of the world. Racism, oppression, sexism, exploitation, war, peace, violence are social issues that have concerned society for ages. Many of these macro problems have significant impact on the micro problems faced by the individual as he seeks to fit his actions with the actions of others. Very few therapists include these matters in an attempt to understand the context of the clients and the specific problems that emerge therefrom.

One of the misconceptions in the literature is that if an individual is facing difficulties in living, he is having psychological problems. There are those in society or have varying degrees of difficulty with various routine everyday life issues and affairs. Even the person who is displaying bizarre and dramatic kinds of behavioral disorders, anxiety or depression is really having problems with living. Certain problems of living for one individual, however, might not be problems of living for another individual. Many persons respond to issues and events differently and will behave in ways they think are appropriate to their situations. For some, coping with routine, everyday life is difficult and/or impossible. There may be various kinds of blocks to persons functioning effectively and well.

One of the problems facing the social science therapist is that certain problems of living have already been labeled and categorized since these problems have been shown to be a result of certain established courses (Szasz, 1961). Certain problems of living are assumed to have specific causes. However, the causes of social problems cannot be predetermined, and we cannot classify them in terms of their causes. Neither can we treat social problems like heart disease or any other organic problems. Hostility, frustration, personal conflict, deviance, depression, anger, stress and anxiety are human responses to certain conditions in the experiences of living. All of these responses are social in nature and have social aspects. Search as you may, people who express these responses are not suffering from some specific disease, but may be appropriately responding to their conditions or situations as they perceive, define or interpret them, or may be the object of the definition and label of others who apply rules about how the individual is supposed to behave. We have come to be surprised that anyone would violate commonsense customs, therefore, when it happens, we quickly label them "sick" or "mentally ill" not deviant. In reality, what is deviant for one is conformity for another.

Social problems have their origin in relationships and interactions. The nature and character of the problems, and their strength cannot be determined and understood outside of their nature. Some social problems may have psychological, economic, political and religious consequences, but they are social in nature. All problems of living are of a social nature and cannot be fully understood from a psychological and psychiatric perspective. There are psychological implications of social problems, but this should not suggest a way or ways for understanding and dealing with problems of living. In The Social Setting of Mental Health (1976:3), the point is made that: Our lives, our worlds, are defined by our relationships to others, both as individuals and as groups. Out of this complex matrix of interactions and relationships come forces which affect our values, our behavior, even our sense of who and what we are.

The therapist who employs GET realizes and recognizes the social nature of all problems of living. That means that the problems are not individual even though their impact might be individualistic. Consequently, to tackle the impact of the problem does not mean that the problem has been tackled. Most of the so-called therapies today are impact therapies of treatment and often fail because of this. Those with a background in psychiatry and psychology have emerged from training systems dominated by an individualistic orientation so intense and so comprehensive as to permit or even make inevitable the ready assumption that the individual is an island unto himself and that his behaviors, his problems, his concerns can be understood almost exclusively in terms of data about his own mental and emotional processes (Dean, et al, 1976:3).

In spite of how bankrupt this orientation has been, there are therapists who hold on to this background and training because it has been legalized and legitimized. Further, the problem has been reinforced by the medical tradition. Arising from the medical tradition, psychiatry has emphasized the diagnosis and treatment of the individual, sought cases of illness within the individual, and developed methods of amelioration essentially focused on the individual (Dean, et, al, 1976:3).

For the most part, this tradition tends to dominate clinical activity today. Social science therapists are tempted to follow this tradition in their clinical practice, even though they apply or attempt to apply sociological or social psychological knowledge. Social science therapists must always remember that our lives and experiences consist of a set of connections which are tied into institutions, groups and other people. Sociology and social psychology are now no longer peripheral disciplines in clinical matters. They have become basic sciences especially for psychiatry, clinical psychology, psychiatric social work and psychiatric nursing. They have all come to the conclusion that there can be no real understanding of human social behavior without the employment of sociology and social psychology. Sociology, and especially sociological social psychology, are "fundamental building blocks for understanding human behavior" (Dean, 1986; Stephan and Stephan, 1985).

When the problems are organic and medical in nature, they are not and should not be the clinical concern of the social science therapist. Such problems are not within the context of the content focus of the knowledge to be applied by sociotherapists and/or psychosociotherapists. If and when there is no recognition of this fact, there is bound to be disjuncture between the context of the problem and the application of knowledge. This happens often when theory and therapy are not grounded in the context of the problem of the clients. For the most part, however, clients rarely recognize disjuncture even though they realize no change has occurred, or if change is experienced, it is not the direct result of the intervention. GET therapists recognize that human beings live group life, and any understanding for clinical and application purposes must be approached and accomplished within the context of this basic view. Social behavior must be seen as a product of interaction. Few of our activities are truly solitary. Human beings are social beings, and everything we do we do in relation to others. How we are able to fit our actions to the actions of each other; how we are able to interact with one another, and what is the process and result when we do, is the fundamental concern regarding human social life, and should be the sociodiagnostic and sociotherapeutic concern of the social clinician.

Naturalistic explanations of social behavior argue, on the one hand, that human behavior, including social interaction, is a product of inherited dispositions we possess as human animals. On the other hand, individualistic explanations argue that we are all individual and different, thus the particular and unique psychological qualities of individuals are significant. However, both the inherited dispositions and the psychological qualities are activated, shaped, refined, and expressed as behavior within a social context.

GET recognizes that there are organic disorders which have clear cut physical causes, but those disorders identified as functional, without proven organic causes, are clearly grounded in the experiences of living and are social in nature, and must be understood and treated within a social context. In this regard, then, naturalistic and individualistic explanations are inadequate for clinical purposes.

Typically, however, problems without proven organic causes are defined as functional disorders. Such disorders fall into the categories of neurosis, psychosis, personality disorders, and psychosomatic disorders. The distinctive characteristics associated with these personal problems are anxiety, feelings of inadequacy, avoidance of stressful situations, the definition of common situations as threatening, hallucinations, delusions, severe personal disorganization, various kinds of bizarre behavior, disorganization in thought patterns and speech, withdrawal from social life, living in a private fantasy world, depression, irrational fears, drug abuse, alcohol abuse, expression of no guilt about deviant behavior, impulsive behavior, self-centeredness and various forms of aggressive and immature behavior.

To give a sense of how GET works, we will present several problems of living, and how GET therapists would view and work with them employing the sociodiagnostic and sociotherapeutic processes advocated by GET. The problems are viewed in a contextual sense, not in individual terms. This means that the problems are viewed and treated as being specific to their contexts; otherwise, there would be disjuncture, misdiagnosis and misapplication. Failure is assured if the social clinician were to proceed differently. The absence of this perspective and methodology from the approaches presently being employed is the fundamental weakness they share and cannot be corrected; therefore, they should be abandoned. To reconstruct, or refine them will only weaken them further. There are those who recognize this weaknesses, but are unwilling, for a variety of reasons, to do anything substantial about it. Some have switched from the weakest, in their opinion, to one that is not so weak. When an approach is faulty, perceptually and methodologically, it is dangerous to use it in creating knowledge about, and application of that knowledge to problems that are lodged in a social context.

Stress and the Job

Stress has acquired a dual meaning. Internal and external forces that create pressure on the individual is the more general use, and the internal reaction or response of the individual to these forces is the more technical meaning of stress. In the very technical sense, stress may be viewed as the wear and tear on the body resulting from any activity. One may then experience stress under varying conditions, such as reprimand from one's boss, or demands of one's work defined as exorbitant. job stress may be defined as a condition in which job-related factors interact with the worker to change his or her own psychological and physiological state so that the person is forced to deviate from normal functioning. It must be understood that conditions under which one person will experience stress may not be the conditions under which another person may experience stress.

There are those who believe that contemporary industrial societies tend to create conditions that place enormous stress on their citizens. These conditions put workers under constant pressure to meet deadlines and quality standards. There are certain occupations that are defined as stressful, and these people who occupy such occupations are believed to be more likely to suffer from a variety of health problems. Air traffic controllers, dentists, lawyers, physicians are such occupations that are specialists associated with stress. There is unexpected stress associated with sudden changes in living patterns. Stress, therefore, is experienced out of a set of conditions to which individuals respond psychologically or emotionally, physiologically and behaviorally or socially. It is the set of conditions out of which these responses are experienced that defines the context of stress.

Physiologically, stress produces a chemical response within the body which results in a short term physiological reaction. Increased heart rate, blood pressure, respiratory rate, perspiration, skin temperature, blood glucose, blood clotting, etc., are a few of the physiological reactions. These reactions to sudden pleasant or unpleasant incidents can create an internal response within the body on a temporary basis. Some may think of this as tension which will go away after the tension producing experience disappears. However, if the experience is continuous resulting from the short term physiological changes, stress sets in and can result in life threatening conditions. Heart attacks, strokes, hypertension, migraine headaches, ulcers, allergies, skin rashes, itching, etc., are some of the conditions.

There are those who believe that a certain amount of stress is necessary for some people to meet difficult challenges and drives them to achieve great things and experience high level performances.

Tension, anxiety, discouragement, boredom, prolonged fatigue, feelings of hopelessness, and various kinds of defensive thinking and behavior are examples or evidence of the psychological consequences of stress. However, there are substantial individual differences indicated in the consequences. The firing of one individual may trigger a depressed mood, anger and hatred, while another person may accept the firing as an opportunity to change professions. Psychologically, when some people are experiencing stress, they display feelings of apprehension and fear of losing their jobs, not really knowing the implications and consequences. Some tend to deny that a problem exists hoping that such attitude and behavior will assist them in coping with the situation. Some fantasize, rationalize and search out socially approved reasons to explain why they are acting the way they do. Others may project undesirable or unacceptable feelings from themselves by attributing them to others.

The physiological and psychological symptoms of job stress tend to lead to actual behavior such as restlessness, agitation, decrease in job performance, drastic changes in eating habits, increased cigarette smoking, coffee drinking, alcohol consumption, illegal drug use, panic, impulsive decisions, errors in judgment and concentration. It is not always possible for people to escape stress on the job. There are conditions over which people have no control and did not create themselves. These conditions and situations are created by the coming together of individuals to perform a task or a set of objectives. This is the context out of which stress emerges and is experienced.

For some people the optimal amount of stress does not exist; consequently, they become overwhelmed by exorbitant demands, conflicting tasks, and high expectations. Many people who are faced with these matters in the job environment tend to respond by trying to cope with a stressful life. Very rarely do they attempt to deal with their stress by getting to the root of the problem. This can only be accomplished by diagnosing the context of the individuals within the work environment. This must be done in a very systematic manner before treatment is devised. Unfortunately, we have attempted to treat stress as a cause in itself, rather than dealing with it as a symptom of something else that is happening. There are treatment approaches that are in existence especially devised for stress as if it were a disease to be treated in a specific way. Even though there are certain physiological, psychological and social/behavioral evidences of the condition of stress, the reason for the stress of each person might be lodged within a different context. Stress, therefore, is regarded by GET as a presenting problem, which suggests that there is a real problem out of which the presenting problem of stress emerges. Consequently, in order for stress to be properly addressed, the social context out of which that stress emerges must be subjected to the sociodiagnostic process. The effectiveness of the sociotherapeutic process is dependent upon the adherence to this perspective which undergirds the sociodiagnostic process. Stress is a problem of living and must be viewed, understood, and treated as such. There are a number of sources of job stress. Where people work or the social situation or context of the work place is the primary focus in understanding the creation of stress that leaves people tense and anxious. Although primary emphasis is placed on the work place, the people involved are significant to the milieu of the work place.

A client who was experiencing stress reported being fatigue and unable to tolerate annoyances and irritations. GET argues that these are merely presenting problems. After investigating the work situation, it was discovered that the client had been experiencing fatigue for a long time. She felt that she was perpetually behind schedule which made her anxious, tense, uncomfortable and uncertain about her future in her company. When all of the data were collected, organized and analyzed, it was discovered that the real problem was one of exorbitant work demands and a burdensome workload. These conditions constituted the context for the creation of stress. Once this was discovered, it became possible to prescribe or devise a plan of action to deal with the condition of stress. It would not have been helpful to assist the client in developing coping strategies for dealing with her fatigue or her anxiety related to her feeling of being perpetually behind schedule. For GET therapist the concern is with treating the conditions of stress rather than having the client learn how to cope with stress. The client will simply be placed in the position of having to always cope with stress rather than affecting and changing the conditions under which she is experiencing it. Once the sociodiagnosis is made a sociotherapeutic strategy can be devised. This is in keeping with the process of grounding which requires therapy to be grounded in theory which is grounded in the data discovered in the sociodiagnostic process. In this way both theory and therapy have direct utility.

The way in which we dealt with the stress in the client was not in the way it manifested itself in her, but how it expressed itself in the workplace. First, we determined that the organization had a genuine concern for the welfare of its workers. In no instant did we find a disregard for the feelings of the employees. Given the discovery, we introduced the need to modify the organizational design. In order for the exorbitant work demands to be reduced, we introduced a rearrangement of the organizational structure so that the demands could be reduced to a healthy level for the client. We realized that someone else could have functioned normally under the conditions we changed. Therefore, we monitored the situation to determine whether anyone else had deviated from normal or optimum functioning as a result. No one had deviated. Another client in a small profit organization was placed in a situation where the job expectations were sloppily defined. Further, he was receiving conflicting demands from two persons which made it difficult for him to comply, thus creating substantial stress for him.

During the sociodiagnostic process it was discovered that the demands were not exorbitant, but confusing and conflicting. Compliance with one demand made it difficult to comply with the other. The client was certain he would be fired after a series of unsatisfactory reports. It was also discovered that the real problem was that of role conflict on the one hand, and role ambiguity on the other hand. There were times when he was asked to accomplish two objectives that were in apparent conflict. In another case, he was expected to accept certain tasks that were in conflict with certain other expectations in another role.

GET argues that therapy must be administered in the direction of the context of the real, rather than the presenting problem. A problem has to present itself in a particular way in order for the traditional therapeutic approaches to be of help. If the problem does not fit their philosophical views they are of no use. In GET, the problem presents itself for its roots to be determined and for its most appropriate treatment to be discovered. Selecting various techniques for doing so is the professional task of the GET therapist. The data, explanations, and knowledge about the problem and its situation or context dictate the therapeutic and the techniques to be used.

For this client, we determined that clarifying responsibilities would effectively deal with the ambiguity in his role, and a precise definition of his job would enhance his functioning and reduce his stress. With regards to the interrole conflict, we determined what the specific matter was about. The requirement of his job assignment meant that he would be traveling and away from his family fifty percent of the time. If he expected to be promoted he would have to comply. On the other hand, his wife would not assure him that she would accept his being away so often and so long. The threat of divorce and the possibility of her relating to another person were present realities. Primary concerns were determined, priorities established, and decisions were made resulting from his process.

GET therapists avoid telling clients what must be done. What must be done has to be discovered and determined resulting from the sociodiagnostic process. This point was vividly noticeable during a brown bag seminar. The presenters were talking about "Humor and Laughter in Therapy." No distinction was made between humor used as a technique in the process of therapy, and funny things, that might be funny to one and not to another, that happen in sessions. To many of the therapists in attendance, they had not thought of the distinction and the others were not sure what was being done. They were simply enjoying the jokes being made by the presenters who made no indication as to how the funny incidents were used in the therapeutic and diagnostic process.

A videotaped session was presented which had to do with a couple who reported having problems regarding sexual activity. The woman did not want to have sex more than once a month and the man wanted to participate in sex three times per week. The therapist immediately assumed that they were having miscommunication problems and recommended that when the husband made advances towards her in bed and she did not want to participate, she should spray him with a water pistol she had prepared for the task. In this way, she was told, he would really get the message. The result of the session was that they participated in sex once per month with the woman taking the initiative. The couple may have had miscommunication problems, but the conflict over when she was willing to respond and when she was not could have been a symptom of something else going on in their relationship which got expressed in what they presented to the therapists as a problem. It could be that the wife was resisting something, or was becoming distracted in the relationship. The problem could have been more serious than miscommunication, but we will never really know if we focus on the presenting problem without employing the sociodiagnostic process to locate the context of the presenting problem. Only then do we really discover the problem, its context, explanations, and ways to deal with the matter. Any other approach will come up short and be ineffective.

Parents who have had to deal with their children with fever have come to realize that giving their children Tylenol might have helped in controlling the fever, but did not treat the real problem that expressed itself in a fever. Most therapists, like those in the case cited above, often treat clients' fever, trying to bring the temperature down and never get to find out what the real problem is. This is the reason that problems keep coming back along with their carriers— the clients. This is a legitimizing process for the therapist, but very expensive and frustrating for the clients.

Depression and the Individual

Depression is a universal problem of living which is experienced by all human beings, regardless to social status or race. Some people seem to be more frequently depressed than others. An interesting question is: why? Another question that many therapists ask is: What is the true cause of depression? The most effective question is: What are the conditions and situations out of which depression emerges, and how do those who experience depression view and respond to such conditions and situations?

Everyone becomes depressed at some point in his life. One may not be so despairing as to attempt suicide, but he has had an attack of depression. There are those who argue that depression is a physically induced illness, thus relieving individuals of any responsibility for it. There are others who see depression as an emotional or attitudinal response to a set of conditions and situations that present persistent difficulties for the individuals who find themselves in such conditions. Sometimes these conditions are understood by the individual, and sometimes they are not. Proper understanding tends to enhance the chances of recovery.

When certain people begin to think seriously about their situations and conditions, they often end up feeling sorry for themselves and entertaining self-pitying thoughts. When this kind of thinking becomes a pattern, changes in circumstances and situations must precede the change in thinking pattern. Some argue that the more one indulges in self pitying thoughts, the deeper the depression becomes. If this thinking pattern of self pity is not arrested, they argue, the person is hopeless. Consequently, the therapist tends to attack the thinking pattern of self pity in an attempt to solve the depression of the client. The depression of an individual should not be simply placed at the doorsteps of self pity. The problem could be deeper than that. Some people do not want to face the real problems, and are happy to accept the conclusion that self pitying thoughts or feeling sorry for themselves is the problem.

GET therapist suggests that there is a reason for such thoughts and that there are conditions out of which these thoughts emerge. It is only when we understand these conditions and situations as the proper context for diagnosis and therapy, that we can address the presenting problems of self pity and depression. The effects of depression are experienced physically, emotionally and mentally, and tend to interfere with social relations and interactions. We should not treat effects as such, but those conditions that produce, or are the social context for the effects, should get our full attention.

A client contacted our GETS office for an appointment. She had heard the Director on his radio program and liked what he was saying about family relationships. After getting acquainted with the process of GET, the sociodiagnosis started with the client reporting what she thought was the problem. She accused her husband of having a girlfriend. She offered several incidents which aroused her suspicions. He was frequently tired and could not adequately respond to her sexual needs. The second session was conducted with the husband alone, after which they both entered the third session. Through the sociodiagnostic process we discovered that the wife wanted to have a relationship with a co-worker who was distracting her by his attention. She was very displeased with the relationship with her husband and felt herself disengaging from him but was afraid to explore the relationship possibilities with her co-worker. She met with him on occasions for lunch and dinner, but was afraid to commit herself to any other contact. We discovered that she was dissatisfied with the way her husband conducted the family's business transactions and how he used the resources of the family. She was especially unhappy with the way he left her out of family matters as if she were not an equal partner in the relationship. She identified the particular skills she had developed which were most appropriate to the business transactions of the family. She was angry about the exclusion and the private way in which he operated. We also discovered that the husband was uncomfortable with his wife's ability and skills, but did not know how to include her in the transactions without losing a sense of power, control and his manhood. He felt it was his responsibility to assure the financial success of the family. He tried to cover up the several failures resulting from his actions and inaction, and tried to explain them away after she discovered them.

Although the real problems were being revealed and discovered, the wife was so dissatisfied with the relationship that she wanted her original accusations to be true so she could feel justified in her having sexual contacts with her co-worker. She even reported having thought of getting a divorce. After realizing that there was no proof for her accusations, she shifted her complaint to problems of sexual relations. However, she was significant in the discovery of her need to be treated as an equal in the relationship and expressed this need in their sexual contacts and relationships. She expressed how she had lost her sexual desire for him; she was no longer affectionate to him. She was sad most of the time around him, and often was hostile. He also expressed fear of what was happening to their relationship, and reported being anxious and worried all the time.

As we worked on the discovered problems, progress was realized almost immediately. There were engagement exercises and the establishment of transactions that included her as an equal in the relationship. We developed ways for him to see and accept her as one who wanted to enhance his sense of self and manhood. He discovered he had certain necessary skills that she did not have and that she had certain necessary skills that he did not have, all of which were necessary to the success they both desired and worked for. Initially, she was tempted to deny the progress and confessed that she was not getting anything out of the relationship and really wanted out. However, as she participated in the nonverbal engagement exercises, she was less distracted by her co-worker and began to disengage from him. Gradually, their relationship began to grow and become satisfying to both of them. They were encouraged to continue the nonverbal exercises to enhance and enrich their emotional contact.

As was determined, not only was the woman depressed, the man was just as depressed and frustrated because he did not understand the accusation. His time was always accounted for, and he made every attempt to please his wife in ways he thought would satisfy her. However, we viewed the presenting problems as symptoms or indications that something else was happening in their relationship. Once there was disclosure and discovery, explanations were developed and the knowledge gained became the basis for the sociotherapuetic process. Their willingness, desire and commitment to do what they discovered needed to be done allowed them to reestablish emotional contact and the possibility for a stronger relationship.

Crime and the Community

One of the pressing and persistent problems of living that confront society today is that of crime. The fear of crime at the community level has forced many community members to change their patterns of behavior and interactions with others. Law enforcement agencies have had little or no success in reducing crime or in controlling it. Consequently, community members have tried to organize themselves to understand and manage the problem.

One community sought our services in helping them deal with the problem resulting from a survey they conducted which indicated that there was a high and persistent level of fear among community members. Every report that was released by the city showed crime increasing. Some professionals recommended and developed a program to work with community members in helping them cope with their fears. Several protective measures were recommended which dealt with their behavior on the streets and in the homes. The idea was to reduce and eliminate the fear of crime by community members by employing a psychological orientation to develop coping skills of such members.

In this particular community, the fear of crime and the increasing likelihood of victimization had caused community members to alter their lifestyles in order to deal with increasing criminal activities in the community. The first thing we attempted to do was to collect data regarding the extent and nature of the crime in the community. This was obtained from community members through interviews, observations, from various surveys and studies conducted by a few agencies in the community, including the police department. After doing a comprehensive evaluation and analysis of the materials, we discovered a number of things:

The community members felt helpless in establishing protection against criminal activity in their community; the response time of the police was too long, members felt that the police lacked functional knowledge of the community; there was a sense that the perpetrators of crime in the community perceived the community a powerless and helpless in dealing effectively with the situation of crime; the members felt that the perception of the police of the community and the nature of policing deterred the reduction and elimination of criminal activity in the community. Even though apprehension was high, it came too late after the commission of the crimes and did very little to reduce the fear in the community (Swan, 1984: 52, 53).

The GET therapist realizes that crime must be understood within the context of the nature and character of the national social order. Further, apparent crime is not an induction of real crime in the social order. Consequently, the emphasis on apparent (street) crime, committed primarily by the oppressed and exploited, tends to distort the rate, nature, and explanations of crime and criminality, and the image of who are the real criminals in society. It also gives a false picture of who benefits most from crime; who are the primary victims, and deters efforts to create real solutions. Data from a broad context suggest that where the ethnic group has undercut white domination, apparent crime rates and the perception of crime appear to be low. There are communities in America, and countries in Africa and the Caribbean where crime rates are extremely low. However, where white domination is bureaucratically administered (the complete form of domination—cultural, social, educational, political and economic) and ethnics are processed by a variety of agencies, apparent crime rates and the perception of crime appear to be high.

After collecting data from community members, it became evident that the definition of crime was too narrow and did not include death, harm, injury, and danger resulting from acts of exploitation, racism, imperialism, capitalism, sexism and other such acts of capitalists and white supremacists. These criminogenic systems bread and promote repressive and exploitative relationships and social injury. The real solution to the crime problem, given these observations, is the employment of a different philosophical/ behavioral orientation from individualism, on the part of the community, to collectivism, and the transformation of the arrangements of the social order to remove the criminogenic systems and their conditions. This means that the present structure of the social order and the political economy which tend to bread crime, would have to experience transformation and radical change not reform to deal effectively with the problem of real crime.

What we attempted at the community level among the powerless, oppressed, and exploited who are victimized and do victimize each other is only sufficient to have us realize how intimately crime is involved in the very nature and character of the social order. Once we understood these facts, we understood how limited our efforts have been, are, and shall be in controlling crime at the community level. Our efforts are meanwhile solutions; nonetheless, they are grounded in the social context of crime at the community level.

From the data we collected, we concluded that the situation of crime in the community, the context of which was the basis for the fear had to be changed by first redefining or changing the philosophy of policing from apprehension, which requires the commission of crime, to the prevention of the occurrence of crimes. This change could occur only by establishing a structure in the community out of which policing would be done. The benefits we identified were: 1) having protection close to and as a part of the basic service to the community; 2) a reduction of the response time; 3) the training of many of the community youth as parapolicemen; 4) reducing the after-the-fact nature of the police presence and policing; 5) maximizing police-community interaction and relations; and 6) restoring a sense of community to the police who live and work in the community and to the members of the community.

An Area Agency was recommended to fulfill these needs. This was the community mechanism for dealing with the situation of crime in the community, and the fear of its members. The Area Agency as a community mechanism had to incorporate the ability to deliver two umbrella functions: 1) protection of the community members and their property, and 2) prevention of the occurrence and continuation of crime. It was also recommended that the Area Agency be accountable to a Supervisory Board, the composition of which would reflect the various characteristics of the community. The details of the Community Area Agency, and the specific functions and powers of the Supervisory Board were to be worked out with representatives of various organizations in the community and the downtown police department, in consultation with us.

The attempt and focus was to treat the situation of crime out of which community fears emerged. Dealing with members' fear without addressing the situation was thought to be useless and secondary to the problems of crime in the community. Developing an ability to cope with fear did not remove the situation of fear; the presence and function of the Community Area Agency did. The fear of the members of the community emerged out of the crime situation in their community. Consequently, the community and the situation of crime in the community became the context for the application of knowledge to the crime situation out of which the fear of community members emerged. This is an essential perspective and process of the GET therapist. The scientific process must be employed if grounding is to be effective; and application direct and specific.

Conflict in Relationships

Human beings are social in nature, and they form social relationships for a variety of reasons and under all kinds of circumstances. Good, strong, and enduring relationships have to be carefully established and nurtured; they do not just happen. Relationships, no matter how good and strong, are not conflict free. Depending on how close the relationships between and among individuals are will determine the nature and extent of the conflicts and how the individuals manage the conflict in their relationships. Too much conflict is not good for any relationship whether it's the family or friends. Conflict should not dominate any relationship. Some conflict is thought to be necessary and challenging but all conflict in relationships should be managed and/or resolved.

People in relationships have conflicts in virtually anything and everything. For example, in their relationships, husbands and wives might have conflicts about where to live, which car to buy, how to discipline the children, what to do about in-laws, how frequently to have sex, how much money to save, how to entertain friends, who said what, who ate the last piece of pie, who messed up the checkbook, where to go on vacation, etc.

In relationships there are situational conflicts which emerge out of disagreements about matters that arise in everyday life. For example, one person might want to watch a championship sporting event on a particular channel; the other might want to see reruns of Dynasty or Knot's Landing. Then there are what some call personality conflicts where the coming together of two different selves magnify the differences between people. Different habits, beliefs, and attitudes, and the most subtle ways of those in close relationships are difficult to overlook. The presence of differences does not automatically lead to conflict. Many times conflicts in this area have focused on small matters. Failure to replace toothpaste cap; going to the bathroom in the dark are small matters persons may get upset about in close relationships.

Who makes the decisions, who's got the power to define the area of structural conflicts. Interactional conflicts arise when the individuals in close relationships fail to fit their actions to the action of each other. The absence of joint-action characterizes the conflicts. These various conflicts can lead to frustration, anger, quarrels and fights. Conflicts can threaten relationships and cause individual participants to ignore it; refuse to acknowledge its presence; repress feelings related to it; force feelings and emotions underground and can run from it. Conflicts that are ignored and are allowed to remain, tend to become more difficult to manage and usually create other problems that have the potential for independence.

A couple contacted our office and made an appointment for a marital check-up. We talked with each person individually and then together. The marital check-up form is divided into four basic areas with specific questions related to the areas. One area has to do with finances and it is the third area on the form. This couple was doing very well with the questions as we identified and discussed discrepancies and possible conflicts in responses. However, when we got to the area of finances, they began to argue and quarrel. The dispute started with accusations regarding the desire of the husband to get the wife working, and her concern for her health. She reported having two ailments that prevented her active involvement in work outside the home. Further, she expressed her outrage at his lack of concern for her condition and his selfish disposition in this regard. After they had argued and quarreled for a while, we stopped them and asked a few questions, including: "Do you all have a budget in place?" The response was, "What, a budget?' The reply was, "Yes, a budget." They did not have a budget nor any other plan or mechanism for helping them manage their finances. There are various ways we can get clients to disclose so that we can discover. In this case, arguing and quarrelling was the way these clients disclosed, providing us with data which indicated the real problem regarding their finances. They admitted that quarrelling about their financial situation was a frequent occurrence. The couple was instructed to collect all of their statements of financial obligations and income and return with them the next session. At the next session, we organized the material so that it became crystal clear what their monthly financial obligations were and what their income was to meet their obligations. To their surprise, after calculations, they had a balance of thirty five dollars on the income side. The wife was so surprised that she requested that we do the calculations two additional times. It was only after the third time and her following the steps closely that she was pleasantly convinced that their monthly income was sufficient to take care of their monthly bills. Our next step was to evaluate each item on the budget raising questions about the amounts. Finally, we reduced several items and added two items to the budget, yet allowing them to have surplus income of seventy-five dollars. The couple expressed relief, happiness and a willingness to work hard, from that point on, to reestablish their emotional closeness. They had started to disengage, but several sessions later they were growing rapidly. We watched them as they went to their car holding hands and being happy, happy, happy.

In another case we worked with, a group of ten people had organized themselves to provide services to their community. At the initial meeting, officers were elected to provide leadership and direction for the group. At all business meetings discussions were free and open. Many of the suggestions were executed, and others were not. The group was becoming relatively successful in the services they rendered when one member began to raise several questions about the role of one or two members and their influence on the group. The influence was admittedly positive, and the other members were confused as to the validity of the voiced concerns. Initially, we were lead to think that the "concerned member," who by now had the sympathy of two other members, had made the concern of the group primary in her life. However, upon investigation, and the disclosure of ideas about the activities of the group and the role of key members, it was discovered that the "concerned member" wanted some leadership role in the group. She felt she could conduct the business of the group in a more organized manner. She was also suffering from low self-esteem and low self-worth and needed to be involved in the group in a leadership capacity in order to feel worthwhile. Her home life and her work situation did not provide for this experience. In fact, it was discovered that it was her family life experiences that afforded her the sense of worthlessness. Her abilities in the group were appropriate and suited the primary activities of the group, but there were others who had more experience in the roles they were chosen to function in the group. Another factor discovered centered around the relationship between two persons who gave leadership to the group, and how this "concerned member" perceived the relationship. These two leaders had a strong personal relationship which influenced the decisions concerning the group. These members talked often with each other and the "concerned member" thought she was not included in the calls and the decisions made. What was recommended helped the group as a unit and the individual members. The leader was encouraged to have group meetings where each person had an opportunity to impact the agenda, thus having a sense of being involved in the affairs and decisions of the group. The operating perspective was that, the degree to which each person felt a part of the group was to that degree will the person assist or resist the group. The relationships have grown since then and the members seem to be functioning at a higher level than before the conflict in relationships between these members. Group meetings now include time to deal with personal relations in the group in addition to the business of the group.

The change in the way in which the group conducted its business, and the group session which lasted forty-five minutes, helped all members become closer and more collective. However, the "concerned member" was encouraged to deal with the problems discovered that related to her relationships elsewhere; those that had their origin outside of the context of the group. Several attempts were made to include her husband and children in the process, but the husband resisted arguing that she had a personality problem and should seek help for whatever personal problems she was having. No time did he want to become involved. He had come to the firm conclusion that he, nor the family setting had anything to do with the difficulties she was experiencing. In fact, he remarked "when she gets herself together, everything will be just okay. She needs to get her act together." The group sessions are helping and the individual is learning how to redefine the situation in her family and how to establish joint-action with members of her family, even if she perceives their behavior and actions to be incorrect, selfish, and demeaning.

Family Violence

Any act which is carried out with the intention or perceived intention of causing pain or injury to another person is considered violence. In the family, violence ranges from slight pain as in a slap to murder. Slaps, pushes, shoves, and spankings are thought to be normal and ordinary. However, the more severe and abusive violence are punches, kicks, bites, chokings, beatings, shootings, stabbings, or attempted shootings and stabbings (Straus, 1984). The tradition of male dominance in society and the home has led to the belief that women are the only targets of violence in the family. Children are targets of violence in the home.

Violence in the home is not rare and is not confined to the mentally disturbed, nor sick people. Neither is it confined to the lower-class, even though it is more likely to be reported among the lower income or lower socio-economic status families. Because family violence occurs in all social groups does not mean that social factors are not relevant and it does not mean that children who have been victims of abuse will grow up to be abusers themselves. Often wives find themselves entrapped socially, legally and materially in a marriage and find it difficult to leave their abused situations. Because they find it difficult to leave does not suggest that they liked being abused. Alcohol and drug abuse are not the real causes of violence in the home, and the abused person did not have to have done anything to cause the abuse.

A case was brought to our attention by a woman who was being abused by her husband. Initially, she sought counseling for herself because she had accepted the views of her husband that she provoked him to hit her. She wanted to find out how and why she was provoking her husband to abuse her. She expressed in strong terms her dislike about the situation and her desire to seek relief. We agreed to invite the husband to join the next session and he gladly accepted the invitation. After exploring their social situation, we employed the encounter process for discovery of the real problems. Initially, they both agreed that it was only when he had a "few drinks" that he displayed this violent behavior. On several occasions she did not come in close contact with him upon her discovery that he had been drinking. After encountering for about thirty minutes, status inconsistency and status incompatibility was very evident. He was a seasonal worker after being fired from a well-paying job which allowed him to respond completely to their financial situation. Now he was unable to do so and felt he had lost his manhood in the process. There were times when he was unemployed for long periods having to depend totally on his wife who was better educated and skilled in several areas which allowed her to make extra money aside from her fulltime employment. The area he felt he could dominate and hold on to his manhood and a sense of self was sex, but she was not responding in a satisfactory manner, as far as he was concern. Upon further inquiry and encounter, it was discovered through disclosures that he was always concerned about the fact that his wife's educational attainment and occupational status was higher than his and he felt he could do nothing about it except to find a job that paid more than she was being paid. However, he was finding it more difficult to find such a job without a high school diploma and/or a college degree. In fact, his reading and writing skills were poor and he believed he had evidence she was ashamed of him because of this.

From the data which revealed the real problems, we devised a plan of action which involved preparation to secure the GED, and the organization of a cleaning service that would establish him as an independent business man. He liked the idea very much and was given an assignment, which required his collecting and organizing names, and contacting all of the possible clients. The wife agreed to assist in this regard and use her skills to secure the extra money needed until his project started paying off. It was not very long before he landed two contracts to clean two large banks. His sense of self was restored and his manhood revived as he saw the results of his plans. He was finding it difficult studying for the GED, but the challenges were motivating and his commitment was strong. There were no reports of abuse, and during the last encounter session, he voiced amazement how he allowed himself to become abusive to his wife. We put in place some nonverbal encounters which were demonstrated and practiced during the session, which we felt would enhance their emotional contact. They were instructed to employ the nonverbal exercises twice a week, and establish a "family meeting" session once per week. A sheet with instructions was given to the family in this regard and they were to report on a weekly basis the progress made in all areas.

Conclusion

Most of the problems human beings face are problems of living. There are times when these problems express themselves in ways that are not very clear to persons who are experiencing them. Sometimes, they are not really known because the symptoms are believed to be the real problems. We have come to the understanding and conclusion that symptoms should not be the primary focus of treatment of problems of living that are lodged in social context. The context of the problems must be addressed so that the real problems, or the difficulties that produced the symptoms might come forth.

Not all of the therapeutic approaches available today have the necessary characteristics to be effective in dealing with problems of living. By definition, all of them are therapeutic in nature and intent, and not diagnostic. This is the reason that the majority of the clinicians who employ the present approaches treat symptoms of problems and very rarely deal with the real problems. If the approaches do not have diagnostic capability then they cannot produce relevant data to produce explanations about the presenting problems of clients. Consequently, the theory and therapy will not have direct utility, and any application will create disjuncture.

Problems of living must be solved in the most direct manner as possible. Many clients are not instructed and guided into the process of solving problems. Some of their problems get resolved, but seldom in the most direct manner. Often solutions come after considerable internal stress resulting in negative attitudes, dispositions and irritation to those involved. Some learn and others do not after experiencing the trauma. It is the unknown qualities of the problems that tend to overwhelm clients and some therapists and counselors.

By following certain steps, all problems of living can be managed and/or solved. There is no need to stumble and wander around out of control until we blunder ignorantly through a process hoping our clients' problems will get solved. Successful solutions of any problem can be navigated if the following steps are followed.

It is not uncommon for clients and therapists to become caught up in efforts to solve a problem that is not the real problem at all. They often find themselves dealing with only a symptom or an aspect of the problem. We need to be very clear what the real problem is and the nature and extent of the problem. Few problems are as simple as they first appear. Most are a mix of several difficulties and conflicts and usually involve two or more people. Thinking we know what the problem is does not always mean we do. Although cutting through our biases, prejudices and preconceived ideas to find the real problem can be a time consuming process, it is essential and well worth the time invested.

The next step is to gather all relevant data from everyone involved. Good and sound decisions are based on good data. Therapists must realize that in a counseling setting, especially a group setting, they are usually surrounded by people who have more information about their situation and problems than therapists have. It is here that they are wise to ask questions, listen and take advantage of their clients' insights. We must be selective and discriminating in the end, but we need to have our clients impart all of the information about their situations and problems they have. Problem solving works best when supplied with the best possible data.

Establishing a clear picture of the problem and knowing from the data what the situation or context of the problem is, allows the clients and therapists to map out or list the possible courses of action. There are alternatives for solving problems. At times clients get so mixed in the quicksand of their immediate, almost instinctive or reflective responses to their situations that they do not even consider that there might be other ways to do something besides the way they have always done it. We should list possible courses of action we might take, whether or not they appear, at this point in the process, to be the best course to pursue. Exercising a little creativity allows us to identify a course of action that might never have been considered before and would satisfy and meet the requirements of everyone. In giving this process this kind of structure and process, we can capture the attention of all so that the problem can be solved in an objective and creative manner. The ability to anticipate consequences, both good and bad, leads us into the next step. We should list the consequences of each course of action. At times, there might be no really good course of action available. In such a case, we should select the one that produces the least damage. We may ask ourselves, "What is the worst thing that could happen if I select this course of action?" Follow the cause of action with the fewest negative results.

We must help our clients learn how to recover from bad situations, and get out of them what they can, giving up more than they must. Even when they are doing their best they can get burned, but they must develop the ability to see enough of the probable consequences of their actions to make prudent choices.

There comes a time in the process when we must allow our clients to act. Sometimes we have to resort to a solution rather than the solution. The wisdom in this position is that in real life situations, they may make a mistake in selecting a course of action, but they cannot wait to indefinitely act. What might seem right at the time might not be right later, but they must consider the alternatives and choose the one which, in their judgment, looks to do the most good with the least damage. We must in the process create within our clients a bias toward action. Problem solving demands a willingness to do something. The knowledge gained in the process of collecting relevant data, must be translated into action.

Learning from the problems they have, allows them to get off the roller coaster sliding from one crisis to another. Problems usually signal something they need to address, and struggling through the problems helps them to reorder the situation; the way they live and prevent the rise of similar or the problems in the future.

Finally, we should encourage clients to be thankful that they have what they have, whatever it is; family, friends, a job, a church, a car, the ability to love, care, etc. They can be thankful they even have some problems so that if they have the appropriate attitude and the right perspective on life, they can see them as opportunities, challenges, and privileges to grow and serve others through their experiences and encounters with them. Our clients must share and be involved in this process and perspective.

References

Dean, Alfred et al (ed.) 1976. <u>The Social Settings of Mental Health</u>. New York: Basic Books.

Swan, L. Alex 1984. <u>The Practice of Clinical Sociology and Sociotherapy</u>. Cambridge, MA: Scheakian.

Stephan, Cookie White and Walter G. Stephan 1990. <u>Two Social Psychologies</u>. Belmont, Calif.: Wadsworth Publishing Co.

Szasz, Thomas 1961. <u>The Myth of Mental Illness</u>. New York: Dell Publishing Co.

Straus, Murray 1984. Explaining Family Violence. <u>In Marriage and Family in a Changing Society</u>. 4th ed., James M. Henslin, ed. New York: Free Press.

Making Discoveries:
Training and Supervision

Chapter 11

* * *

Making Discoveries:
Training and Supervision

Introduction

The need to train and supervise Clinical Sociologists and Sociotherapists in clinical or sociodiagnostic and sociotherapeutic matters is increasing in importance and significance. It is being realized that training by psychiatrists, psychologists and other such clinicians who practice psychotherapy is unacceptable and inappropriate even though some clinical and therapeutic skills might be acquired in the process. The fact is that these professionals are not trained in the subject matter that Clinical Sociologists seek to apply to problems that are lodged primarily in a social context that require their sociodiagnostic and sociotherapeutic attention and intervention. Clinical training and supervision must be related to and grounded in the theoretical and methodological principles of the content-focus of the academic and professional training of the Clinician. Since Sociology is the content-focus of Clinical Sociologists their training and supervision must be grounded in its body of knowledge, yet flexible enough to enjoy secondary relationships with other principles that are lodged primarily in other bodies of knowledge. It is also important to note that other clinicians use the body of knowledge of sociology in clinical matters. Some professions have no body of knowledge of their own that is provided by their area of specialization, and their academic training is not grounded in the social context of the problems of their clients. Clinical sociologists should be trained in sociology and sociological social psychology if they are to make application to problems of their clients that are social in nature. The training should encompass four (4) primary components: theory, methodology, clinical and therapeutic skills and techniques, and the relevant content areas, such as family relations, family therapy, industrial sociology, human relations, group dynamics, community organization and development, criminal justice systems, school sociology, etc. This academic program should be the basic content areas of the discipline, at the graduate level, which should be the fundamental requirements for becoming Clinical Sociologists. Once this foundation in knowledge is established, or is in the process of being acquired, practical experiences in the acquisition of clinical skills and therapeutic techniques should follow.

The several works regarding training and supervision of clinicians, especially psychotherapists, present various debates regarding the merits and limitations of a great number of training programs and methodologies. What seems to be the conclusion is that many therapists are generally dissatisfied with the quality of training they receive (Dies, 1974, 65-79). This is the case because a fundamental content or body of knowledge is absent from their academic training. Sociology is the scientific study of human behavior in group life and is essential for understanding and explaining human problems of living. Clinical Sociologists and Sociotherapists are in a unique academic position to become very effective clinicians. What is required beyond the academics are skills in sociodrama, contextual analysis, developing interpretative and empathic abilities, intervention techniques, and developing facilitating and monitoring skills whether their clients are couples, individuals, families, groups, industry, the community or the society. The training procedures and practices, therefore, should be especially suited to the social situation and context of the group and the individual's behavior within the context of the group. The training must be comprehensive enough to provide sound foundation in academic and practice to assure a certain degree of competence, integrity, and skills. This foundation in knowledge and skills will allow the Clinical Sociologist to grow through continued practice experience.

When the clinician is able to establish an appropriate working relationship with clients, and demonstrates an ability to translate theoretical knowledge into intervention strategies for change, the results will be meaningful. Although the practical training for most therapists today takes place outside of the formal regular degree-granting program, practical training for Clinical Sociologists must be integrated with the regular formal education. The canons of the craft of social diagnosis must be integrated with therapeutic activity. No doubt, there will be those who can provide evidence of equivalent competency; such persons should be exempt from parts or all of the formal experiential requirements.

The choice today for Clinical Sociologists is to enter the established training programs after completing graduate work, or for Sociological organizations and associations to establish programs which give primary attention to the application of sociological or sociological social psychological knowledge and thinking. Presently, many sociologists who attempt to practice are relying upon reading, attending seminars workshops, and conferences, and by receiving whatever formal or informal supervision they can secure from others trained and/or experienced in their area. The best posture is to have the practical training built into the formal academic experience. The relationship anticipated process must be structured for the outcome or product to be of real quality. The training program should guarantee the delivery of certain competencies and skills that are grounded in the body of knowledge of sociology. This can be accomplished if certain characteristics and elements dominate the training process.

Sociologists have technical competencies and have developed techniques and skills which they have effectively used to study human behavior in group life and the nature and content of group process. Statistical, methodological, conceptual and theoretical tools are all part of their technical competencies they have demonstrated in gaining understanding of various problems of group life and the quality of life in society. Community organization and development, industrial relations, family, martial, political, economic, and social problems are part of the quality of modern society, and sociological knowledge and thinking must be applied to these problems to assist people live growing and more productive lives as they participate in group life. The Clinical Sociologist must be trained to be competent in applying sociology to daily life affairs, and for purposes of effecting personal and social change. Sociology programs that attempt to train Clinical Sociologists will include in their program knowledge that focus on cultural background, heritage, life experiences, feelings, emotions and meanings that would compliment formal training in sociology. Students will gain knowledge through structured experiential training workshops and small group experiential sessions where they will gain valuable insights about the dynamics of small groups and group life. All of these avenues of learning will be expressed or demonstrated in practice and be informed by sociological theoretical perspectives, whether it is the symbolic, exchange, conflict, structural-functional, dramaturgical, or labeling perspective. The connection or relationship is made when students understand and analyze human behavior in group life in society; the aspect of human life represented by each perspective, and how these theoretical perspectives can be applied for clinical purposes to achieve meaning of self and others in group life.

Sociological perspectives have relevance for daily living, and for change toward improving, fulfilling, and satisfying interpersonal relations and social interactions between individuals and among people in groups. Not only is the clinical sociologist trained to understand human social behavior in society, but is trained in ways and methods to take action to solve problems of living. In the process, they learn what to look for, and their theoretical frames of references are guides for noting symbols, interaction, exchanges, conflicts, drama, branding or labeling, structures and functions which are recorded and analyzed for purposes of change and growth. The theoretical posture of the clinical sociologist is complimented by scientific methodology which is a way for the clinician to make discoveries about life's conditions, and problems of the clients, or in their problems of social living. We have structured and given direction to these experiences and are training sociology students to determine what is happening, what it all means, and what can be done to change or improve the situation.

To put emphasis on the clinical aspect of training in graduate programs, since we have come to see clinical as social diagnosis, or as a process of disclosure and discovery, does not do violence to the "academic" and "pure" scientific concerns of sociologists who are scientists and practitioners who apply their findings to the real life situations of clients. This means that programs that train clinical sociologists must structure the experience of social diagnosis, treatment and improving relationships, to social situations, and persons. The primary purpose of the added and special emphasis in the present sociology programs is to train sociologists how the body of knowledge of sociology can be used for personal and group understanding and improvement. Clinical Sociologists are obligated to know the technicalities of the perspectives in Sociology and how they are used in a scientific way to be effective in the clinical process. In other words, technical sociology compliments the use of sociological perspectives in clinical matters to understand and improve personal well-being and functioning in group life in society. In those cases where insights are drawn from other areas and fields to provide greater or fuller understanding, the program of clinical sociology must have a synthesizing approach.

Clinical sociology programs must provide professional training and occupational role experiences that focus on the application of sociological thinking and knowledge to programs faced by individuals, groups, communities, and organizations that are lodged primarily in social contexts. Once the programs are designed and do function to accomplish this purpose, clinical sociologists are being produced. Students must gain skills for understanding, discovering specific information about human social behavior in group life, and for making application of what is discovered so that they can assist their clients understand and "fix" things. The data discovered are shaped by theoretical perspectives without which clinical sociologists will function in darkness in an attempt at understanding and getting their clients to understand or in assisting them to improve their situation.

Although clinical programs to train clinical sociologists may differ in emphasis, there should be certain basic course content and experience to assure the delivery of certain skills and competencies.

Courses in Clinical Sociology, Group Therapy and Dynamics, Sociotherapy and Psychotherapy, Industrial Sociology with a human relations emphasis, Martial and Family Relations, Martial and Family Therapy, Theory, Methods and Sociological Statistics, the Sociology of Mental Health, Clinical and Therapeutic Techniques; and an opportunity to develop intervention skills, and learn how to make behavioral assessments, and situational analysis should be the primary formal and experiential training for all clinical sociologists. Merely being dissatisfied with traditional academic sociology; or writing about the evils of the "medical model" in mental health; or being disappointed in the way traditional clinicians attempt to apply sociological knowledge and thinking; or simply realizing a need to see the discipline broaden its base will not be enough to establish clinical sociology as an independent field of practice. It must be structured so that it is not absorbed into other behavioral and social sciences. Once it is structured, it can amass more and better documented information through research and theory building. There will also come social and political alliances with other health care disciplines or fields. This is the process for survival and growth. Those who are interested in such training must be dedicated and committed, and willing to be involved socially and politically. This posture is required if clinical sociologists are to be involved in changing entire social systems, including their rules and hierarchies, especially if there are those who believe that this is a fundamental way to affect the lives and objective conditions of people whose oppression and inequality are the basic causes of social and psychological distress.

The Challenge for Clinical Sociologists

Part of the struggle of Clinical Sociology and Clinical Sociologists to be established is the capturing of those applications of sociological thinking and knowledge that are now made by clinical social workers, clinical psychologist and psychiatrists. This is indeed a formidable task because in many cases it would mean the demise and/or weakening of certain professions and professional influence, and the questioning of the effectiveness of present clinical applications. So, those who question the need for another distinct clinical profession with no real professional programs and specific sociological curricula might be suggesting that other clinicians are making applications of sociological thinking and knowledge. This attitude by other established clinicians might be the greatest drawback to standardization of the practice or accreditation of programs for training clinical sociologists. The warrants for clinical sociological practice are very evident and have been discussed by a number of persons (Glassner & Freedman, Glass, Swan, Straus). Sociologists, properly trained are more capable and appropriate to conduct specific research, diagnose and engage in therapeutic activities that have the group or the social situation as a focus. If this point is firmly established and settled, then the legitimate role of Clinical Sociologists can be well established, even if the sociodiagnostic and sociotherapeutic techniques are identical to those of other clinicians, especially those of clinical social workers, clinical psychologists, social psychologists, and community psychologists. The crucial difference is that the Clinical Sociologist brings to social diagnosis and sociotherapeutic intervention a difference theoretical view, different methodological connections, and knowledge-base for clinical sociological practice. The need for professional programs which would provide this kind of training and certification is imperative. However, those who have been trained both in academic settings, and at various centers, institutes, clinics; in seminars and workshops, must provide a dimension to the legitimate role and place of Clinical Sociologists in clinical and therapeutic matters. These Clinical Sociologists can pave the way for those who will be trained through programs to be established, and those that are established, to enter the larger clinical environment into which Clinical Sociologists will locate themselves whether in the private or public environment. A variety of roles may be assumed by Clinical Sociologists, and to confine their roles to being researchers, consultants, or as a part of a team within the clinical environment, is to limit the role and functions to the traditional skills acquired by Sociologists. To add a clinical dimension means that clinical sociological diagnostic and therapeutic skills must be acquired to combine with the traditional theoretical and methodological skills are combined with clinical training in specific sociological curricula which will facilitate sociological diagnosis and therapeutic intervention in problems within a social context or of a social nature. The sociological curricula must include theory practicums, research experience, and clinical field experiences.

Aside from the development of certain professional skills, such as interpersonal skills, abilities to make accurate observations, assessments and measurements, and acquiring abilities in social diagnosis, intervention, and in situational analysis and interpretation, the Clinical Sociologist should in the process, acquire certain personal attributes. We have mentioned earlier that he should be committed and dedicated; she should also be energetic, open, confident, resourceful, tolerant, good-willed, honest, curious, enthusiastic, self-aware, have personal integrity and even be humble. Both the personal attributes and professional skills, provided by a competent and strong faculty, teaching relevant courses, in a curricula that provides for field-based training and internship experience in various places, are essential for effective clinical sociological practice. We must come to see the overlapping of the professional and the personal as we see the overlapping and interrelating sociological perspectives that capture the interrelationships reflected in the nature of social life. This is important for Clinical Sociologists so that they grasp the nature of multidimensional interlocking networks of social interaction and relations that constitute group life. One real danger to establishment of programs to train Clinical Sociologists is to continue to debate the validity and legitimacy of Clinical Sociology and clinical sociological practice and not make it happen with or without the support of "Establishment Sociology", or the cooperation of other clinicians and clinical professions, especially those whose base must be broadened to include clinical sociological practice, and various accrediting agencies who must redefine the nature of mental illness and relationships to include the social context or dimension. What must be avoided is a hap-hazard attempt to develop programs to train students for roles as therapeutic agents without careful evolution of the impact on the discipline of Sociology; the mental health delivery system; the target populations; the social systems, and the possible reaction, resistance and/or assistance of other therapeutic agents. A significant portion of the concern of clinical sociologists must be with the content of training issues and the efficient utilization of Clinical Sociologists. There must exist, therefore, a training and research paradigm which will facilitate the production of competent and skilled clinicians. There must exist and educational model that would utilize frontline sociologists who are teaching, writing about and practicing the application of sociological knowledge and thinking as clinical sociologists. This model must have a theoretical (conceptual) and methodological schema for understanding and evaluating sociological applications in various social settings and multiple levels of society. The model should also allow for the division of labor to which many Clinical Sociologists will subscribe in their professional life after training. It is possible to develop a scientist-professional model where the individual assumes the clinical services role, the research services role, or a combination of both. The educational model for training Clinical Sociologists would operate with experienced Sociologists serving as teachers, consultants or advisers and supervisors, and graduate students serving as research assistants, training and supervision coordinators of a number of persons in the program and trainees in other settings where students and others are used as therapeutic agents. The persons being trained can be divided into small groups for purposes of supervision. What is being argued is that a systematic plan be developed with clearly conceptual and process components for the training of Clinical Sociologists who can function effectively in various clinical and therapeutic settings applying sociological knowledge and thinking. What is required is the organization of a program model that allows for the acquisition of clinical and therapeutic skills in addition to theoretical and methodological competencies. The Theoretical-Methodological-Clinical schema is basic to the educational model that would provide a framework for a comprehensive understanding of the social order and social relations within the social order. Further, it would provide a mechanism for rigorous and systematic evaluation of the impact of sociological applications at various levels in society, and in various group settings within a social context. Implicit in the educational model would emerge design and measurement of organization, group, community, and societal change.

Clinical Supervision of Sociologists

The primary purpose of supervision is to assist trainees develop clinical skills, and, in the process of learning, how to translate and apply theoretical and technical knowledge to the problems of living in group life. The supervisees learn how to establish helping relationships with those who seek their services. This helping process is greatly influenced by theoretical orientations, including the content, structure, and process of the supervision. Consequently, the future of the supervisees is shaped, for the most part, by the nature of theoretical orientation of the supervision. Where the established clinician is in a different field, the influence is beyond style and reaches into content, knowledge base, theoretical perspectives and methodological approaches. Personal and professional attributes of individual supervisors are important, but should not dominate the nature of the supervisory relationship. Therefore, clinical supervision should be thoroughly conceptualized and systematically conducted if it is to be effective and productive.

In the supervisory process, the less experienced clinician develops professionally in expanding and applying clinical knowledge and techniques under the direction of a more experienced clinician. If this education takes place in a group setting, the supervisees can assist each other in developing their professional identity. An objective of supervision should be to assist the supervisees develop internal properties and qualities so that they can independently monitor and critically evaluate their own work and establish a posture that fosters growth and development. The learning process will not stop at the end of training and supervision, and growth will require continuous examination of self and work.

Teaching and supervising the acquisition of clinical skills requires that there is established knowledge regarding the qualities clinical sociologists should possess. How the transition from novice to trained is facilitated is a real challenge, and the various problems in supervisory sessions must be identified and analyzed to assure that specific task and demands of the interventionist role and other stumbling blocks are dealt with. Most of these issues must be resolved if competencies are to be learned for the supervisees to participate in intervention. Having the supervisees supervise less experienced trainees should be a part of the supervisory training which should help in the process.

As supervisees struggle to master various tasks and demands, there are certain challenges that must be given special attention. First, there is the sense of authority or the lack thereof, and marginal status which requires that a new set of rules be employed to govern a different kind of relationship and interaction. The supervisee is given some authority to develop and execute plans and strategies for intervention. At the same time, this degree of independence is being monitored and influence given. This experience can be particularly troublesome for those who are suffering from role ambiguity and marginality who seek to define their role without tangible authority. This challenge is also particularly problematic especially if there are conceptual difficulties with the power of the therapist and the status of marginality. The anxiety that can result from this experience can be managed if supervisees are assisted in creating or constructing their own authority. Some supervisors define their role in terms that withhold authority and the exercise of authority by supervisees. Being effective in the process of social diagnosis and intervention becomes more difficult when the clients perceive the conflict or the restraints on the role of supervisees. Supervisors are perceived to be in a position to confer authority. In the case where this is true, conferring authority is crucial to the supervisees creating the necessary authority for effective action.

Secondly, the clients involved in this process are real, and have demands and expectations. There are also professional expectations of the supervisor that might or might not be those of the institution. When clients, and even the supervisees, perceive conflicts between institutional and professional expectations, there is a loss of faith by clients and supervisees that weakens the effectiveness in the process of social diagnosis and intervention. The role of the supervisor is to influence the belief that these conflicts are either not real or that they are being resolved, and that there is collective effort to work together to demonstrate competent action. In this regard, the work of the supervisor is challenging. Supervisees must be assisted in learning how to deal effectively with the various expectations, where and when they exist, and at the same time, deal with theirs that are constantly undergoing change. There is usually, constant redefining, refocusing, and reconstructing of the rational for being involved. In the process, the supervisees' activities receive some degree of validation from the clients, the supervisor and acceptance by one's self.

There are times when supervisees, in an attempt to explore the complexities of problems within a social context, develop a tendency to perceive the problems as being too immense to tackle. The supervisor, on the other hand, who has tackled such problems before and was successful in solving them, is tempted to provide assistance which disallows a real opportunity to learn, especially if there is evidence of impatience on the part of the client or the supervisor in the time that is taken by the supervisees to solve the problems, if there is a display of disposition which questions the ability and perceptibility of the supervisees. Patience, tolerance and a careful evaluation of where the supervisees and a productive relationship between them and the supervisor, and between the supervisees and the clients. At times it is best to provide the supervisees with the opportunity to clinically focus on a single matter rather than a complexity of issues. If the supervisees are made to feel or perceive the problems to be unsolvable, this disposition can be easily and quickly conveyed to clients, and the results can be an unwillingness to intervene and meaningfully participate in seeking solutions. The supervisors' role in this instance is to assist the supervisees to be clear as to what can and cannot be accomplished, and help to avoid the vacillation between a sense of futility and hope so that a set of realistic goals can be developed. The successful resolution of these issues facilitates the development of competences and skills that can be assessed by supervision and live observation. The supervisor and the supervisee must come to know, and the supervisees should demonstrate the perceptual ability required in sociodiagnostic assessment. Further, the ability to formulate one's observations of the situation, relationship, and interaction, demonstrates the conceptual skill supervisees must possess to satisfy the goal and objective of the supervision. The achievement of this skill can be determined by evaluating and reading case notes, supervisory notes and other materials that are collected and used to determine progress in supervision. Executive skills must also be determined in supervision: The way in which supervisees negotiate situations and how they function as they intervene to help alter situations, relationships, and interactions. Supervision and observation are imperative in assessing these competencies and skills.

Supervision is a helping relationship influenced by theoretical and methodological orientations. The primary intent in the process is to assist supervisees maximize their abilities and knowledge, based upon their training, for social diagnosis and intervention. Although the supervisory process is experiential, it is clearly educational. The more experienced, and in most cases the more knowledgeable clinician, helps the less experienced and knowledgeable develop professionally in applying clinical knowledge, thinking and skills.

The issue with regards to Clinical Sociologists is what is being applied. There are sociologists who have psychological and psychotherapeutic training, and have been supervised by professionals whose theoretical and knowledge base are different from that which distinguishes Clinical Sociologists from other clinicians, even from Community Psychologist. Clinical Sociologists do not seek to apply psychological and psychiatric knowledge and thinking. There is no need to become established as sociological clinicians if this is the intent. There are established clinicians who are making this contribution. Clinical Sociologists make the point that the body of knowledge of sociology is most appropriate and applicable to group life, human behavior in group life, social relations, and interpersonal connections. There are professionals in the clinical field who have no theoretical base for their applications. From their inception, they have borrowed from Sociology. Other professionals focus on the individual and personality systems in both their training and supervision. Those professionals whose formal training is rooted and grounded in medicine promote the medical model to which Sociologists should identify. Sociologists have sociological and sociological social psychological thinking to make applications. Now there is the need for training and supervision for the development of clinical skills to make clinical social diagnosis, and to facilitate sociotherapeutic intervention. It should be expected that those professionals who possess diagnostic and therapeutic skills, but have traditionally leaned on sociological thinking and knowledge for application, will challenge the move of sociologists to establish programs for the development of competencies and skills in clinical and therapeutic matters. Because there are sociologists who are dissatisfied with the traditional posture of sociology, and have decided to practice sociology clinically, those professions and professionals that are closely related feel threatened and have attempted to resist Clinical Sociologists' entrance into the clinical field. There are those who are raising serious questions and objections. One of the reasons that the present posture of those who call themselves clinical sociologists "includes diagnostic and therapeutic techniques virtually identical to those used by psychologists and social workers" (Glassner, 1981), is that most of these sociologists were trained and supervised by psychologist, psychiatrists and other clinicians who practice psychotherapy, and apply psychoanalytic thought in their practice. In order to feel legitimate these sociologists have not attempted to be difference from other traditional clinicians. Some have even been tempted to refer to themselves as psychotherapists, because clients and consumers do not know who is a clinical sociologist, or what clinical sociotherapists do. This is understandable because clinical sociology is not well established, and there will be continued resistance to its establishment. Some sociologists who want to practice clinical sociology are tempted to avoid the resistance and challenge by focusing on the individual or personality system, in an attempt to do otherwise brings conflict, especially from supervisors in the process of supervision. It must be clear that what distinguishes clinical sociologists from other clinicians is that they combine sociological knowledge and thinking with certain sociotherapeutic techniques that are based upon group, social-system, cultural and societal perspectives. The theoretical orientations are different and the content-focus, (social situation/context), and sociological variables (class, sex, race, ethnicity, etc.) are different (Cohen, 1981). Presently, other clinicians perceive the field of sociology as a discipline which studies a set of conceptual problems with activities that are basically confined to research and scholarship, the aim being to build knowledge. It is this knowledge that others have attempted to use which clinical sociologists laid claim to for application. This can be done and is being done, even when the techniques employed in the process of social diagnosis and treatment are similar to those used by traditional clinicians. Again, the sociotherapeutic techniques used by clinical sociologists are not in question relative to the distinction to be made. The theoretical perspectives, and the focus on the sociocultural and societal context of the problems provide the distinction. Nonetheless, there are methodological approaches for discovery and social diagnosis that also make a difference in the practice of clinical sociology. Clinical Sociology has been defined in such a way that there are those who actually practice clinical sociology who have some training in sociology but are not called sociologists, neither do they see themselves as sociologists. A clinical role for sociologists in such areas as family therapy, marital therapy, organization development, community organization, etc., will not be fully realized until there are designed programs to train clinical sociologists, and an established supervisory process so that clinical competencies and skills can be developed. This is crucial in order to gain consumer confidence and provide services that are creditable and legitimate. Sociology must restructure itself to include the opportunity and potential to train practitioners in clinical fields and social change. This should be a welcome move, especially at this point when other clinical professions are beginning to recognize, in a more significant way, the sociological context of the various problems they seek to diagnose and change. The present change agents who deal with organization, martial, family and community problems do not lodge the problems in the same social context as do Clinical Sociologists (Swan 1981; Glass and Fritz, 1981: 352).

Conclusion

The basic elements exist for the growth, development, and establishment of clinical sociology. The need to look as the process and structural variables that underlie human behavior must be given primary attention rather than trying to change the behavior directly. In organizational terms, focusing on the individual and providing psychological strategies for solving stress is not the posture of Clinical Sociologists; neither do they think this approach gets at the real cause of job stress. Clinical Sociologists looks at the organizational structure and the social-environmental context of the stress to avoid treating the symptoms and consequences of the stress. Once this approach is firmly established, and results become distinctly evident, client groups will demand the services of clinical sociologists. Finally, with the development of academic programs and an established supervisory system to assure the development of special competencies, clinical sociologists will have the techniques and skills necessary to provide distinctive clinical service. It is only as a distinct clinical role is established through training and supervision will there be an opportunity for a multidisciplinary practice. Small-group dynamics and interpersonal skills; modes of intervention in groups and sociodiagnostic skills for groups must be central to the training supervision, inspite of the designation of the degree. Further, since sociology is the study of group life, and human behavior within the context of the group, the training and supervision of Clinical Sociologists must take place within a group setting. The supervisory process can also be enhanced by the presence of two or more supervisors who would co-facilitate the process, and the training can be done with a peer in a co-therapy model. It will, no doubt, take time to fully translate ideas and positions into established programs for the training and supervision of Clinical Sociologists, but this is exactly what should be accomplished if established programs are to be developed, grow and become creditable and legitimate. Such strategies as using audio-visual feedback in the supervision process are also very useful within the group setting. Ideas are everywhere; they simply have to be collected and organized.

As others think about, and write about, and practice clinical sociology, an established set of arrangements will emerge and take their place for the training and supervision of Clinical Sociologists. If not, the effort to establish a practice that focuses on knowing and offering knowledge; doing and offering service, will fail, and will not meet the human needs that Sociologists are and can be trained to meet.

References

Dies, R.R.
   1974 Attitudes Toward the Training of Group Psychotherapists: Some Interprofessional and Experience-Associated Differences. Small Group Behavior 5: 65-79.

Glassner, Barry
   1981 Clinical Applications of Sociology in Health Care. The Journal of Applied Behavioral Sciences. 17/3 (July, August, September).

Cohen, H
   1981 Connections: Understanding Social Relations. Ames Iowa State University Press.

Straus, R.A.
   1979 Clinical Sociology: An Idea Whose Time has Come . . . again. Sociological Practice, 3/1 (Spring): 21-43.

Glass, John and Jan Fritz
   1981 The Development of Clinical Sociology: Response to Glassner. The Journal of Applied Behavioral Sciences 17/3 (July/August/September).

Swan, L. Alex
   1981 Clinical Sociology: Problems and Prospects. Mid-American Review of Sociology, Vol. 6 No. 2 (Winter), 111-127.

Glassner, B. and Freedman, J.
   1979 Clinical Sociology. New York: Lougman.

Discovering Essential Facts

Chapter 12

* * *

Discovering Essential Facts

Introduction

We have argued in this work that in order to be effective in treating problems that are social in nature, or problems within a social context, we have to ground the theories (explanations) and therapies (treatments). In order for this process to work well, it is imperative that essential facts are discovered. We have also argued that this process of discovery is achieved through disclosure by the clients. The skills of the therapist in this process of disclosure and discovery are crucial to the outcome. The entire process is facilitated by the techniques of Encounter, Interpretation and Situational or Contextual analysis. Initially the Sociotherapist assumes the role of a scientist as he engages the clients in the Encounter process for discovery. This is the basic nature of GET, and everyone who employs this approach might have her own style of engaging the clients, but must employ the scientific process in order for the essential facts to have theoretical and therapeutic utility.

What we want to accomplish in this chapter is to present a few cases to demonstrate the process of Encounter which leads to disclosure and discovery. We maintain this posture in GET because presenting problems of clients are not always the real problems; they are simply symptoms or indicators of the real problems. This is the reason for the scientific posture in the process of GET which happens prior to the therapeutic posture. The probing and questioning, however, must be in the direction of the presenting problems. The scientific process and the therapeutic process are interrelated and interdependent because the creation of specific knowledge about the presenting and real problems is crucial to intervention and application of that knowledge.

As stated earlier, it is best to have all persons who are involved in the situation, also involved in the sociodiagnotic process. This is vital to the collection of the essential facts. It is also best to have each person encounter the sociotherapist individually before the collective encounter. Clients are often agreeable to do this only after the process is fully explained and assurances given that their frank and open disclosures will not be told to others during the collective setting. They are assured that the information will not be shared with others, and that their disclosure is simply preparation for the construction of questions for the collective encounter. If questions are to be raised in the direction of the presenting problems, the data the clients provide in the sessions must give direction and lay the foundation for discovery in the sociodiagnostic process. Discovery also takes place during the individual sessions. Three cases are presented here to demonstrate the process of "Discovering Essential Facts."

Case Number One

A man called the office and talked with me about a relationship problem he was having. As is often the case, he like other callers wanted to discuss the matter over the phone. I asked him when he wanted to visit the office to discuss the matter. He gave me a time and asked about the cost when he realized I would not diagnose his situation on the phone. When he arrived for his appointment a few days later, I gave him information about my qualifications and the approach I use in counseling and therapy. He shared his knowledge of me and the fact that he listened to my "Family Forum" program on radio. After I had collected some demographic and general data about him, I asked him to tell me something about the person with whom he was in relationship. Before me was an African American who was a high school coach who had entered into an intimate relationship with an Anglo woman whom he said had little employment skills, out of work, with two teen-aged girls, who lived in a trailer. Her financial situation was not good, neither was his. I continued the Encounter with the question:

T.	What do you think is the problem for which you are seeking assistance?
Claude.	The woman is really jealous. I have tried my very best to let her know that I care about her, but she is so suspicious.
T.	How long have you known her?
Claude.	Not very long. I met her earlier in the year before we started going together this summer.
T.	Has she talked with you about her feelings and why she might be jealous?
Claude.	See, she does not like what I'm doing with my daughter who lives with my ex-wife.
T.	What is that?
Claude.	Well, I buy all my daughter's clothes and I pay half of the rent on the house as an investment. If and when the house is sold, I will have my equity in it. I don't want to lose that at all. She can't seem to understand that.
T.	What does she say about it?
Claude.	She does not see why I continue to do what I'm doing. She gets mean and nasty about the whole matter. I'm very close to my daughter, but the ex and I don't have a thing going.
T.	Does she believe you?
Claude.	I don't think so. She calls me as I leave her place. If she can't find me she will call over to my ex's, or go looking for me like she's trying to catch me in a lie or something.
T.	What have you done about the matter?
Claude.	I have talked with the woman many times, but I can't seem to get through to her the fact that the ex-wife and me are through. This was a fact long before I met her.
T.	What do you know about her and her relationship?
Claude.	I know she was seeing this guy who fooled her and did not tell her he was married. She said she has stopped seeing him and they are just friends now.
T.	Do you believe her?

Claude.	Yes, but I have heard about the guy. He tries to con women. He's a real jive turkey.
T.	Does she talk to you about this guy?
Claude.	Sometimes. He comes around or calls her sometimes and she would tell me about it.
T.	Do you want the relationship with her?
Claude.	Sure. That's why I called you for help. I don't know what to do about this wo man and her jealousy.

At this point I told the client that I would have to see both of them for a session after which we would decide what direction to take. He agreed and assured me that there would be no problem getting her to come because they had discussed that possibility and she was willing to come. Further, he disclosed that she admitted to him that she had some personal problems for which she might get help if she came. "Maybe you can help her, Doc, if she came," he remarked, "I don't know what to do or how to relate to her."

I assured him we could get to the bottom of the matter when we came together for the next session. He called her from the office and established a convenient date for the next appointment and left, anxious to return. I had gotten from him enough information to start the next session, and when they returned, we agreed that I would talk to her first. The entire process was explained in his presence. They voiced their consent to the process and he left the room and closed the door. She seemed anxious to start, but I started by telling her that he had called seeking assistance concerning their relationship and that he had had a session with me. Before she said anything, I asked:

T.	What do you think is the problem with your relationship with him?
Carol.	He says I'm jealous.
T.	Are you? What do you think?
Carol.	I'll say yes I am. I'll say I'm jealous.
T.	How do you demonstrate your jealousy?
Carol.	I call him to see if he is at home when he says he's going home, or when I think he should be at home.

T.	And if he's not at home?
Carol.	I think he's some place with someone else.
T.	Another woman?
Carol.	Yes, another woman.
T.	Have you ever talked to him about your feelings?
Carol.	Yes, but he thinks I'm crazy to think and feel the way I do.
T.	Why?
Carol.	He says he's not doing anything.
T.	What do you believe?
Carol.	I don't know. I just know what he says.
T.	Have you ever caught him in a lie?
Carol.	No. He tells me that he's open and honest with me, but that I get mad and start an argument with him when he is open and honest with me.
T.	Do you want him to be open and honest with you on personal matters?
Carol.	Yes; sure I do, but I don't think I can handle it at times.
T.	When are some of those times?
Carol.	When he goes to see his daughter who lives with his ex-wife.
T.	What about that, that makes you upset?
Carol.	I just don't see why he spends his money on them and gives them so much attention.
T.	Does he spend much time with you?
Carol.	Yes he does. I give him that. He likes spending time with me, but we don't go out any place. He's always broke.
T.	Would you like him to take you out more often?
Carol.	Yes.
T.	What is stopping that from happening?
Carol.	Maybe I don't dress like he wants me to dress. I don't know.
T.	We can ask him about it when he comes in. Do you have anything you want me to know that I have not asked about? I'm about to invite him in for the collective Encounter session.

I had enough of the presenting problem to start the collective Encounter session. There were other questions I could have asked, but they could be asked during the collective session.

When he came in, I informed him that we had a productive session, and that I did not spend quite as much time with her as I did with him because of the relatedness of the responses and that he had initiated the counseling process. I instructed them to position their chairs so that each was directly facing each other and was comfortable. I observed their facial expressions and body movements and asked him if he was comfortable with the position. She seemed at ease and anxious to get on with the session. He appeared uneasy and I wanted to check it with him before I started. He said he was okay, but he kept shifting in his seat for a while.

T.   I want each of you to look directly into the eyes of each other when you speak to each other. Call each buy the name you are accustomed to calling each other. Speak directly to each other when I ask you to do so. At times I will stop the process to take note of something, or clarify, or make observations with you concerning certain things. If you are not doing as I want you to, I will stop you and ask you to do it the way I have explained. Do you think you have caught the nature of this process?

Carol.   Yes, I think I have it.

Claude.   I have it.

T.   Look at each other. Tell her how you feel about her. Remember to call her by name and talk directly to her. Look at her and tell her.

Claude.   I feel frustrated and confused about our relationship and how you are behaving Carol. I have tried my best to treat you with concern and care.

Carol.   That's true and I do not know why I behave the way I do, except I don't think you mean what you tell me.

Claude.   That's your problem, Carol, you have been fooled by guys who didn't mean you any good so you think I'm just like the rest of the persons you dated, but I'm not. I can't get you to relate to me on the basis of what I say and how I treat you.

T.   Do you trust Claude, Carol? Tell him if you trust him.

Carol.	That's what I have been trying to get over to you. I don't trust you, Claude, and I guess it's going to take a while for me to do so.
T.	Tell him what he's doing that gives you reasons not to trust him.
Carol.	Nothing, really. You are not doing anything that causes me to not trust you, except how you related to your daughter and your ex-wife.
Claude.	That's what frustrates me, because . . .
Carol.	I know you say nothing is going on with you and your ex, but I get nervous when I know you have been over there; that's just the way I get Claude and I don't know why I get that way.
Claude.	I've told you that woman does not mean anything to me anymore. I have to keep in touch with my daughter because we are very close and I want to keep the equity in my house so I pay half of the rent. I treat it as an investment.
Carol.	He doesn't take me . . .
T.	Tell him. Tell Claude.
Carol.	You don't take me anywhere. You spend time with me, but we don't go out to eat or anything. I don't think he likes the way . . .
T.	Talk to him.
Carol.	I don't think you like the way I dress.
Claude.	Well, I wish you would dress better than you do, but you know my financial situation; it is tight.
Carol.	I'm not working and I can't get my financial situation together and you wouldn't help me do anything about my property.
T.	What about your property?
Carol.	I have some property that was taken from me and I told him about it, but he hasn't done anything to help me.
T.	Did you promise to help, Claude?
Claude.	Yes, but it is not that easy, and we have discussed what the problem is and I don't think we can do much about the matter. It's been so long ago.

T.	Let's deal with that later. Tell Claude how you see yourself, Carol.
Carol.	What do you mean? Tell him who I am?
T.	Yes, how you see yourself.
Carol.	Well, I'm a kind woman, Claude. I'm affectionate and would give away my last dime if someone needed it. I am afraid of being hurt by you. I like going out and meeting your friends.
T.	How do you feel relative to him?
Carol.	I don't think I'm adequate for you, Claude. I don't dress right; you have your middle-class friends, and I'm angry at myself for being inadequate. Why me? I'm not in your class. Why me?
Claude.	I care about you, and want our relationship to grow.
Carol.	I don't think I'm what you want.
Claude.	Is that why you keep these two guys coming around in case I leave you?
Carol.	No, they are just friends I enjoy.
Claude.	You know what that Evans guy wants because he's the one you had a relationship with and the other night when he was there, you know why he was over there.
Carol.	He's a nice person. He's a lot of fun and I just enjoy his company.
Claude.	But you know actually why he had come over?
Carol.	Maybe, but that does not mean anything was going to happen.
Claude.	But I told you about him. He doesn't mean you any good. I just don't like him coming around you.
T.	Let me go back to a couple of things. Carol, you say you don't trust Claude, right?
Carol.	That's right.
T.	You would say then that you lack trust, not that you are jealous.
Carol.	That's right.
T.	Something else you disclosed we should look at. You said you are inadequate, or that you feel this way. Do you feel he could get someone else in his class? What do you mean by what you disclosed?

Carol.   Well, I wonder why he doesn't date a black woman in his class. I'm sure he can get someone more sophisticated. I dress in jeans and so forth, and I guess that's why he has not taken me around any of his friends. I don't feel up to his standard.

Claude.   Wow, that's real heavy. I didn't know you thought like that. I don't mind taking you out. It's just so expensive these days.

T.   Would taking you out help, Carol?

Carol.   Some, but I still don't see why he wants me. He probably could get several women in his category.

T.   You asked him and he told you he cared about you. You don't think you are worth his caring?

Carol.   Yes, but maybe if he meets somebody better, he'll just quit.

T.   Are you afraid of that?

Carol.   Yes, Sure I am.

T.   Do you have what it takes to keep him?

Carol.   I don't know.

T.   Ask him what it will take to keep him.

Carol.   What will it take to keep you, Claude?

Claude.   Trust me. Believe in me and stop letting those guys, especially Evans, come around the house.

T.   Evans' name has emerged before. Tell me about Evans.

Claude.   Who?

T.   Anyone.

Carol.   Evans is this black guy who comes around every once in a while. He's just a friend. And this other black guy is nothing to me at all. He is a nice guy who stops by now and then.

Claude.   Tell him that Evans was your boyfriend who made a fool out of you and took advantage of you, but you still let him come around, and he only wants one thing from you and you know it. Sometimes I think she wants him to come around.

Carol.   Yes I do, Claude. He's a lot of fun.

Claude.   You called him to come over the last time. When I called, he was there and I came on over and made him leave.

T.	Are you protective of her?
Claude.	Maybe, because I know that kind of a guy. I was the one who told her some things about him and when she checked, they were correct. He was trying to pull the wool over her eyes.
T.	You said he is a lot of fun, Carol; more so than Claude?
Carol.	Sure. Claude is serious, Evans is a lot of laughs. He makes me feel alive.
T.	How do you feel about that, Claude?
Claude.	The guy is up to no good. He is a trickster.
T.	Would you prefer Evans to Claude, Carol?
Carol.	In some ways, yes. In most ways really. But Evans has other involvements and can't give what I need at this time. But he comes around and has conversation.
T.	Do you think he comes around for something else?
Carol.	Maybe, but that's okay. I know how to handle him.
T.	Do you think she could, Claude?
Claude.	The guy is a con. I can't see why she would want to have him around when he did to her what he did, and still comes around looking for more.
T.	Do you think he could get her to be intimate again?
Claude.	Yes.
T.	How do you feel about that?
Claude.	Confused and angry.
T.	Have you ever asked her how it is that she has all black boyfriends in the last few years?
Claude.	No.
T.	Would you like to ask her?
Claude.	I guess I could. How come Carol?
Carol.	I don't know. I guess I just run into them. I don't know.
T.	Has that been a concern of yours, Claude?
Claude.	At times. I figure that if Evans and those others could get her, any other brother can. It makes me really nervous at times.
T.	Could that have been influencing your decisions regarding taking her out and not the lack of finance?

282

Claude. Maybe. I guess that played a major part. I don't want to get into no mess over no woman. And you know how some brothers are. They see you with her and they want to be all over her.

Carol. Sometimes, I just can't believe he's serious. Cause all the others wanted was one thing. I thought he wanted just a fling; that is what the others wanted.

The session ended here and we scheduled another collective Encounter session. At the next session we started where we ended. I recalled what we had discovered in the last session and complimented them for being so open with what they disclosed. I asked them how did they feel about the relationship and its possibility and they assured me that they wanted to continue until they were helped. I read to them what we had discovered in two areas during the Encounter session.

T. We discovered that Carol does not trust you Claude, and that it has nothing to do with what you have done, but rather who she thinks she is. She is apprehensive about the relationship and keeps raising the question, why her, since she does not think she is in your category. We discovered then that the problem was not one of jealousy. So far, is that what you remember we discovered?

Claude. Yes.

Carol. Yes.

T. Claude, we discovered that you were protective of Carol and believed she was vulnerable to brothers, especially those who could con her into a relationship. We need to explore this a little more and look more at Carol's concept of herself in relation to you and other relationships. Are you all ready?

Claude. I am.

Carol. I think I am.

T. Is there anything either of you wishes to say before we start?

Claude.   This thing about my being protective is interesting because I was never this way before or with my ex-wife. This is rather interesting.

T.   Let's explore that some more. You want to feel special with Carol?

Claude.   Yeah. Sometimes I do and sometimes I don't.

T.   Do you get angry and confused about this?

Claude.   All the time. Here I am trying to make the relationship work, and she is still making contact with these con artists.

T.   Earlier you tried to explain that behavior, Carol; try it again.

Carol.   These guys make me laugh. They are lots of fun.

T.   Are you not uncertain about your relationship with Claude?

Carol.   That's true. I am uncertain.

T.   Would that also have anything to do with staying in touch with these other guys?

Carol.   Maybe. I guess so. In case he just left me, I'll have somebody around. He can get better than me. Sometimes I figure he just wants a fling. He can't be serious about me.

Claude.   I'm not going anywhere Carol. I've told you that many times. What must I do to convince you?

Carol.   Help me with my problems.

T.   Tell him what problems.

Carol.   With my property and things.

T.   You really want him to help you with this problem?

Carol.   Yes.

T.   Will you or can you help, Claude?

Claude.   I don't think there's anything I can do, but I will try.

T.   Is that okay, Carol?

Carol.   That's all I want him to do is try.

T.   Back to her uncertainty about the relationship with you and her behavior with these other guys. That does not make you feel special Claude, does it?

Claude.   Not at all. These guys are not good, and they mean no good.

T.   They are all black guys? No white guys involved?

Claude.   No white guys. These are black guys.

T.   How does that make you feel? Tell Carol. Talk to her.

Claude.   Well, that makes me feel that I'm not special to you. Anybody can get you. Since you been dating all these brothers, any brother out there on the street can get you. That does not make me feel special at all.

T.   Do you think she has a preference for dating black men?

Claude.   It seems so.

T.   Ask Carol.

Claude.   Do you?

Carol.   Do I what?

Claude.   Have a preference for dating blacks?

Carol.   I like Evans.

Claude.   See, that makes me mad. He's nothing but a con artist. I'm trying to treat you like a lady.

T.   That does not make you feel special, does it?

Claude.   It sure doesn't. That's what makes me mad with you Carol. I'm trying to make this thing work for us and you can have this Evans guy over there laughing and going on, and you know what he's after. He does not want it to be over with you all.

Carol.   He's a lot of fun to be around.

T.   More so than with Claude?

Carol   Claude is more serious.

T.   Carol said earlier, Claude, that this is her protection against the possibility of your leaving. Did you hear that?

Claude.   Sure did. I didn't know she felt that way. I try to tell her I'm not going anywhere.

T.   Evidently, that' not working. Tell him, Carol, what you need.

Carol.   Well, I guess time, and doing things together. Going out more will help. Meeting his friends and letting them know we are dating.

T.   Would that create the certainty you need so that you don't need to have these other guys around?

Carol.   If I knew he meant what he says about me and the relationship, it will do a world of difference.

285

T. Would this help you also with your concern about her having these guys around, Claude?

Claude. Sure seems so.

T. What do you think of yourself, Carol, in relation to Claude?

Carol. Wow, that's a tough one.

T. You disclosed earlier that you didn't think he was serious about a relationship with you because you were not in his category.

Carol. Well, I don't have anything. He's going to school and is educated. I know he meets educated women, and I just don't think he really, I don't know.

Claude. You're a good woman Carol. You are kind.

Carol. You don't like the way I dress with these overalls and stuff.

Claude. That can change. That's no problem.

T. We have to stop now, but let's see what we have discovered and what it tells us we have to do or what direction to take.

T. We have discovered that Carol's insecurity and uncertainty are related to her perception of herself in relation to her perception of you, Claude. She confirms her perception by your lack of taking her out. This seems to be the reason that she holds on to the friendships of these guys, especially Evans. On the other hand, we discovered that this is the very thing-the holding on to their friendships—that upsets Claude.

Claude. Let me see if we are on the same track. Carol's view of herself is influencing her behavior towards me. So if I make her secure in her view toward herself, she will change her behavior toward me and those guys?

T. How do you see the situation, Carol?

Carol. Like Claude, my view of me is in the way of relating to Claude. I must believe that he cares about me for me. Once I can come to this belief, I would not need these guys' friendship, or put their friendship in competition with Claude's friendship.

T. Good. What does this say about what actions to take? What is the real question?

Claude. How could I make her feel secure so that she does not have to think negatively about herself where I'm concerned?

T. That's okay. How are you to view yourself, Carol, if you are to feel certain and secure in Claude's friendship and love for you?

Carol. I don't know really, but that seems to be the key to the whole thing. I can accept Claude's love and friendship if I display a positive view of myself. Is it also true that I hold on to the others' friendship to feel positive about myself?

T. To start, accepting Claude's love and friendship on the basis of who you are will provide the sense that you are special to him. This should help you accept his relationship with his daughter and ex-wife. Claude, you can do what we discovered Carol needs from you to feel special. Take her out and introduce her to your friends. There are a number of non-expensive things that you both can do that can become special to you both. Can you all think of some things to do together that would not be expensive, or that will not require any cash?

Claude. Sure we can.

Carol. I would like that very much.

T. That is not to suggest that that's all you do. Planning a special time away from the home could require the setting aside some cash for that special purpose. There are some other things I think you can do that are suggested by what we have discovered.

T. How do you think you interact with Claude, Carol—On the basis of what you really think of yourself, or on the basis of what you think he thinks of you?

Carol. I guess the last one—how I think he thinks of me.

T. Does it conflict with what you think of you?

Carol. What do you mean?

T. Is your concept of yourself in conflict with your concept of Claude's concept of you? Are they different?

Carol. I think I understand. Let me repeat it to see if I really get it. Is my thinking of me in conflict with what I think he thinks of me. Not really. No, there is not conflict. They are about the same.

T.	But there is a conflict between what you think he thinks, your view of yourself, and how he says he views you.
Claude.	That's what it is because Carol, you would not accept what I say and how I feel about you.
Carol.	I just don't know.
T.	Let's establish a plan of action to get some things changed. What do you think the situation calls for, Claude?
Claude.	I need to demonstrate to Carol that I mean what I say and how I feel about her.
T.	Carol, tell Claude how he can do that.
Carol.	Take me out. Show me to your friends and relatives.
Claude.	That's no problem at all.
T.	Do you think his doing these things will help you change the way you think of yourself in relation to him, Carol?
Carol.	I think so. I will also have to accept myself for who I am. If he says he accepts me, I should do the same.
T.	There you go, Carol. Evidently, Claude sees something in you that he is responding to. Apart from the other things we will do in our future sessions, we will work on self-acceptance and locating those integral qualities that you and Claude see in each other, but especially in you Carol, that you can celebrate. You need to have a sense of internal celebration and a genuine sense of self-acceptance. I want to start some non-verbal exercises with you all to enhance the expression of your feelings for each other and the way you relate to each other. How does that sound to you?
Carol.	Wonderful.
Claude.	Great. I'm ready.
T.	Okay. Is there anything else you think we might do that's related to our discoveries?
Claude.	No, not really.
T.	Carol?
Carol.	I was thinking, but I can't come up with anything.
T.	Let me show you what to do as home assignments. After we have done the various exercises during our sessions together, I will ask you to continue them at home.

After demonstrating the exercise I wanted them to practice at home, I gave instructions regarding things we agreed upon. I went over Claude's tasks and behavior changes. I then focused Carol on her tasks and behavior changes. A time was established for the next session and they left hopeful and happy.

It is very evident in this case that the presenting problem was not the real problem. The sociotherapist should not deny the presenting problem but use the problem to give direction to the discovery of the real problems. The presenting problem is viewed as a symptom of something else that is happening, and the sociotherapist is to assist the clients in making discovery through disclosure. After or during the discovery process, plans for change may be developed.

Regardless of how successful this process might be, there is no guarantee that the clients will follow through with their tasks and responsibilities, even when there is collective agreement and personal discoveries. Another problem is the temptation clients have with going over the problems by themselves at home, starting in the car on their way home. I usually discourage this activity in strong terms noting the possible dangers to the desired outcome. If they care to talk about the discoveries and how they plan to carry out their assignments, it should be done in session with the therapist. Confirming and reaffirming discoveries and their commitment to follow through is the desired posture for clients to assume. This posture is usually a good sign that change has taken place in disposition and that it will take place in behavior and in the clients' situation.

Crucial Observation

Before presenting another example for discovering essential facts, let us look at a situation found in another work. The authors attempted to discuss confrontational interpretation under the heading Psychodynamic Techniques. The client was asked a question, and the reply was:

Wife: The reason that I'm not pursuing my career is that Leslie
            doesn't want me to work.

Therapist: Karen, I agree that Leslie's opposition is part of the
            explanation for why you're not pursuing your career.
            However, I don't think that's the whole story. I suspect
            that part of what's holding you back is that you have
            some feelings about this that don't have much to do with
            Leslie.

It is evident that no grounding is taking place in this process. This is the typical way clinicians relate to clients and their problems. Notice that the client has provided a reason, an explanation, or a theory, if you please, for her not pursuing a career. While it might be true that Leslie's opposition might be the reason or part of the reason, it might not be the whole story. However, to be guessing, and saying I don't think, demonstrates that the discovery process is incomplete. When the client offers explanations, the therapist is to treat them as part of the disclosure and allow the data to indicate to the client what the reasons are or what explanations are emerging. No time during the sociodiagnostic process should there appear to be a difference or conflict in theoretical or explanatory perspective. It causes clients to become defensive; it eats at their confidence and ability to see things, and tends to confirm in their minds the superior perspective and knowledge of the therapist. This is never the case when we allow the data to tell us what is the matter and how to address the situation. The posture of the therapist should be that it is not known until and unless it emerges from the data collected from the clients as they Encounter each other and the situation or the context of the presenting problem(s). Most therapists, however, tend to need the reliance they establish in their clients on their perspective and knowledge about what the problem is, how it is to be explained and how it is to be treated. This is the reason that they have such awful results and why clients are in sessions with them over such long periods. They guess and apply common-sense knowledge through the whole process because they are not appropriately trained nor do they have the skills to engage the scientific process to do otherwise.

Often the therapist is operating on the basis of his or her predeterministic theory of the problem. A great number of books have been published which outline a variety of ways to treat family problems and marital conflicts. Many of these books are said to be guides through the labyrinth of strategies for resolving marital difficulties. Some purport to have investigated the seeds of the various problems and offer explanations for them. One work (Strean, 1985) argues a new theory which says, "that every chronic marital complaint is actually an unconscious wish."

What we need to remember always is that every problem has its own context in time and space, and that theory and therapy must be relevant and have direct utility. This is achieved only when the theory is grounded in the context of the client's problem, and when the therapy is grounded in the theory of the problems—presenting and real. There should be no disjuncture between the creation of theory and knowledge and the intervention and application of knowledge. This means that the knowledge being applied must be specific to the problem and its context. The above case demonstrates this process, and every case one assumes must follow this process if the outcome is to be effective.

Case Number Two

The next case to be presented has to do with a client who attempted to commit suicide. The case of the client was brought to my attention by a nurse after a seminar/workshop I conducted at a church. She said while I was talking, the woman came to mind and that she was certain, as I continued, that I could help this woman. I agreed with her and asked, "What is the woman's problem?"

"She attempted suicide four times, the last time she poured gasoline over herself and set herself afire. Before that she had cut her wrist twice and attempted an overdose."

I said, "Oh! How is she doing now?"

"She needs help. Let me give you her number so that you can give her a call." I quickly refused the offer of the number and asked that she give the person my number and suggested that she ask the person to call me. For three weeks I heard nothing about the matter until one day at the same church, the nurse asked if I had heard from the person, and I said no. It was not long after that the person contacted me and we started to work together. After getting in touch with her psychiatrist, it was determined that he had labeled her suicidal and depressed. He had placed her on a variety of drugs which were not doing much to help. It was also determined that she was abusing alcohol. After her release from the hospital, the woman had never left her house to do anything, including going out to pick up the newspaper. It became very obvious while talking with her that there were serious self-image problems. She had a fixed notion of how she should be and was not becoming.

Almost all attempts at suicide can cause the death of the individual if there is not discovery and intervention. All such persons tend to have problems with their view of themselves as objects. The Sociotherapist, however, has to determine the social context out of which the attempted suicide emerged. The attempted suicide behavior viewed as the presenting problem will provide directions for questions for disclosure, discovery and intervention. It is, therefore, logical for the psychosociotherapist to ask questions in the direction of the presenting problem. It is not useful to start treating the presenting problem without locating its roots which helps us to avoid maltreatment. Most therapists tend to immediately treat presenting problems without checking or even having a way to do so.

At the first session my concern had to do with establishing trust between the client and myself. She had to be comfortable with me and the questions I would ask for our sessions to be meaningful. The attempt is to ask questions in a way that the clients see and understand that they are carefully asked. The progression from general to specific, from impersonal to personal and from remote to intimate is significant to the success of the process. It is always important to bear in mind that questions are asked also in the direction of the presenting problem, and in the process, other relevant questions emerge. This point is especially true because GET does not promote a philosophical statement about human beings and the nature of human problems. It seems unwise to pre-determine the explanation of specific problems and their theoretical contexts. Again, it is crucial to make the point that GET simply provides a scientific way for discovering the nature of the social situation; explanations about the problems emerging from the social situation; and ways for making adjustments and different choices; changing concepts, behavior and the situation. The GET therapist must always remember that GET is an approach which allows for the discovery of the problem(s) and its context which must be addressed theoretically and therapeutically if the problem is to be solved. The treatment and the therapeutic techniques employed in the process are dictated by what is theoretically discovered about the problem and its context. Therefore, any approach which promotes a predetermined theory or explanation about a problem creates disjuncture between theory and therapy which is dysfunctional to the resolution of the problem.

Pointed questions and those questions that are regarded personal must be asked in the process of discovery.

My first question to this client addressed her family.

T.	Tell me about your family.
Susan.	I have no children, but I have a husband who really does not understand me.
T.	Tell me more about your husband.
Susan.	He's Asian and quiet. He does not say much and he works very hard to achieve. He is a kind person but distant in our relationship. He is a very nice person and very kind. He provides for me very well.
T.	Do you all plan to have children?
Susan.	Yes, later we plan to have two or three children.
T.	What about sisters and brothers?
Susan.	Yeah, I have a sister and two brothers. The brothers are in another state, but that sister is here making my life miserable.
T.	You refer to her as that sister?
Susan.	She is a mess. She worries me to death.
T.	How so? Tell me how she worries you.

Susan.	Well, it's a real problem dealing with my sister. She makes me feel like I'm nothing.
T.	How long have you felt this way about your contacts with your sister?
Susan.	Ever since she and I had a falling out.
T.	What does she do that causes you concern?
Susan.	She treats me as though I am nothing, and no good. She runs me into the ground.
T.	How did you perceive her before the falling out?
Susan.	She was a kind person who cared about people. I never thought she would turn on me the way she has.
T.	Did you admire her and the qualities you just identified?
Susan.	Yes. She was my idol. I saw a lot of good qualities in her and wanted to be like her.
T.	Is she older than you?
Susan.	Yes, four and a half years older.
T.	Are you disappointed with the situation the way it is?
Susan.	I'm not just disappointed; I'm often depressed. When I first attempted suicide we were involved in a big falling out. She called me all kinds of negative names. I felt so hurt and rejected by my sister who I thought was a great person.
T.	Have you ever discussed the matter with her?
Susan.	She would not talk with me in a way that we could get at the problem.
T.	Why?
Susan.	She would cut me off when I tried to talk to her about our relationship and her negative comments to me.
T.	How often does she make these comments?
Susan.	Everytime she comes over to my house.
T.	Why do you continue to let her in the house?
Susan.	I don't know. Maybe I am hopeful she would be different.
T.	Have you taken her comments seriously?
Susan.	I think so because I feel badly everytime she leaves. I would feel so sad and depressed that I would want to do away with myself.

T.	She has an impact on you. She is evidently very significant to you!
Susan.	I guess so.
T.	Do you have to guess?
Susan.	Well, no. She is and has always been significant to me. Now it seems to be affecting me adversely.
T.	What do you think is the problem?
Susan.	How she sees me.
T.	How do you see yourself? Is it different from how your sister sees you?
Susan.	I guess so because she has a negative attitude toward me and she thinks I am hopeless.
T.	Has she ever told you that you are hopeless?
Susan.	Many, many times she has said those exact words to me— you are hopeless, or you are a hopeless case.
T.	How long ago did she start telling you this?
Susan.	About three years ago. Every time we got into a heated discussion, she would close the discussion or argument with that statement.
T.	Other than trying to talk to her about it, have you talked to anyone else?
Susan.	No. I would talk to my husband about the arguments we would have, and he would simply ask why we could not get along.
T.	What would be your reply?
Susan.	I would just say she is a mean person and miserable in her own life.
T.	Has he ever blamed you for any of it?
Susan.	Maybe in his mind, but he has never said he blamed me!
T.	Tell me how it all happens. Give me an example of an incident—how it starts, and how it ends. I don't want details, just provide some sense of the situation.
Susan.	Okay, I'll try. She would call and ask me what I'm doing, or even how I'm doing. Before she is through talking, she would invite herself over.
T.	What would you have to say about her self-invitation?

Susan.	Nothing after a while because she would come whether I object or not. Anyway, when she get there, we would talk like sisters and human beings for a while, then she would get off on me about something. By then she would not go until she had had her piece and had run me into the ground. One time, or there were times when I would counter her arguments and statements, but she always gets the last word.
T.	Are you saying that she dominated the situation all the time?
Susan.	All the time. It would drive me up the wall sometimes.
T.	You looked up to her as a big sister, and respected her views on matters.
Susan.	I would say so.
T.	How did you regard her views of you?
Susan.	At first I did not pay much attention to what she said about me, but they seemed so constant that I started thinking about them after she left. After a while, I was crying about the matter and began drinking hard.
T.	Did drinking help?
Susan.	No. It made the situation worse because she now had another thing to get down on me about. It got to the point that I did not care what happened to me. I got so sad and depressed that I stopped doing anything around the house. All I did was drink alcohol. Two of the times I tried to commit suicide were right after having a run-in with her.
T.	What do you see as the problem?
Susan.	Taking her views about me too seriously.
T.	What about how you see yourself and its importance?
Susan.	Seems as though her opinion of me is more important to me than my opinion of me.
T.	How could you deal with this conflict in views and difference in the importance of opinion?
Susan.	I can stop her from coming over to my place, and I can talk less to her on the phone.
T.	Would that solve the problem in total?

Susan.	No. Seemingly, I will have to pay more attention to my opinion of myself rather than giving her opinion so much credit.
T.	Do you believe how she has characterized you?
Susan.	I'm not sure. She has called me so many things, and has said I am this and that, that I might have come to believe some of it, if not most of it.
T.	How do you think you can get her to change her views?
Susan.	Impossible. It's hopeless.
T.	That means?
Susan.	That means I have to put more emphasis on my opinions of me.
T.	Do you know what they are?
Susan.	I think so. Yeah, I think I know.
T.	Identifying them is a beginning, do you see?
Susan.	True. I can do it.
T.	What is next?
Susan.	Believing them.
T.	What if they resemble what she thinks or says about you?
Susan.	Anything I don't like I will try to change it.
T.	Whenever one accepts how others view him or her, the others have control over their thinking and their behavior.
Susan.	I want to control my own thinking and my own behavior. I sure don't want my sister doing it.
T.	Would you say you allowed her to tell you how you should see yourself?
Susan.	I guess so. At least I can see where I allowed what she thought of me to affect me in a bad way.
T.	What do you think you have to do about it?
Susan.	I know I don't want to attempt to hurt myself anymore. I also realize that I am not what she says I am.
T.	Rejecting her views of you is the first step. What's next?
Susan.	Well, you tell me.
T.	What is suggested by what we have discovered?
Susan.	I have to accept myself and create my own sense of importance.

T.	How are you going to avoid your sister's contact and negative input?
Susan.	I will tell her and be firm about the matter. If she does not stop, I will take whatever action is necessary to establish distance between us.
T.	We can also work on identifying the qualities you think are positive and good about you.
Susan.	That should be real interesting.
T.	Your assignment for next week will be identifying several of such qualities. We will look at each one at the next session and how you may develop a style to convey each when you interact with your sister or any other person.
Susan.	That sounds good. I guess I don't know how to convey my good qualities. I know I have them, but . . .
T.	We have work to do for our next session.

What is always important in GET is that the clients are encouraged to disclose or search themselves to discover and participate in determining what is to be done. The clients must discover what the problems are and it becomes easier to determine what to do. Their willingness and persistence in doing what must be done is usually the real concern. This client went on to do the assignments and developed a positive concept of herself and developed various styles appropriate to the conveyance of the several properties or qualities of herself.

Clinical Sociologists are also invited to work with problems of the community. In this case, a community-based organization was concerned about crime and the fear of community members expressed in becoming victims.

In every case, the Clinical Sociologist must be especially concerned with devising ways to get clients to disclose and discover. Further, how to determine in the process of discovery that the presenting problem is or is not the real problem is also a special challenge for the Sociotherapist.

Case Number Three

The fear expressed by community members has changed the behavior of almost all community members. Psychotherapists had been consulted about the matter and coping programs were recommended; various sessions were conducted with community members and a survey was conducted to determine the concern of citizens regarding crime and the fear of crime.

The Clinical Sociologist who was called in to conduct the survey discovered that citizens regarded police protection as a severe problem in their neighborhood. Crime was also a severe problem to them and their fear was great. Citizens feared the police; complained about their response time and the downtown nature of policing in their community. The need for anti-crime seminars and workshops in the neighborhood was expressed along with the desire to support neighborhood watch programs.

The group sessions that provided the information were conducted by the Clinical Sociologist who met with ten different members of the community at a specified location twice per week. This was done until members stopped coming. Nothing really new was said by the different groups, but the repetition of certain ideas and themes suggested that the matters discussed were valid. The last group session dealt with a review of what was discovered and the various intervention strategies.

T.   You all and others have come to the conclusion that there is too much crime in your neighborhood?

John.   It gets so bad sometime we don't know what to do. And we've been here so long we don't want to move, and some can't move even if they wanted to.

T.   Kind of locked in aren't you?

Pete.   That's the feeling you have around here. But something can be done if the community wanted to.

T.   Do you think the community wants to do something about the crime problem?

Pete.   Well, let me put it this way. You wander sometimes.

Maude.   I tend to agree with Pete. We tend to talk about the problems more than we organize to do anything about it. And when we do anything, we argue about how it's being done. We never stick to anything. I am afraid of what's happening in my area of the neighborhood. Every time you turn around, somebody is robbing somebody.

T.   Are you afraid of the criminal activities?

Maude.   Yeah. I try to watch my house and keep myself to myself. I also have some more locks on my doors.

Jane.   What I'm concerned about is how long the cops take to get here when you call them. Man it's like forever waiting on them to come.

T.   What seems to be the problem?

Jane.   They don't seem to care.

Henry.   They know where the call is coming from. So if it comes from this neighborhood, they take their time. If the call comes from, say "the man's" neighborhood, they get there in a hurry.

T.   They, the police, respond differently to different calls base on the neighborhood; that's what you are saying?

Henry.   That's it. You got it.

T.   Do you feel protected in your neighborhood, Henry?

Henry.   Yeah, but not because of the police, but what actions I have taken, know what I mean?

There was laughter. Seemingly they all knew exactly what he meant and it did not only have to do with putting extra locks on his door.

T.   I get where you're coming from.

Henry.   Ha, got to do what you got to do.

T.   Let's look at what we have. Crime is rampant; fear is widespread, and the neighbors do not feel safe from criminals and even from some police. With all this information, what have we discovered about the issue of crime in the community?

Tate.   I've been sitting here saying nothing, but what all this says to me is that we don't have any control on the matter. Crime is all over us, and we are afraid. The police who are to protect us and prevent this mess are discourteous to everybody, sometimes abusive and rude in just dealing with the average citizen. I thought this police/community relations thing would do something, but things done got worse around here. Folk are doing their thing right out in the open. They ain't hiding nothing. We need something right here in our community that will deal with these problems.

T.   You have summed it all up, Brother Tate. What do you think will accomplish what is discovered to be the problems?

Tate.   I don't know off the top of my head, but we need a service that is in the community like we have banks, food stores and other such service stations, we need a police station or department in our community; maybe that will do it.

T.   Interesting, because crime is low in communities where there is a permanent physical presence of the police. Tate, you mentioned control. You think that is important to deal with crime in this community?

Tate.   I think so. We have to do it. Nobody is going to do it for us. In fact, I don't think they care or even want to do anything.

T.   Any mechanism that is established to deal with crime, the fear of crime and protection and safety must be accountable to the community. It must offer protection to the members of the community and their property and also prevent the occurrence and continuance of crime.

Bob.   A lot of other things got to go along with the mechanism as you put it. But I can see a whole lot of benefits to us if we have a department for policing right here in the community. We would not have to wait until the police felt like coming out here when you call them. We can have prompt responses and twenty-four hour visibility of the police.

T.	Who would you all want to staff the station or department?
Tate.	We have a whole lot of folk around here to staff the place. We have young, old, and in-between.
T.	That means those who run the station should come from the community. That sounds like community control, Tate. What do you say, Bob?
Bob.	Sounds that way, but it's sounding too good to be true. We may finally have something here; I do hope so.
Tate.	I think so. It's going to be up to us to make it work.
T.	A proposal will have to be developed to present to the City Council with the police chief's endorsement. People and programs will have to be identified. There are para-medics and para-legal, and we can create para-police for the station. They can work different shifts under the supervision of regularly trained police officers. It would be good if they lived in the community also, but it might not be possible at the outset. After a while, many of the para-police can be further trained to take over the station.
Tate.	How could the community get involved?
Jane.	I think we can get all these community agencies involved. The NAACP; the Urban League and the others. We can have a representative from each one to make up a Board to supervise the operations and plan programs to assist the community and for training the workers. Refresher courses, workshops seminars, survivals hotline and other such things can be developed. You know what I was thinking while you all were talking; the thing I see here that is also good is that when you have people working in the station from the community, they already know the community and know what's happening in the community.
T.	A Supervisor Board seems to be a good idea. I think we are doing great in dealing with this problem. All we have to do now is put together our discoveries and what they say about what will get the job done.

The agreement among the group was to identify a few persons from the various groups to write the proposed plan of Action. The cost and benefits were to be included. The members were to find a most appropriate place to house the station's operation.

One of the problems of dealing effectively with the issue of crime is the many attempts to treat the problem without locating and examining its context. At those meetings we attempted to discover the community's context of crime and allowed what was discovered to dictate to us ways of treating the problem. This chapter is simply designed to show how to get clients to disclose, discover, and devise plans of action to treat and change the situation and resolve some of the problems.

Crucial Observation

The primary focus of this work is the presentation of GET as a sociodiagnostic and sociotherapeutic approach and process in Clinical Sociology. Sociology had always demonstrated itself as the scientific study of society and of human behavior within the context of group life. We view group life as human beings interacting and relating to and with one another. Clinical Sociology, therefore, has to do with the scientific (discovery) study and treatment of group life and of humans interacting and relating with one another in group life. GET is an approach which establishes a process and mechanism that defines a method for the discovery, identification and treatment of those problems of living within the context of group life. As is shown in this work, the problems can be at the micro level as well as the macro level. No doubt, there are other sociological or sociological social psychological approaches that need to be developed that will have the potential for discovery, identification and treatment of problems of living in group life. Clinical Sociology will not be able to maintain its credibility in the absence of developed and refined sociodiagnostic and sociotherapeutic approaches and techniques for discovery of data and explanations of problems relative to that data and the emergence of ways from the data for the treatment of those problems.

In order for us to develop adequate and appropriate diagnosis and therapies for human services, we have to place the human being within a social location. The task for clinical purposes is to understand the creation or emergence of the social location or situation and its importance and significance relative to the persons involved. One of the many reasons for the failure in dealing with problems of living is that there has been the exclusion and ignoring of the sociological nature of persons' problems. The experiences of the individual are formed and structured by groups. The group experience is the context for individual choices. Language, communication, interacting and relating are group processes. Schools, families, churches, the workplaces, prisons, the freeways and highways, and the market places are all social settings. Neighborhoods, communities, cities, and societies are not individual creations; they are the collective creation of group life. There are, therefore, sociological components and a sociological perspective that have direct bearing on discovery and therapy. Discovery and therapy derived exclusively from any other perspective is logically incorrect and inadequate.

All therapeutic models have explicit or implicit views about human beings and the human condition. Some views are totally false and some have partial truths about human beings and the human situation. It is crucial that therapists operate from a correct perspective of human beings and the human situation. Human beings have the ability to make choices. This ability is exercised interacting and relating with one another and in creating social situations. The choices of the human being, or the exercise thereof, may be limited by circumstances that are not totally controlled by the individual; this simply limits the individual choices.

GET requires a broad perspective of society and social behavior that provides a point of view for the determination and treatment of specific problems. Once the specific problems and their contexts are discovered, any appropriate technique or set of techniques dictated by what is discovered are used to achieve the goal. Nothing is really known except the problem presented to the sociotherapist and no predetermined explanation is held except the broad theoretical perspective that provides direction for the discovery process with the presenting problem as a point of departure. The explanations or theoretical perspectives about the specific problems and their contexts emerge during the sociodiagnostic process which also tells the sociotherapist and the clients what must be done to achieve adjustments and changes. This is why we argue that therapy must be grounded in theory and theory must be grounded in the data disclosed by the client and discovered from their social situations or contexts. This must be done in order for the explanations of problems and the treatment of problems to have direct utility, and to avoid disjuncture between the discovery, intervention, and application. Grounded theory facilitates the identification of human and organizational problems and suggests possible strategies for solution.

In GET, there are techniques used for discovering what the real problems are, and there are techniques or approaches used that are dictated by what is discovered during the sociodiagnostic process that are used for treatment and achieving adjustments and changes in choices, beliefs, thinking behavior and situations.

As is now understood, GET stresses discovery and understanding first, and intervention and application afterwards. Such techniques for discovery and understanding the problems and situations of the clients are: Encounter, Confrontation, Interpretation, Analysis and Assessment, Interviewing, Active listening, Clarification, Situational or Contextual Analysis, Explaining, Dialoging with Self and Others, Behavior Analysis, Probing, Reflection on Feelings, and Exploration of the Social Dynamics, Patterns and Styles of Interacting, Relating, and the Presenting of Self. The sociotherapeutic techniques that might be dictated by the sociodiagnostic process are: Cognitive Restructuring, Challenging Beliefs, Role Taking, Role Playing, Resocialization, Role Reversal, Reflection of Feelings, Non-verbal Actions, Contracts, Formulation of Action Plans, Modeling, Homework Assignments and Behavioral and Situational or Contextual changes. Any other techniques for discovery or change will emerge during the sociodiagnostic and sociotherapeutic processes. The sociotherapist has to be alert and observant, ready to shift from on technique to another as the discovery dictates.

Case Number Four

The case of the Cheaks was brought to my attention when Mrs. Cheaks called to make an appointment to see me. She said she had heard me on radio, and was impressed with my comments on the various issues callers raised regarding marital and family problems. When she came to the office for the first session, she was without her husband. I started the session by telling Mrs. Cheaks what I did, and how I practiced counseling. I asked if her husband knew she was seeking counseling and she informed me she had invited him to come and he agreed to be present the next time. I quoted my fee and we agreed to start the next week with her husband present. A time was agreed upon and she left. The next session started as soon as I explained to the husband how I planned to conduct the session. We agreed that Mrs. Cheaks would be first when I explained my approach to talk to each one individually before I counseled with them together. The diagnostic process started with Mrs. Cheaks.

Swan.	Do you mind if I refer to you by your first name?
Simona.	That's fine. I'd prefer that.
Swan.	Thanks. What is your view of the situation you wish to address?
Simona.	I feel like my husband is withdrawing from me. He's not how he was when we first got married.
Swan.	Was he more intimate?
Simona.	Yes. He was attentive and caring.
Swan.	Do you think he is changing in his feeling towards you?
Simona.	Yes, but he says no, that he's just tired and is working too much.
Swan.	I notice from the information you shared with me last week, you both are pharmacists. Do you work together?
Simona.	No. He works at a shopping center, and I work at a hospital.
Swan.	Do you all have conflicts in schedules that interfere with your spending time together?
Simona.	Yes, but we have some time to ourselves.

Swan.	What you all do during these times?
Simona.	Nothing really. We may watch a movie together, or go to the store, that's all.
Swan.	What else would you like him to do with you?
Simona.	Anything that makes me feel he still cares about me, and wants to be around me.
Swan.	Have you told him about this?
Simona.	Yes.
Swan.	Have you asked him to do something specific?
Simona.	Not really, he should know what to do.
Swan.	Is his withdrawal more evident now than before?
Simona.	I think so.
Swan.	How?
Simona.	He is staying out later, and making a lot of excuses.
Swan.	How have you responded to your perception of his behavior?
Simona.	I decided to leave him alone and stay to myself. I even thought about asking him to leave until I heard you on radio. If he is going to treat me as if I'm not apart of his life, then he can go.
Swan.	Would you be surprise and afraid if he is being distracted by something or someone which is causing him to disengage from intimate interaction with you?
Simona.	Yes, but if that is what is happening, then he should tell me and we can decide what to do.
Swan.	Do you have a question or a comment at this point?
Simona.	No, not really.

Mrs. Cheaks went out and invited Mr. Cheaks to come in. As he sat I said:

Swan.	That did not take long, did it?
Mr. Cheaks.	Not at all. Actually, I did think it would take longer.
Swan.	We will spend about the same amount of time together before we invite Mrs. Cheaks back.
Mr. Cheaks	That's fine.

Swan.	What is your view of what is happening in your relationship with your wife, Simona?
Mr. Cheaks.	She's not as affectionate as she used to be and she's putting on too much weight.
Swan.	What are you feeling about her weight? By the way, may I call you Charles?
Mr. Cheaks.	Sure. About her weight. Well it does not make her look attractive. She is getting out of shape and I feel distracted by the way she looks. My emotions are dead.
Swan.	Have you told her how you feel about her weight?
Mr. Cheaks.	Not really. I made comments a couple of times. She seems sensitive about the matter.
Swan.	So she does not really know how you really feel?
Mr. Cheaks.	Not really.
Swan.	What do you think she would do if she knew?
Mr. Cheaks.	(He smiles). I don't know really.
Swan.	Take a guess or two.
Mr. Cheaks.	Get mad and withdraw.
Swan.	Has she done this before because of something she did not like?
Mr. Cheaks.	A couple of times.
Swan.	How did you feel when this happen?
Mr. Cheaks.	I could not communicate with her. I felt uncomfortable in the house in her presence.
Swan.	What would you do during this time?
Mr. Cheaks.	I would leave, or go in a room by myself.
Swan.	What would she do?
Mr. Cheaks.	Nothing. Just stay sad.
Swan.	Let's get Simona in here.

Charles went to invite Simona in as I arranged the chairs to face each other for the encounter. I asked them to sit facing each other so that they can look at each other as they talk to each other as I direct the encounter. I instructed them that I would stop the encounter at various times to highlight a point, engage them in interpretation of what went on, establish clarity of a matter, identify problems, and discover explanation.

Swan.	Simona tell Charles why you are here. Now tell him not me. I want you to talk to each other. Have and exchange and I will jump in to keep it on track, or shift it, etc. Tell Charles why you're here.
Simona.	I felt that we needed help in our relationship.
Charles.	We?
Simona.	Yes, we Charles. That's the main problem, he . . . you think I have a problem.
Charles.	You're the one that's complaining.
Simona.	But I've told you what is my problem.
Swan.	Tell him now.
Simona.	Ok. Well, you, I feel like you are withdrawing from me. We don't spend enough time together. We don't do anything together anymore.
Swan.	You all spent time together before Charles?
Charles.	Yes, we did.
Swan.	Tell Simona why things have changed. Tell her how you see the situation.
Charles.	Well, a few years ago she . . . you just seem to let yourself go. You have let your weight get out of hand and I don't like how you look.
Simona.	Oh, so you think I'm too fat?
Charles.	Yes, and it turns me off. I cannot get close and be affectionate to you with all that weight in the way.
Simona.	I have always been on the heavy side.
Charles.	Not as big as you are now.
Simona.	Maybe, but that is not the reason you are withdrawing from the relationship.
Swan.	Do you know of a reason why Charles is withdrawing Simona?
Simona.	I guess he's being distracted by his work or something.
Swan.	Could it be someone?
Simona.	Could be.

Swan.	Ask him.
Simona.	Right now?
Swan.	Yes. Do you feel afraid of what you might find out.
Simona.	Somewhat. I do not want to know the truth.
Swan.	I can ask him, but you don't want me to do that, do you?
Simona.	You can, but I guess I can do it.
Swan.	Do it, and remember to keep looking at each other.
Simona.	Are you being distracted by something or someone?
Charles.	I do work late and all that, but I could cut that out if you were more affectionate. You know I need that from a woman.
Simona.	I can be affectionate, but if you keep withdrawing, I am not going to chase you down to be affectionate.
Swan.	Have you got any affection from Simona in the past month?
Charles.	Not really.
Swan.	Did you hear what Charles said about needing affection?
Simona.	Yes.
Swan.	Do you want to ask him a question or two about that?
Simona.	What do you mean?
Swan.	He said he needs affection. He must have it and you are not supplying it.
Simona.	You mean he must be getting it somewhere else?
Swan.	Do you think you should ask him?
Charles.	She doesn't have to ask me, I can tell her. It's a simple yes.
Swan.	Tell her about it.
Charles.	Well, there is this lady at the store who is very loving and affectionate. She knows how to treat a man. It started a few years ago, but at first it was just talk and nothing to it, but later on she started really caring and I simply responded. You know what I mean?
Simona.	No not really. What about your family, me and you.
Charles.	We are still together.
Simona.	But you are having a relationship with another woman.
Swan.	How do you feel Simona?
Simona.	Betrayed, angry. It's a big let down.

Swan.	Tell him. Tell Charles.
Simona.	I feel angry and betrayed. I feel like a big let down.
Charles.	I'm sorry, but I just responded.
Simona.	Just responded! That's how you would behave if any woman related to you? Where is your self control? I can't believe this.
Swan.	What is it you cannot believe?
Simona.	That he is so weak to fall for any woman who shows him some affection.
Swan.	What did the weight matter have to do with your response to the other woman?
Charles.	Nothing really. Maybe I was not getting enough love and affection from Simona.
Swan.	Could you terminate the response today if you wanted to do so?
Charles.	Sure.
Swan.	Would Simona have to do something to help you?
Charles.	Yes and no.
Swan.	Explain.
Charles	Well I could just stop and that will mean I will have to do without the things she does for me. On the other hand if you would be more affectionate and loving, I could make it back.
Swan.	How does that sound Simona?
Simona.	I don't know. I feel so hurt.
Swan.	Do you love Simona?
Charles.	Yes.
Swan.	Do you think she knows it?
Charles.	I think so.
Swan.	Ask her.
Charles.	Do you know that I love you?
Simona.	I don't know anymore. How could you do what you are doing?
Charles.	Need the affection.
Swan.	Is the weight the problem or an excuse?
Charles.	Maybe an excuse.
Swan.	Do you want the relationship?

Charles.	Sure. Yes indeed. We get along real well otherwise.
Swan.	Do you want the relationship Simona?
Simona.	Not if there is another woman.
Swan.	Tell him what you want him to do.
Simona.	Give her up.
Swan.	Would you do this for the relationship?
Charles.	Yes, but she would have to help me.
Swan.	Tell how she can do this.
Charles.	Show me some affection. I do think she could do so better if she took off some pounds.
Swan.	Tell her what you just told me.
Charles.	I want you to show me some affection, and I want you to take off some weight.
Swan.	Do you hear what he is saying?
Simona.	I think so.
Swan.	Tell him what you heard him say.
Simona.	First, you want me to give you more affection and get rid of some weight.
Swan.	Do you hear him say that the weight is in the way of his warming up to you?
Simona.	I guess so, but why.
Swan.	Ask him.
Simona.	Why is the weight thing so important?
Charles.	I like you better with less weight. You are more flexible and I can handle you better. Plus you can handle yourself better in intimate situations.
Simona.	I see. So you think I can't be affectionate to you as I am?
Charles.	You have not been.
Simona.	That's because you withdrew. Now I know why.
Swan.	Tell him what you are willing to do. He has indicated what he will do.
Simona.	I can give you affection, and you know that, and I don't like my weight either, so that's no problem. I knew your working late was distracting from the relationship, but this other lady was only an occasional guess.
Swan.	Would that continue to be a problem?

Simona.	No if it's over, or will be over soon.
Charles.	That's no problem, there were no expectations.
Swan.	Do you love Charles?
Simona.	Yes, I love him.
Swan.	Do you love Simona?
Charles.	Yes, sure I do.
Swan.	Are you willing to make a commitment to what you need to do?
Charles.	Yes.
Simona.	Yes.
Swan.	Have we looked at everything you wanted to deal with?
Charles.	Yes.
Simona.	Yes, and more.
Swan.	Let us look at what we have discovered. Charles, you started withdrawing and recognizing the affectionate responses of this other lady as you recognized that Simona was gaining weight. You accepted these responses from your co-worker and explained you acceptance of her affection on the basis that Simona was gaining weight and as such was incapable of being as affectionate as you wished. At the same time, Simona, you withdrew because of his late working hours and a suspicion that there was someone else. You felt rejected and got careless. Is that the situation so far?
Charles.	Yes.
Simona.	Yes.
Swan.	Charles, you need the affection of your wife to feel special and somebody important. Your sense of worth is tied up in the expression of love and affection from the woman with whom you have a relationship. It makes you feel good when you are shown love and affection.
	Simona, you can function without such expressions and not seek these from another man. But you withdraw and keep your feelings inside. You told me during our introductions before the sessions that you have been married thirteen years. Are you tired of the relationship?
Charles.	No.

313

Simona.	No.
Swan.	Do you agree with my view of what was discovered about the situation?
Simona.	I agree.
Charles.	That seems to be accurate.
Swan.	Do you want to add anything?
Simona.	No.
Charles.	No.
Swan.	Do you have a set aside time to talk about family problems?
Simona.	Not really.
Swan.	This is the first thing I am going to recommend you put in place. A special agreed upon time to deal with issues in the family. In fact, I want to put that in place today. What time is best?
Simona.	Well, we are home during the week-end, so Sunday is a good time.
Swan.	About what time on Sunday?
Charles.	Between ten and twelve.
Swan.	Select an hour.
Charles.	Eleven to twelve.
Swan.	Is that ok Simona?
Simona.	Sure.
Swan.	The next thing I will suggest is that we work on some non-verbal gestures that are affectionate in expression to reestablish emotional connection, or to build on what is there already. Initially, we can start here in the office for two sessions and then you can continue them at home whenever you get together. Getting into a weight loss program will help and can be scheduled at a time when both of you can go. Make this a joint effort. Something you are both doing or encouraging one another to do. This means that you will have to schedule specific time to spend together for the next several weeks. Hopefully, this could become a part of your family situation. With no children to account for, this should not present too great a problem. How do you feel about what I have outlined?

Charles.	Great.
Simona.	Good. I hope it works because I am tired of playing around.
Swan.	Let us meet here next week at the same time for the next session. Here is your assignment. Identify and write down seven things you like about each other which you don't want to change. Okay!
Charles.	Okay.
Simona.	Okay, and thanks
Swan.	See you next week.

Sociological Practice and Sociology: Survival and Viability of a Discipline

Chapter 13

*   *   *

Sociological Practice and Sociology: The Survival and Viability of a Discipline

Attempts to "save" the discipline of sociology from stagnation and irrelevance have captured the concerns and efforts of many sociologists, especially sociological practitioners, as well as some academic sociologists. A number of issues with establishment sociology have been identified along with what is believed would successfully address the problem. The activities of sociological practitioners have brought into question the limitations of the discipline of sociology calling for the inclusion, promotion, recognition and advancement of sociology practice. Others have suggested various models of sociological practice to be employed, including social engineering which is designed to make the discipline more useful and relevant.

What is offered in this work is a view of the role of the sociological practitioner as a scientist-practitioner that necessitates the integration of the essential elements of sociology in a parasitical manner to fulfill the mandate of the sequential process of "knowing and doing." This would resolve the disconnect problem among theory, research, and practice. The practice-continuum conceptualizes the process where explanations are driven by data, and application, intervention, and practice are driven by the explanations. Specific contextual data is the essential base and its context is the foundation of specific knowledge resulting from the practice-continuum.

A number of things are suggested in order for sociological practice to be viable and sociology to enhance its usefulness and relevance. Identifying and claiming territorial rights to sociological knowledge; enhancing the training of sociologists to emphasize equally sociological knowledge and skills for solving problems and meeting the needs of the community and society; identifying primary and secondary user of sociological knowledge, and closing ranks until sociological practice is properly grounded and well established, to name just a few.

Introduction

The Key elements of any discipline, especially a social science discipline, are theory, methods of research, and knowledge—the body of which defines its territory, its explanatory and methodological boundaries. However, sociology never really developed an application or a truly practice element which seems very difficult to establish at this time. Although the discipline of sociology began in America as a field of study concerned with the application of knowledge to matters that have to do with the improvement and enhancement of society and the lives of humans, it quickly became involved in competing with other sciences, social, physical and natural, in the creation of knowledge for the sake of knowledge. For a new and growing discipline, the attempt to understand the social world was essential, however, a more active involvement in creating knowledge, via a relationship between theory and research, for the purpose of intervention, application, and practice to reduce and alleviate social problems and to improve the conditions of society would have avoided or prevented the disconnect presently evident among theory, research, and practice (Tomasi 1998).

Efforts To Save The Discipline

Attempts to save the discipline from stagnation and irrelevance have the attention of well established academic sociologists who are trying to rescue and liberate sociology from its history of repression, oppression, and philosophical idealism. The resistance of establishment sociology to give recognition to sociological practice—applied and clinical—has impeded the discipline immeasurably.

There are those who recognize the dilemma in which the discipline has found itself and are removing the blinders in order to creatively address the problem. What must be realized is that knowledge can be created demonstrating scientific legitimacy to enhance an increase the territory of the discipline, and at the same time establish utility and viability of sociology and sociological practice. The knowledge has to be created specifically for the purpose of social intervention and application, or with the express purpose of addressing specific human social problems. In this sense, there is no need for scholars to divorce themselves from roles as change agents, or insulate themselves from the social, political, and socio-economic context, and create socially detached knowledge for its own sake (Feagin and Vera, 2002, Weinberg, 2002). Social practice activities of sociologists, grounded in sociological knowledge, are broad, from changing individuals, situations, and society; and are socially responsible. The very fact that we believe and know that there are things, conditions, patterns of behavior and a social trend that must be changed suggests that we can create the knowledge and develop there from the strategies appropriate to the particular situation. To our thinking, sociology is in the midst of an identity challenge, if not a crisis. We must reframe and rethink the identity of sociology if it is to claim the prominence and creditibility it deserves. We can start by including as part of the statement of identification and definition that "knowledge/knowing is the beginning of application/doing, and application/doing is the completion of knowledge/knowing." All too long we have learned on the notion that knowledge is power, and so we created knowledge, but failed to realize that knowledge put into action (application) is power. There would be no need to address questions regarding relevancy if the knowledge we created had immediate and specific applicability. Sociology and sociologists face a real challenge when they are asked, at this point in the development and history of the discipline, to answer questions such as—"what do sociologists do?" "Of what use is sociology?" "Whom do sociologists serve?" "And where do sociologists work?" Many students and most of the general public are still not sure of the distinction made between common sense knowledge and sociological knowledge.

L. Alex Swan

Sociological Territory/Boundary and the Practice-Continuum

Sociology as the study of group life and human behavior in society has much to offer the society, but it must liberate itself from routines and start growing the area of sociological practice. In this way, sociology will be felt and have its impact on the lives of individuals, groups, communities, organizations, industries and societies. Bill Hauser (1999) argues that "we must continue to cultivate applicable sociological knowledge ... we must make sure that our sociological tools are applicable to those who need them ... we must strive to find applicable solutions, whether they are helping a business create new products, helping an agency improve its progress, or helping society deal with its problems" (p. 17). Jim Hougland (1989) reasoned "that while all social science disciplines have something to contribute to policy decisions, sociology's emphasis on structure, its efforts through (sociological) social psychology to understand individuals and groups in their social context, and the efforts of social demographers to understand changing population trends can provide broad, societally based insights that are unlikely to come from other disciplines" (p. 225).

This is a territorial matter which has not really been seriously addressed. We have paid lip-service to arguing territorial rights. This is one of the reasons that other professionals attempt to use sociological knowledge without giving proper credit to sociology and sociologists. Our claim to sociological territory is best made and demonstrated in practice. Sociological concepts and perspectives must not be distorted, and when done by others, we must dispute and challenge it forthwith.

Jonathan H. Turner (2001) argues that "sociological practice and clinical sociology need to be supplemented by an engineering wing in the discipline. Engineering is ultimately, the application of general theoretical principles to concrete problems and there is no reason why sociology cannot also be an engineering discipline. There is nothing inherent in the subject matter of sociology that prevents this engineering orientation from emerging" (p. 99). Turner explains that "engineering involves the application of knowledge about properties of the universe to practical problems of building something or in many cases tearing something down. Whether a road, building, port, canal, bridge, heating plants, electrical system, or whatever is being built, engineers try to say what is possible to build and how to build it" (p. 101). Turner provides several points that he believes would allow for an "engineering wing" in sociology. "The key to engineering, then is having (1) powerful theoretical principles, (2) confidence that these principles are correct as a result of systematic empirical application to real-world problems, and (3) knowledge of how to translate empirical findings and theoretical principles into rules of thumb that can be communicated to fellow engineers". Making sociology an engineering discipline is dependent on each of the steps functioning all together to produce "quality social engineering" (p. 101).

Melvin L. Fein (2001) agrees with many of the points made by Turner, especially that theory and practice need to be better integrated. However, he argues that "social engineering has more negative baggage than Turner supposes." He asserts that "it assumes an ability to control events that is normally lacking and which cannot be attained by following "rules of thumb". Fein concludes "that the sort of social engineering that Turner recommends is a fantasy." Although it might be difficult to accomplish, he suggests instead a "reflexive sociology that utilizes the difficulties encountered in practice to shine a light on its theories than to revise and retest these in the crucible of practice." This position holds out the promise of a cumulative science and many more enlightened applications than Turner's suggestion which is "too arrogant to serve as a paradigm for actual interventions" which he believes "is an invitation to petty totalitarianism" (p. 121, 125).

Robert J. Dotlzer also agrees with Turner that the various "wings of sociology (theorist, researcher methodologist, and practitioner) need to be better integrated." He offers, however, "major revisions to Turner's engineering manifesto." Dotzler presents a couple of reasons that Turner's social engineering is important for the discipline of sociology. The first is the encouragement it gives to the various wings of sociology to build bridges to address the "disconnect." The other reason is the significance sociological practice has in the activities of sociologists. The question that begs addressing is: "would social engineering facilitate the disconnect and achieve the integration of the work of sociological theorists, methodologists, researchers, and practitioners?" It would seem that the role of the sociological practitioner, especially the clinical sociologist, must change from a narrow perspective to one as a scientist-practitioner which necessitates the successful integration, in a parasitical manner, to fulfill the mandate of the sequential process of "knowing and doing." This process and posture would solve the disconnect among theory, research, and practice (Swan 2005).

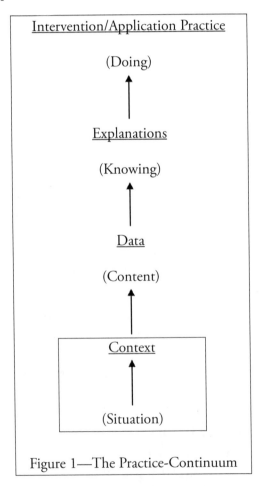

Figure 1—The Practice-Continuum

The practice-continuum (Figure 1) helps to conceptualize the process. Explanations are driven by data; and application, intervention and practice are driven by the explanations. Data is the essential element, and its context is the foundation of the practice-continuum. It is expected that within the context of the continuum the clinical sociologist or the sociological practitioner will have some knowledge of theoretical perspectives, research methodologies, and therapeutic and application skills and strategies. Even though explanations (theories), research, and practice are independent entities, they are parasitically joined in the practice-continuum. In this sense, the sociological practitioner is a researcher/scientist who collects data, the content of which produces or yields explanations for "knowing and doing," and the same sociological practitioner assumes the role of a theorist and a therapist/ practitioner. Although the training of sociologists tend to prepare one to assume all of these roles, nothing in the process facilitates their integration except a practice focus. Therefore, the focus should be deliberate and structured to accommodate the practice-continuum. This focus would also liberate sociologists from intradisciplinary conflict and identity challenges. This does not negate the independent development of theorists, researchers and practitioners who are skilled at different levels of preparation and readiness, but are professionally focused on one area. The practice-continuum also allows for verification of explanatory discoveries. In other words, in the process from knowing to doing, descriptions and explanations are required; verification and plausibility are achieved and validity is obtained. Grounding the explanations and the intervention/ application takes care of this concern and sociological practice establishes viability and relevance. Our position is that sociological practice requires the marriage of theory or explanation and research or scientific discovery. This is the reason that we argue that the sociological practitioner, and especially the clinical sociologist, must be a scientist-practitioner in the sense that Grounded Encounter Therapy (GET) suggests (Swan 2005, 1988).

Five suggestions for revising Turner's manifesto are offered by Dotzler:

1). Dropping his negative caricatures of the various wings.
2). Giving greater recognition to the uses already made of sociology.
3). Moving away from the traditional positivistic models of science and practice toward a more open, eclectic one that views theory and practice as independent activities that are both enriched through strong interaction.
4). Considering the need for an autonomous sociological practice occupation.
5). Inventing or selecting an alternative expression for "social engineering" because of the heavy negative baggage it carries (p. 127).

In response to the rhetorical question in Turner's topic—"Social Engineering: Is This Really as Bad as it Sounds," Tabori (2001) argues that "the answer must be a resounding "yes!" Several reasons are provided. "First, the title is misleading because the suggestion to borrow a specific technique or method from the field of engineering for the conduct of applied sociology . . . is a far tamer proposal than implied in the title." The second reason given is that "even within its own terms, the argument for a "rule of thumb" methodology does not hold up. The relationships between science engineering and "rule of thumb" are not clear, and this carries over into the discussion of developing rules of thumb for use is applied sociology (p. 143). His final reason is that Turner does not seem to show any "awareness of the continuing debate concerning the application of hard science models to social science research, especially represented by the works of Peter C. Ordeshook (1996), and Jeffery Friedman (1996).

In introducing the concept of social engineering, Tabori also points out that "Turner raises expectations about a discussion of a much larger issue than the one which he eventually addresses . . . his discussion of social engineering . . . represents a straw man that he uses to beat up sociologists for being overly ideological, antiscience, and narcissistic rugged individuals. His dismissal of the concerns that surround the concept of social engineering is somewhat cavalier" (p. 144).

Tabori references works from political science and economics where for a couple of decades an examination of social engineering, social regulation and state behavior is discussed (Scott 1998). What has been discovered is that "large-scale social engineering soloution are often inefficient and frequently do harm even when well intended and anchored in social research" (Ostsoom 1990).

The claim "that social engineering would force sociologists to be more rigorous and discipline . . . and become less ideological, more scientific and less narcissistic (rugged individualists)" is strongly questioned and challenged "as gratuitous hyperbole and really not worthy of Professor Turner. Some of the most dangerous, destructive, and ideological regimes in the history of the world have been served by social engineering concepts" (p. 144).

The Role of Sociological Practice

Turner and others have engaged all sociologists, directly or indirectly, in the necessary debate regarding the role of sociological practice in the discipline of sociology. Consequently, or as a result, there is also debate about the value, importance and role of sociology in society. There is no doubt that sociology has developed its key elements—theory, methods of research, and sociological knowledge/context. We can easily fix the disconnect recognized or evident as has been suggested in the presentation of the practice-continuum. The problem or challenge is not only a lack of a practice wing and the disconnect among the elements. Another real problem is the nature of the knowledge being created. For the most part, the knowledge being created is primarily general, and therefore not applicable to the specific problems faced by individuals, group, communities, organizations, and industries. Many of these problems are being addressed by other professionals whose content is not sociological, who attempt to translate sociological knowledge and findings for practical use, or they attempt to understand and address problems that are social in nature using perspectives that are incongruent with the nature and content of the context of the problem. Usually these professionals distort concepts, misuse sociological findings and knowledge because they are not trained in sociology, or they are not sociologists. The intradisciplinary and interdisciplinary conflicts are not productive in solving the problems and meeting the challenges. As a matter of fact, it is rather late to resolve the conflicts without engaging in agitated confrontation.

Sociology missed the opportunity to have its knowledge define the content of the significant licenses and certifications that legitimize and validate what has come to be defined, narrowly, I might say, as practice. Demonstrating its utility could have been its marketing strategy. There is no doubt that sociological products are in society and sociologists must identify, claim, and promote them for sociological credit. Establishment sociology as well as sociological practice will benefit. When sociologists become advocates and announce and spread in the market-place the value and utility of sociology and sociological knowledge and its application to the well-being, growth, and development of society and the public, public support will be forthcoming and sociology and sociological knowledge will take their rightful place among their natural customers, clients, and users. No doubt, there will be intellectual confrontations and challenges, but the context and nature of the issues and problems are within the territory of the discipline of sociology. There are sociologists who have been significant in the development of sociological knowledge who can identify and note the impact sociology had had not only in "knowing", but also in "doing." There are those who teach sociology but are not sociologists and not really aware of its impact and utility except for the knowledge it provides. The perceived lack of impact or the lack of its recognition is related to the nature of its findings and the problem of applicability. Instead of, or in addition to addressing the questions: "What do sociologists do?" and "What can sociology do?" We should be addressing the questions: "What has sociology done and is capable of doing?" and "What have sociologists done?"

The conversations engaged in by many sociologists today regarding sociological practice suggest that a strong practice component in the discipline will significantly and substantively allow for theoretical and methodological benefits for the discipline and society. Indeed, a strong practice component in sociology will enhance the survival and prosperity of the discipline. When we change the way sociologists are trained to allow for the development of scientists-practitioners who are skilled in theory, research, sociological knowledge, including consulting, marketing, presentation, contextual analysis, mitigation, and expert witnessing, etc., sociologists and the public will come to view the field and practitioners, not only as users of the wealth of sociological knowledge, but also as creators of that knowledge. Sociological practitioners and clinical sociologists accomplish this as they practice discovery, creation, and application. Sociology students, undergraduate and graduate, and those who teach sociology, especially those who are not sociologists (creators and applicants of sociological knowledge) and the external customers, various social (entities) organizations, and individuals who use sociological knowledge for various reasons or purposes will testify and attest to the utility of sociological knowledge and the relevance of sociology.

What Must Be Done? Going Forward

The debate and discussion of the role and presence of sociological practice to the survival and progress of sociology as a viable and useful discipline will continue for some time to come. In the meantime, there are a number of things we can, and must do.

- We must identify and claim territorial rights to sociological knowledge.
- In addition to creating general sociological knowledge, we must also create specific contextual knowledge for the purposes of application since general knowledge is not contextually applicable.
- We must change the way we train sociologists to produce scientists-practitioners whose role is to create the specific contextual knowledge and understanding for application and social intervention.

- We have to identify primary and secondary users of sociological knowledge (a market) and develop marketing and presentation strategies to meet their needs. The disconnect among theory, research, and practice will be resolved by adhering to the "practice-continuum" which dictates a parasitical relationship among the disconnected elements of the discipline.

- Sociological practitioners should close ranks and determine, over a period of two to three years, how they want to or must relate to other professionals once it is clear as to their role and function. The presence and dominance of non-sociologists who inject perspectives and concepts that are not sociological, and are not healthy to growth and development, especially on the process of addressing the needs of our customers, must be curtailed. There is no need to be sociological practitioners or clinical sociologists if we have to rely upon, and depend on, or borrow perspectives and concepts, to practice, that are not sociological. Presently, there is too much confusion in the literature or writings of those who define themselves as sociological practitioners, especially clinical sociologists, who are still wed to the purely academic. Additionally, too much of what is not sociological knowledge or influences of non-sociologists are evident among practitioners. This is not to say that in the future viable relationships cannot or should not be developed with closely related professionals.

- Sociologists must fully understand that sociology is the study of social life, social change, the context and social "causes" and consequences of human behavior. Since all human behavior is social, very few fields have such broad scope and relevance for research, theory, and the application of knowledge.

- The territory and boundaries of the discipline need to be differentiated and protected from professional distortions by those who question its utility and significance. There are too many problems of a social nature that need addressing not merely from the perspective of scientific understanding, but also from an application and intervention perspective. The trained, or otherwise established sociologist, as scientist-practitioner is in the best possible position or role to completely address the matter.

- Sociologists, and especially sociological practitioners, must seek to correctly understand how human behavior emerges. Some of the explanations presently being cherished should be questioned and challenged, even though they have been around for years and seem to have some validity. The same thing is true of the proper use of concepts and the greater use of the "social self" instead of the concept of personality in discussions and analysis of human behavior.

- Sociological knowledge should also define the content of major licenses and certifications that have to do with human social behavior. Presently, there is conformity to the culture of psychologists and psychiatrists. In private and public settings, clients and employers must know and expect that sociological knowledge is being applied. We should not conform to the culture developed, nor should we merely inject sociological knowledge and understanding into the culture as token participants with little or no professional significance. We must do more. What dominates should conform to the sociological knowledge which is consistent with the definition of sociology and how it defines and explains human social behavior and the context of that behavior. The labels must also be consistent with how we define our roles and the way we make determinations of human social problems.

- We need to develop discovery and social intervention approaches that are consistent with being scientists-practitioners which allow the therapeutic intervention to be guided by an analysis of the situation rather than imposed from the outset by the therapist/clinician/practitioner. All relevant issues should be derived from the methodological encounters between the scientist-practitioner and the client or clients. The encounters with the clients must define what the relevant problems and issues are, what explanations or theories are relevant for understanding them, and what intervention strategies are appropriate. This is a dramatic contrast to psychological theories, particularly psychoanalysis which impose a specific causal theory at the outset. Our theory must emerge from the client-defined social context, not the other way around (Swan 1988).

Conclusion

No doubt there are serious problems with the way sociology, as a discipline, has been allowed to present itself and its utility. Its key elements are not well integrated; it is too idealistic; too philosophical; mainly irrelevant to the needs of the masses, and lacking in practical application to real-life situations. Sociological practice holds the key to the progress and utility of the discipline. All of these challenges can be successfully addressed as various forms of social intervention are created.

Because of the complexity of human social situations, and the ability of human beings to change and adapt to altered circumstances and life-events, they are more apt to learning new ways of doing things. Social practice requires that sociological practitioners be in constant contact with the complexity and human ability (Tabori 2001). This is the reason that Grounded Encounter Therapy provides a more useful approach and method that can solve the particular problem of sociology and other social sciences in developing empirically and contextually well grounded theories for intervention. From the questions being raised and the statements made regarding the utility and relevance of the discipline of sociology, it seems very clear that the discipline never created society's dependency on sociological knowledge to solve human social problems. Sociology has been promoted as a discipline creating descriptive an explanatory knowledge for understanding of various social issues, but not as profession with skills for intervention and application for change. Therefore, the professional market for students trained in sociology which is driven by available careers was never really developed and established. When talking with students and even members of the public about sociology and how it defines itself, there are expectations because it seems to suggest so much. There is therefore, no need to re-label the discipline, however, there is a desperate need for sociology to demonstrate in specific ways, relevance in association with the expectations the definition suggests. The public must evidence a more skilled and practical professional who can demonstrate what can be accomplished through the use of both sociological knowledge and skills in the workplaces of the community and society. In a few instances, changes in the structure of the curriculum are taking place to emphasize sociological knowledge and skills providing insights into solving problems and meeting the needs of the community and society. A practice perspective must be reflected in a new effort to give students of sociology competency to acquire career positions. As a result, sociologists will be more comfortable and not tend to fumble in attempting to answer the questions: "What can sociology and sociologists do?" and "What can I do with a degree in Sociology?" In the end, sociologists must demonstrate confidence in the methods and approaches they develop that lead to empirically "well-grounded" explanations which are designed for intervention and application to problems faced by humans and society. Theories or explanations which are generated in this manner are sound and do not require trial by "real-world" application. They can be implemented and lead to the development of appropriate solutions. The contextual suitability is determined by the real data and information from the setting or situation. There would be no question in being able to specify how sociologists know what they do, and the techniques used as practitioners. In the process, they would have linked theory, methods of research, and practice.

It is indeed unfortunate that sociology, like other social and behavioral science disciplines, did not follow through in developing a practice component to utilize its insights in practical application as well as to continue basic scientific discovery.

Psychology, Anthropology, Economics, and Political Science have developed practice components. Auguste Comte, Karl Marx, Emile Durkheim, W. E. B. Dubois and Max Weber emphasized the practical use of sociological knowledge. They envisioned sociologists as scientists-practitioners using the scientific knowledge discovered to bring about positive change (Fritz 1991, pp. 18-21; Caser 1977, pp. 12, 13). It is evident that these pioneers and founders held the view of a discipline which provided knowledge as a source of information and analysis and a practical sociology for addressing social problems. Sociological Practitioners honor their original intent to continue the complimentary duality of the discipline of sociology (Ward 1906; Collin 1983; Tomasi 1998). The practicability of the discipline is its viability and value.

Reference

1. Collin, Albert 1983. "The Course of Applied Sociology: Past and Future." pp. 442-466 in <u>Applied Sociology</u>, edited by Howard E. Freeman, Russell R. Dynes, Peter H. Rosse, and William Foote Whyte. San Fancisco: Jossey-Bass.

2. Coser, Lewis A. 1977. <u>Masters of Sociological Thought: Ideas in Historical and Social Context</u>. 2nd edu. New York: Harcourt Brace Javanocvich.

3. Dotzler, Robert J. and Ross Kopel 1999. "What Sociologists Do and Where They Do It-The NSF Survey on Sociologists' Work Activities and Work Place." <u>Sociological Practice: A Journal of Clinical and Applied Sociology?: 71-83.</u>

4. Feagin, Joe and Hernan Vera 2002. <u>Liberation Sociology</u>. Boulder, Co: Westview.

5. Fein, Melvyn 2001. "Social Engineering in Context: Some Observation on <u>Sociological Practice: A Journal of Clinical and Applied Sociology 3:131-125.</u>

6. Friedman, J. (ed). 1996. <u>The Rational Choice Controversy.</u> New Haven, Ct: Yale University Press.

7. Fritz, Jan M. 1991. "The Emergence of American Clinical Sociology." pp. 17-28 in <u>Handbook of Clinical Sociology</u>, edited by Howard M. Reback and John G. Bouhm. New York: Plenum Press.

8. Hauser, William (1999) 2000. "Let Us Now Praise Famous Sociologists." <u>Journal of Applied Sociology.</u> 17: 13-19.

9. Hougland, James G. (1989, 1977). "Giving Voice to the Public: Survey Research Applied Sociology, and Public Policy." Pp. 219-230 in <u>Directions in Applied Sociology,</u> edited by Stephen F. Steele and Joyce M. Iutcovich. Arnold, MD: Society for Applied Sociology.

10. Ordeshook, P. C. 1996. "Engineering or Science: What is the Study of Polities?" in <u>The Rational Choice Controversy.</u> Edited by J. Friedman. New Haven, CT: Yale University Press.

11. Ostrom, E. 1992. <u>Governing The Commons: The Evolution of Institution for Collective Action.</u> New York, N. Y.: Cambridge University Press.

12. Scott, J. C. 1998 <u>Seeing Like a State: How Certain Schemes to Improve Human Condition Have Failed.</u> New Haven, Ct: Yale University Press.

13. Swan, L. Alex 1988. Grounded Encounter Therapy: Its Characteristics and Process." <u>Clinical Sociology Review.</u> 6: 76-87.

14. Swan, L. Alex 2005. "Clinical Sociologists as Scientists-Practitioners: Using Grounded Encounter Therapy (GETS)" Manuscript submitted for publication.

15. Tomasi, Luigi 1998., <u>The Tradition of the Chicago School.</u> Aldershot, England: Ashgate.

16. Tabori, John Rogard 2001. "A Response to Professor Turner's Social Engineering: Is This Really as Bad as it Sounds?" A Methodologist's and Political Economist's Perspective." Sociological Practice: <u>A Journal of Clinical and Applied Sociology.</u> 3:143-147.

17. Turner, Jonathan H. 2001. "Social Engineering: Is This Really as Bad as it Sounds?" Sociological Practice: <u>A Journal of Clinical and Applied Sociology.</u> 3:99-120.

18. Ward, Lester 1906. Applied Sociology: <u>A Treatise on the Conscious Improvement of Society by Society.</u> Boston: Ginn and Company.

19. Weinberg, Adam S. 2002. The University: An Agent of Social Change?" <u>Qualitative Sociology.</u> 25: 263-272.

Conclusion

The primary intent of this work is to introduce to Clinical Sociologists and Sociotherapists, and to professionals in the fields of counseling and therapy The Grounded Encounter Therapeutic approach which allows the clinician and the client, who are dealing with issues of a social nature or within social content, an appropriate, valid, and reliable way of discovering the real problem from the presenting problem and the ways for intervening, applying, and explaining the problem which is grounded in the social context of the client.

This approach was precisely presented in an article published in Mid-American Review of Sociology in 1985. Another version as a chapter in the book The Practice of Clinical Sociology and Sociotherapy, in 1984 and the well noted version published in Clinical Sociology Review in 1988. This work provides all of the dimensions of the approach, its theoretical foundations, characteristics, and its intervention and application techniques.

One perspective is that Grounded Encounter Therapy is a discovery, intervention and application approach which allows the theory which guides the process to be developed from an analysis of the situation or context rather than imposed at the outset by the therapist.

It is a dramatic contrast to psychological theories, particularly psychoanalysis which imposes a specific causal theory at the outset. In GET, on the other hand, the theory emerges from the client-defined context, not the other way around.

The basic assumptions and philosophies of the various therapeutic approaches in the clinical field, capture the views of therapists regarding the nature of human beings and the reasons for their problems. Implicit in the philosophical statements are their theoretical perspectives. Any assumption, philosophy or theoretical perspective outside of their's cannot be accommodated, and is rendered invalid. However, this philosophical and theoretical confinement stifles the scientific process of discovery and makes explanatory and therapeutic applications suspect. Application and explanation must be grounded in the scientific process of discovery which must be grounded in the social context of the clients, not the assumptions and philosophies of the therapeutic approaches. The position or posture does not necessarily deny the validity of the assumptions and philosophies of the therapeutic approaches. However, it does raise serious theoretical and therapeutic questions regarding the utility of the approaches for purposes of social diagnosis or during the scientific process of discovery.

Early development is of critical importance to some approaches since later personality problems are thought to be rooted in repressed childhood conflict. Other approaches argue that human beings are influenced by the expectations and demands of significant others. Because we are dependent upon others as children, our early decisions are made under their influence. However human beings are not passively scripted, it is argued that there is cooperation in achieving these early decisions.

Other approaches argue that human beings are shaped by learning the sociocultural conditioning. The problems that the person has is thought to be a function of his sociocultural conditioning.

Another example of the predetermined posture of the definition of the problem is seen in the approach which argues that all human problems of a personal nature are the result of distorted and irrational thinking that leads to emotional behavior disorders. It is believed that human beings are prone to learning erroneous, self-defeating notions which create problems for them. Humans are viewed as being discouraged needing encouragement to correct mistaken self-perceptions.

It must be fully understood that therapists and counselors are significantly influenced by their theoretical perspectives and therapeutic approaches when they come in contact with clients. What they look for and what they see are dictated by perspectives and approaches which influence their procedures and strategies. Further, the basic assumptions in their perspectives and approaches affect the way they view and work with their clients. Even the goals therapists pursue are determined and dictated by their theoretical and therapeutic assumptions about the nature of human beings and the definition of their problems. It is functional to embrace a general theoretical perspective about human interaction and social relationships, but to predetermined clients problems by applying a theoretical orientation paralyzes the discovery process and the grounding of the therapy. It might be true for some that they are shaped by social forces, or that they are pushed by the need to overcome inherent feelings of inferiority and pulled by the striving for superiority; or that we define ourselves by our choices without realizing or being aware of the factors that limit and restrict the range of our choices. However, this might not be, and is usually not the case for all clients. Every problem of a social nature has it own context in time and space.

Most therapists today are not good scientists, even though their initial task is to collect data from their clients. The collection of data is carried out through the process of discovery to determine the real problem. Most therapists, however, confuse the presenting problems with the real problems of the clients. Moreover, during the intake interview or initial discovery and beyond, they seek to make their clients fit into their approaches or their predefined and predetermined system. The role of the therapist seems to be to convince the client that his/her problems are defined and explained by the particular therapeutic approach held by the therapist. Resistance is never viewed by the therapist as disjuncture between the predefined posture of the approach and the reality of the client's situation. Because clients are made to, and sometime pressured into believing that the therapist knows or should know what his/her problem is after a brief period of encounter, the client gives in to the predefined and predetermined explanations and goals for therapy. The process is not to discover the real problems, but to fit the client into his/her therapeutic scheme. Goals are established in relation to how the approach defines the problems of the clients. The initial struggle with the clients and the information they produce is to force them into seeing their problems and situation for the perspectives defined by the approaches.

There are video tapes of therapists with different therapeutic approaches who have attempted to help the same client. It is very evident, as the therapists conduct sessions with the same client at different times, that the attempts of these therapists, with different approaches and philosophical assumptions, were to fit the client into their approaches. Success was accepted or acknowledged only when the client began to see things from the perspective of the therapist and the particular approach dictating the session. This is not to suggest that clients may not have problems in the area of each of the modalities of various approaches. However, it is not true to the scientific process of discovery for data to be skewed by therapeutic approaches that have predetermined explanations of clients problems. The data discovered must dictate explanations, understanding and possible solutions. To view clients and their situations from the particular therapeutic approach of the therapist to stifle the process of discovery and exclude possibilities that might be beyond the dimensions of the particular approach. The real problem therefore is in the area of discovery and understanding which is a scientific process. After the real problems and the context out of which they have emerged are discovered, it could be that the techniques, strategies, goals, etc. might be used only because the scientific process dictates which techniques and strategies are applicable and appropriate.

Not enough attention is placed on the scientific process and the most appropriate ways of discovering what clients problems are regardless of the therapeutic and philosophical orientation. There are all kinds of possibilities when the discovery process is scientifically conducted; ethnicity, race, class, attitudes, values, dispositions and other important matters relevant to the social context of the clients will emerge. The therapist has to remember that what is significant are these things that emerge in the discovery process. The therapist must therefore be skilled in obtaining disclosure. There should be no fear of erroneous labeling and ethnocentric biases if the focus of discovery is the social context of the clients. The process of discovery, or the scientific process promoted by GET prevents the therapist from grounding the problems of the clients in his/her particular therapeutic approach and assumptions. Instead, the therapist is forced by the dictates of the scientific method to ground the problems of the clients in the social context of clients.

How problems are identified, defined, explained, understood and treated are crucial to the outcome for clients. It is from the context of the clients' problems that explanations are generated, and it is from the explanations and understanding of the problems and their contexts that treatment is developed. Further, it is to the contexts of the problem (presenting and real) that the knowledge and understanding gained is applied. The knowledge and understanding required by GET is specific knowledge for intervention and application because it is recognized that every problem has its own context in time and space. Moreover, presenting problems are but mere symptoms, suggesting that there is a real problem.

Problems cannot be well understood outside of their contexts, and they cannot be effectively treated outside of their causal, and theoretical contexts. The techniques and strategies used in intervention and application should be selected on the basis of what is discovered about the problem and its context.

GET recognizes that the traditional assessment and diagnosis are detrimental because they are basically external ways of understanding the clients. Therefore, the internal along with the external word of the client is captured. Comprehensive interviewing and probing are used to gather specific information about the social situation of the clients. GET requires specific knowledge because specific knowledge is applicable, general knowledge is not.

The subjective word of the client is provided by the client through disclosure and discovery. Predetermined explanations, assumptions and definition tend to block, stifle, and restrict the scientific process of discovery. The process is a collaborative effort with the client and therapist attempting to discover and understand the problem and its context, and their deciding on a plan of action for change, suggested and made evident by the discovery.

There are therapists who place marital conflict within the context of the multigenerational family unit. What if this is not the proper context? We cannot assume that all marital conflicts have such a context, or have the same context. What happens when we embrace such a perspective is that is blinds us from seeing any other context and we are tempted to force all data into that context, regardless.

There are those who argue that many of the personal difficulties for which people seek professional help are social role problems. Confictual relationships, family problems, identity ambiguity and confusion, mid-life crisis or transition and vocational dilemmas are all derived from role failures. If these are to be corrected it is argued that dysfunctional roles must be replaced with more satisfied patterns of behavior. This argument is sound and the proposed solution plausible if the solution is grounded in the explanation of the problem which in turn is ground in the context of the problem. Again, what must be remembered is that every problem has its own context in space and time, and that a problem must be understood and treated within its own context.

If academic training and experience have real value, then the majority of those who present themselves as clinicians to assess social situations, social interaction and interpersonal relationships should find it difficult doing so without the appropriate disciplinary base and content focus. It should also be problematic because they do not have the methodological skills and training to offer theoretical insights and explanations to problems lodged in a social context. For the clinical Sociologist; the Sociotherapist and the Sociological practitioner, we must first assume the role of the scientist whose initial task is to collect the essential contextual facts at the micro, messo and macro levels in which the explanation, intervention and application are based or grounded.

Get is constrained only by its theoretical frame of reference, the context it represents, and the ability of those who use it. All problems of a social nature or social in context can be addressed by the approach. All effective therapies must be scientific to assure discovery - discovery of the real problem, its context, its explanations, the appropriate techniques for intervention, and the possible ways to effect change, enhancement, and growth.

Clients with "metabolic disorders", "psychotic disorders," etc., where manifest symptomatology is of a social or behavioral nature, but the etiology is not socially determined, might not be suitable to the scientific or socio-diagnostic process of GET.

Bibliography

Beger, Peter and Thomas Luckmann
 1967 <u>The Social Construction of Reality</u>.
  New York: Doubleday.

Blau, Peter M.
 1964. <u>Exchange and Power in Social Life</u>.
  New York: John Wiley & sons.

Blumer, Herbert.
 1969. <u>Symbolize Interactionism: Perspective and Method</u>.
  Englewood Cliffs, N.J.: Prentice-Hall.

Brown, A. R.
 1952 Structure and Function in Primitive Society.
  Glencoe, IL: Free Press.

Buar, et al., eds.
 1979 Contemporary Theories About the Family.
  New York: Macmillean.

Cohen, Harry
 1981 Connections: Understanding Social Relationships.
  Ames: The Iowa State University.

Cooley, Charles Horton
 1970 Human Nature and the Social Order.
  New York: Schocken Books.

Coser, Lewis A.
 1956, 1967 <u>The Functions of Social Conflict</u>.
  Glencoe, Ill.: Free Press.

Dahrendorf, Ralf
1958 Act of Utopia: Toward a Recitation of Sociological
Analysis." American Journal of Svc. 64:115-127.

1968 <u>Essays in the Theory of Society</u>. Stanford, Calif.: Stanford
U. Press.

1959 <u>Class and Class Conflict in International Society</u>. Stanford,
Calif.: Stanford U. Press.

Dies, R. R.
1974 Attitudes Toward The Training of Group Psychotherapists:
Some of Interprofessional and Experiences-Associated
Differences. <u>Small Group Behavior</u> 5: 65-79.

Douglas, Track
1973 <u>Introduction to Sociology: Situations and Starvation</u>.
New York: Doubleday.

Dukheim, E.
1951 <u>Suicide</u>. New York: Free Press.

Garfinkel, Harold
1967 Studies in Ethnometerology. Englewood, N.J. Prentice-Hill.

Glass, John
1979 Renewing an Old Profession: Clinical Sociology.
<u>American Behavioral Scientist</u>. Vol. 23, No. 3,
March/April, 513-530.

Glass, John, and Jan M. Fritz
1981 Comments on the Preceding Article.
<u>The Journal of Applied Behavioral Science</u>,
17, 3: 330-346.

Glassner, Barry, and Jonathan Freedman.
  1979 Clinical Sociology, New York: Logman.

Gouldner, Alvin W.
  1954 <u>Patterns of Industrial Bureaucracy</u>. Glencoe, Ill.: Free Press.

Homans, George
  1974 Social Behavior As Exchange: It's Elementary Forms. New York: Harcourt Brace Tovanovich.

Husseral, Edmund
  1859 Ideas. London: George Allen & Unwin.

Malinowski, Bronislaw
  1939 & 1944 A Scientific Theory of Culture. Chapel Hill, North Carolina: University of North Carolina Press.

  1945 The Dynamics of Culture Change. New Haven, Conn.: Yale University Press.

Marx, Karl
  1964 <u>The Economic and Philosophic Manuscript of 1844</u>, Dirk J Struck (ed.) New York: International Publishers.

Marx, Karl and Frederick Engles
  1962, 1964 <u>Selected Works, Vol. 1</u>. London: Lawrence and Wishart.

Matza, David
  1969 <u>Becoming Deviant</u>. Englewood Cliffs, N.J.: Prentice-Hall.

McGee, Reece, et. Al.
  1980 <u>Sociology: An Introduction</u>. New York: Holt, Rinehart and Winston.

Mead, George Herbert
  1934 <u>Mind, Self and Society. Chicago</u>: University of Chicago Press.

Mills, C. Wright
    1948, 1963 <u>Power, Politics in American Society</u>. New York:
        Ballatine.

Schutz, Alfred
    1899/1967 <u>The Phenomenoloy of The Social World</u>, Evanston,
        Ill.: Northwestern University Press.

Strauss, Roger
    1979 Clinical Sociology: An Idea Whose Time Has Come Again.
        <u>Sociology Practice</u>, 3: 1:21-43.

Styker, Sheldon
    1972/1980 Symbolic Interactionism: A Social Structural Version.
        Menlo Park, Calif.: Benjamin/ Cummings.

Swan, L. Alex
    1981 Clinical Sociology: Problems and Prospects. <u>Mid-American
        Review of Sociology</u> (Winter), 2:111-127.

Turner, Jonathan H.
    1975 "Mark and Simile Revisited: Reassessing the Foundations of
        Conflict Theory," <u>Social Forces</u>, 53: 618-27.

    1975 "A Strategy for Reformatting the Dialectical and Functional
        Theory of Conflict," <u>Social Forces</u>, 53:433-44.

Wallace, Ruth & Alison Wolf
    1986 <u>Contemporary Sociological Theory</u>. Englewood Cliffs, N.J.:
        Prentice-Hall.